Remaking the Concept of Aptitude:
Extending the Legacy of Richard E. Snow

The Educational Psychology Series

Robert J. Sternberg and Wendy M. Williams, Series Editors

Marton/Booth • *Learning and Awareness*

Hacker/Dunlovsky/Graesser, Eds. • *Metacognition in Educational Theory and Practice*

Smith/Pourchot, Eds. • *Adult Learning and Development: Perspectives From Educational Psychology*

Sternberg/Williams, Eds. • *Intelligence, Instruction, and Assessment: Theory Into Practice*

Martinez • *Education as the Cultivation of Intelligence*

Torff/Sternberg, Eds. • *Understanding and Teaching the Intuitive Mind: Student and Teacher Learning*

Sternberg/Zhang, Eds. • *Perspectives on Cognitive, Learning, and Thinking Styles*

Ferrari, Ed. • *The Pursuit of Excellence Through Education*

Corno, Cronbach, Kupermintz, Lohman, Mandinach, Porteus, Talbert / The Stanford Aptitide Seminar • *Remaking the Concept of Aptitude: Extending the Legacy of Richard E. Snow*

Dominowski • *Teaching Undergraduates*

Remaking the Concept of Aptitude: Extending the Legacy of Richard E. Snow

*Lyn Corno, Lee J. Cronbach, Haggai Kupermintz,
David F. Lohman, Ellen B. Mandinach, Ann W. Porteus,
Joan E. Talbert for The Stanford Aptitude Seminar
Edited by Lee J. Cronbach*

LAWRENCE ERLBAUM ASSOCIATES, PUBLISHERS

2002   Mahwah, New Jersey   London

Copyright © 2002 by Lawrence Erlbaum Associates, Inc.
All rights reserved. No part of this book may be reproduced in
any form, by photostat, microform, retrieval system, or any
other means, without prior written permission of the publisher.

Lawrence Erlbaum Associates, Inc., Publishers
10 Industrial Avenue
Mahwah, NJ 07430

Cover design by Kathryn Houghtaling Lacey

Library of Congress Cataloging-in-Publication Data

Snow, Richard E.
Remaking the concept of aptitude : extending the legacy of
Richard E. Snow / by the Stanford Aptitude Seminar ; edited
by Joan E. Talbert, Lee J. Cronbach.
    p.   cm. — (The Educational psychology series)
Work completed by the Stanford Aptitude Seminar after the
death of R. E. Snow.
Includes bibliographical references and index.
ISBN 0-8058-3532-6 (alk. paper)
1. Ability—Congresses. I. Talbert, Joan E. II. Cronbach, Lee
J. (Lee Joseph), 1916–   . III. Title. IV. Series.
BF431 .S612   2001
153.9—dc21
                                          00-046613
                                              CIP

Books published by Lawrence Erlbaum Associates are printed
on acid-free paper, and their bindings are chosen for strength and
durability.

Printed in the United States of America
10 9 8 7 6 5 4 3 2 1

Contents

List of Exhibits

List of Figures

List of Tables

Foreword

Rarely do seminars author books. And rarely does a scholar's unfinished book generate posthumously a full-scale publication that realizes some fraction of his hopes. Both are the case here and that deserves explanation. This Foreword sketches the book's evolution over nearly two decades and explains how the seminar worked to complete it. We two write this at the request of other seminar members. (Cronbach managed the production process and Talbert is Dick Snow's widow.)

The seminar tried to capture in print Dick Snow's ambitions to provide a scaffold for future theory, research, and practice organized around the concept of aptitude. As the Preface he had drafted suggests, Snow meant to lay out his own understanding of the aptitude concept in order to ground and inspire future efforts. The seminar took up this project where Dick left off. The reader of the Preface must remember, however, that statements about "this book" represent aspirations of Dick's that we may or may not have realized.

Dick died in December 1997, 7 months after his pancreatic cancer was diagnosed. He gave all his waning strength in that period to extending the manuscript on which we have built. He was convinced that the concept of aptitude is pivotal to understanding individual learning and performance in particular situations. He expressed the hope that his incomplete manuscript could be brought to publication, and the two of us, who had been providing limited collegial support for his final efforts, undertook to do just that.

This book has a long history; jottings for it began to pile up in the late 1970s. In 1982 Dick was awarded a Guggenheim fellowship for the project of starting a book-length theory of aptitude. At that time he had nearly 20 years of experience with research on individual differences in ability and personality, considering both frontier psychological issues and the influences of learner characteristics on response to instruction.

After working on the book project for a year, Dick concluded that the time for putting forth a theory had not arrived. The field was changing rapidly. New questions were being posed—some of them in research he was directing. Many more findings would be needed before enough conclusions were in hand to support a theory. Dick's views evolved, as his research and that of other investigators found ways to track previously elusive mental processes, as he became well acquainted with the work of European scholars, and as, in research on instruction, statistical examination of relations of outcomes to initial characteristics of students gave place to examination of the transactions between the individual and here-and-now problems or lessons.

Dick produced a stream of theory-centered papers with modest titles, most of them starting with "Toward a Theory" (e.g., Snow & Lohman, 1984). In the 1990s he pressed forward with the idea of a book that would offer, not a finished theory, but a prospectus for the work that could be expected to deliver, perhaps in another 10 years, a defensible and sufficiently comprehensive theory. The extent of Dick's commitment is indicated by the thick file of outlines for his book—augmented over the years, elaborated, and sometimes radically amended.

When diagnosed with cancer, Dick was working on two books—one that explicated theory and research on individual differences in abilities and personality, and another that refined the concept of aptitude as the interface of person and situations and defined frontiers for new theory and research. His vision for a book he might complete before his death integrated these purposes and the assembled materials.

Dick compiled a large binder of material written specially for his book plus extracts from publications of earlier years. A few chapters had been through many drafts; a few were at the other extreme, no more than lists of potential topics. For some parts he had assembled a kind of scrapbook of relevant passages from his publications, to be fitted together later and restyled.

After Dick's death, we set out to pull together a complete book. Cronbach organized a panel that included participants in the Stanford Aptitude Research Project in each decade from 1966 to 1997. Most of them had been coauthors with Dick in the 1990s and so are familiar with much of his latest thinking. In alphabetical order, the panelists besides ourselves are Lyn Corno, Haggai Kupermintz, David Lohman, Ellen Mandinach, and Ann Porteus (see list in box on p. xx).

Cronbach, with the help of Jayne Patterson (who had been Dick's administrative assistant), assembled the continuous prose and the fragments according to the latest outline; he imposed a common format, and flagged missing sections. The fragmentary nature and varying style of the material led us to consult as senior advisers two colleagues and admirers of Dick, Richard Shavelson and Lee Shulman. They examined the collated material and encouraged us to develop an approximation to the book that the outline envisioned. They flagged parts of the draft as contributing little, and other parts as meriting fuller treatment. Snow, they said, had always sought reviews of his drafts and made use of suggestions; we should aim to tell a clear story, not treat what was left us as untouchable.

As Dean of the School of Education at Stanford, Shavelson offered support for secretarial and related expenses plus a research assistant. Shulman, as President of Carnegie Foundation for the Advancement of Teaching, offered to underwrite travel of distant panelists for face-to-face meetings (and hosted two meetings). Moreover, he offered to commission a professional editor to lighten the panel's task of revision.

Cronbach altered somewhat the arrangement of the assembled material (following suggestions of the advisers), wrote some needed continuity, and distributed all of it to the panel. Also, he asked particular panelists to draft missing sections or chapters. Sometimes several panelists in turn modified or extended versions of a chapter. The Palo Alto contingent started meetings to review in detail one near-complete chapter after another, but the major work of the Seminar was conducted by e-mail.

Most of the panelists convened in April 1998. They made the first of several revisions of the outline, and exchanged views on the available drafts. The prime goal in editing, they decided, would be to make Dick's ideas readily comprehensible to interested students new to the field. To this end, some complex thoughts were left on the cutting-room floor. The panel hoped that this style would enable the book also to serve teachers and other practitioners (as Dick wished). Although the book can offer them no concise recommendations for their immediate use, a new view of aptitude will, Snow believed, help them rethink familiar practices.

The content of the present book does not reflect Dick's wish to influence policy and practice outside education (e.g., psychotherapy, occupational psychology). Lacking drafts of the innovative thoughts on policy and practice that Dick could have offered, the panel placed the emphasis on educational-research topics. But the panel shared Dick's view that it is important for both professional and nonprofessional audiences to know what has been learned about aptitudes. This book is about what is known, as well as about what remains to be known.

As writing and review went on, a key period in the development of this book was June–July 1998. Dick had expressed great respect for views of Simon, Gibson, and Brown, and for the "cognition is situated" thesis advanced by Rogoff, Greeno, and others. Those views, and how Dick proposed to relate them to aptitude, are best left for certain of the chapters that follow. Dick's call for a major reconceptualization of aptitude as residing not in the person but "in the interface" between person and situation (Snow, 1994) loomed as a challenge for the Seminar. It was an armature for his argument, yet panelists gave conflicting interpretations to this and companion metaphors. Eloquent, passionate e-mail messages flew from one panelist or another to the rest. There was no lead voice; this was truly rapid-fire seminar discussion. Talbert was able to amplify Dick's writings by recalling conversations where Dick told how and why he found these new ideas illuminating. The panel moved to a much better understanding of Dick's final intellectual agendum. But to write about this did literally require "extending the legacy."

In the months prior to July 1999, as chapter drafts were completed by one or more panelists and the substance approved by another pan-

---

Members of The Stanford Aptitude Seminar

Lyn Corno, Adjunct Professor of Education and Psychology, Teachers College, Columbia University (formerly Professor)

Lee J. Cronbach, Vida Jacks Professor of Education Emeritus, Stanford University

Haggai Kupermintz, Assistant Professor of Education, University of Colorado, Boulder

David F. Lohman, Professor of Educational Psychology, The University of Iowa

Ellen B. Mandinach, Senior Research Scientist, Educational Testing Service

Ann W. Porteus, Lecturer, School of Education, Stanford University

Joan E. Talbert, Senior Research Scholar and Codirector, Center for Research on the Context of Education, School of Education, Stanford University

elist or team assigned to review that piece, they went to Cynthia Patrick, a professional editor. She pointed out obscurities, challenged jargon, and flagged (for example) unnecessary use of passives and other wooden writing. Min Li, as research assistant, was an astute member of the Palo Alto review sessions, and took special responsibility for the completeness and correctness of the bibliography. She started with a compendium Patricia R. Jones had made for us from all the bibliographies of Snow papers that were available on disk, including an incomplete list for the 1997 manuscript. In the months approaching May 1999, Sarah Shearer put marked-up text and scribbles into good shape and kept our files. She also produced a near-final version of most of our new figures. Elayne Weissler-Martello picked up the continuing tasks when Sarah left Stanford after her husband's graduation. Patricia Martin, aide to David Lohman, helped with text and figures in chapter 5. All these helpers devoted considerable talents and effort to the project.

In August 1998 the panel decided that it was a mistake to continue as if R. E. Snow would be the listed author. The panel foresaw that after publication in that form (especially when we had been retaining the first-person style of his drafts) any quotation from the work would carry a tag such as "According to Snow, '...'." Yet the panel, having tried to extend his ideas as they understood them, and having reduced the complexity of some Snow statements, could not be sure that Dick would have agreed with the new wording. It would have been improper to put words into his mouth.

The alternative "R. E. Snow et al." with panelists as the *alii* did not remove the problem. Nor would signed chapters fit the facts. Writers and revisers had tried to present Dick's views, and not to express their own views or to strive for consensus where their personal views differed. Hence they did not wish extracts to be quoted as their opinions. Out of much brainstorming in the January 1999 meeting came the welcome idea of attributing the book to "The Stanford Aptitude Seminar." All panelists are or have been affiliated with Stanford, and all had played a role in the seminar-like meetings of the Stanford Aptitude Project. And we had educated each other in the best seminar tradition.

The book contains long passages originally written by Dick. Verbatim quotations are rarely long, however, because of our amendments and paraphrases. Entering quotation marks wherever Dick's exact words appear would be pedantic, but in chapter 8 some direct quotations are identified, to set them off from our attempts at extending Dick's thinking. Footnotes at the start of other chapters assist readers who would like to track down Dick's own words on a substantial part of the chapter content.

We thank each of the persons mentioned in this Foreword; we appreciate especially their loyalty to Dick and the thoughtfulness they demonstrated. We need not amplify on the value of what the project's helpers did. But we must express special thanks to the panelists for persisting with the enterprise even when it intruded into crowded lives. Some did substantial fresh writing for the book, far beyond the amount envisioned when they joined the team. At the same time, they found the Seminar to be an exceptional opportunity to think through their own views on aptitude, by interacting with top-flight colleagues on issues at the core of Dick's frontier thinking.

The Preface and Dedication that follow were prepared by Dick to lead off his book.

—Lee J. Cronbach and Joan E. Talbert

Preface by R. E. Snow

This book is about human aptitudes, the characteristics of human beings that make for success or failure in life's important pursuits. Individual differences in aptitudes are displayed every time performance in challenging activities is assessed. Concerns about aptitudes and their opposites, inaptitudes, have been rising in recent decades because many young people are not well equipped psychologically to succeed in education, or well equipped by education to succeed in employment or adult life later on. Public debates concerning the sources and solutions for this problem use many terms, some focused on the person—intelligence, personality, motivation, social skills—and some on the situation—family environment, socioeconomic limits, educational mistreatment, job design or allocation. The problem seems to be severe and worsening, regardless of the focus or terms of any particular part of the debate. And, as this book argues, it may often be the person and the situation in interrelation—in interaction—that makes for success or failure, not characteristics of persons and situations alone.

In the search for solutions, two values need to be preserved, advanced, and also balanced. Despite important individual differences in aptitudes, society needs to provide equality of educational opportunity so that all persons have the chance to develop their own aptitudes to the maximum each one desires and can reach. It needs also to provide for optimal diversity of educational programs, so that all aptitudes useful to individuals and society can be developed. Resolving these dilemmas and advancing the intelligent development and use of aptitudes for individual and societal good will pose a major challenge for social science and for social policy for decades to come.

I see this book as the capstone report of a research project—I call it the "Aptitude Research Project"—that operated intermittently at Stanford University from 1966. (The story includes also some of my work in 1960–1966 at Purdue University.) I offer here a review and up-to-date summary of the project's main conclusions and the resulting ideas regarding the nature and use of aptitude constructs and measures, particularly in education, in the world of work, and in public policy pertaining to important human individual differences.[1] The research findings from the Stanford project include those from doctoral dissertations and other studies not treated in project reports. The book also draws on ideas and findings from related research activities around the world.

The book does not attempt a comprehensive review of the literature. It is in no sense a revised edition of or a deliberate supplement to *Aptitudes and Instructional Methods: A Handbook for Research on Interactions* (Cronbach & Snow, 1977)—the first and most extensive report from the project. Nor is it a compendium of project conference reports akin to those appearing under the general title *Aptitude, Learning, and Instruction* (Snow & Farr, 1987; Snow, Federico, & Montague, 1980a, 1980b). The book's recommendations for research on human aptitudes, and their understanding and use in public affairs, derive from all that past work as well as from current work. I suggest moves toward much needed reconceptualization of individual differences in aptitudes, and improvements in how they are studied. I hope the book prompts others to carry these ideas further.

[A lengthy description of the intended content of the chapters in the 1997 outline for the book has been omitted.]

Many people have contributed to my work on the Aptitude Research Project over the years. Lee Cronbach established the project at Stanford and invited me to join him as Associate Director. He has been mentor, collaborator, critic, and friend ever since. He turned the project over to my direction after the 1977 book went to press, but he advised on several of the later studies. David Lohman was Associate Director and coworker as the project moved into cognitive-process analyses of individual differences. During the Purdue days, Warren Seibert and I worked together. I have had much fine staff assistance also. Here I acknowledge most particularly the contributions of Jayne Patterson, who kept continually organized the segments written out of sequence for the various parts of the manuscript.

---

[1]See Foreword, pp. xix–xx.

Many doctoral students contributed as project assistants or informally in seminars and class discussions or in their own research. These include: Ray Alvord, Katherine Baker, Mimi Beretz, David Berliner, Charles Bethell-Fox, Yuko Butler, Robert Chastain, David Coffing, Janet Collins, Lyn Corno, Susan Crockenberg, Judy Dauberman, Maria Cardelle Elawar, Michele Ennis, Guy Fincke, Mike Friedman, Lita Furby, Larry Gallagher, Lynne Gray, Jennifer Greene, Laura Hamilton, Robert Heckman, Douglas Jackson III, Jan Kerkhoven, Meg Korpi, Haggai Kupermintz, Patrick Kyllonen, Suzanne Lajoie, Vi Nhuan Le, Marcia Linn, Ellen Mandinach, Nancy Hamilton Markle, Brachia Marshalek, Mike Martinez, Mary McVey, Michael Nussbaum, Akimichi Omura, Pearl Paulsen, Penelope Peterson, Tamarra Pickford, Ann Porteus, Gisell Quihuis, Gavriel Salomon, Evonne Schaeffer, Martin Smith, Nicholas Stayrook, Judith Swanson, John Swiney, Darlene Tullos, Dan Webb, Noreen Webb, Sia Wesson, Sam Wineburg, Phil Winne, Dan Woltz, and Elanna Yalow. There have been contributions also from Visiting Scholars to the Stanford School of Education from the United States and around the world. Among these were John Biggs, Robert Conry, Frank Farley, Jan-Eric Gustafsson, Joop Hettema, Shindong Lee, Hiroshi Namiki, and Enoch Sawin.

Many of the ideas put forth in this book have been taken up in research books and in texts in other languages. In particular, I am familiar with Hiroshi Namiki's *Interaction Between Individuality and Educational Environments: A Task for Educational Psychology* (1997).

This book is dedicated
to my five wonderful children, who taught
me much about individual differences

Erich Alexander Snow
Shenandoah Snow
Alec Anders Snow
September Snow
Ryan Richard Talbert Snow

—Summer 1997

1 Aptitude: The Once and Future Concept

A society thrives on the performance of its members. One of the main questions that applied psychologists ask is "How do we get good performance?" After a century of research, that question remains elusive; a coherent and parsimonious theory of performance is still lacking. Indeed the subquestions are becoming increasingly complex, as scholars focus on the interplay of person and learning situation.

Managers try to arrange conditions to get the best from the people they hire. In the same way, teachers strive to arrange the learning situation to get the best from their students. The conditions that bring out the best in one employee or student, however, may not inspire another. Each person has worked out over many years how to respond in her own way to symbol systems and social cues. Each has aptitude for particular situations. Recognizing specifically the qualities each person brings to a situation, then adjusting the situation to improve the fit—these are major tasks of those who work with people.

THE AIM OF THIS BOOK AND SOME OF ITS FEATURES

How to think about and how to investigate aptitudes is the subject of this book. Richard Snow investigated aptitude for nearly 40 years. As an educational psychologist, he drew evidence almost entirely from studies of instruction or of the management of education and training. For Snow, these studies pointed up the need to design instructional environments that can mesh with the aptitudes students bring to a class, not only to improve short-term performance but also to enhance the aptitudes they leave with. This book retains Snow's emphasis on education, but the ideas generalize beyond education. Other writers could develop the same story with emphasis instead on how business management, or psychotherapy, or parenting should recognize, respond to, and extend the aptitudes of participants.

This book particularly addresses psychologists. The modern profession, from its earliest days, has been helping to shape both public opinion about talent and practice in other professions. Psychologists are in the right position to modify the way the broad public and the decision makers deal with aptitude. In this book we have less interest in transmitting today's conclusions about aptitude than in framing questions for research that will reduce uncertainties, and, in time, weld an adequate theory.

Chapter 1 is primarily a review of the history of thought about aptitude. Here, and at the start of other chapters, we list in a footnote publications by Snow that are predecessors of at least one fairly large piece of the argument in the chapter.[2] The source named may or may not have been directly paraphrased by Snow in his final manuscript, or by us. We list the sources so that interested readers can see a more complete statement (as of the date of its publication), in Snow's own words. Because materials from various sources are blended with each other and with additions, we cannot generally connect sources to particular subsections. The last paragraphs of this chapter sketch the topics of subsequent chapters, most of which are foreshadowed in chapter 1.

Psychologists have come a long distance since Galton's *Inquiries Into Human Faculty and Its Development* (1883), and do have much evidence on some questions. Nonetheless, knowledge about how aptitudes facilitate learning and problem solving is seriously incomplete. The best theory of earlier decades has spoken of the individual working alone. Recent writings emphasize that learning and problem solving are typically carried on in groups. The person is in a social context, except in institutions (or research studies) designed to keep individuals separated. To stretch aptitude theory over its proper domain, new kinds of research and a restatement of traditional concepts are needed.

We have tried to write so that this book can be read by those who have limited acquaintance with psychological and educational research. We have therefore kept technical detail to a minimum. A handful of terms familiar to students of psychological research and

---

[2]Discussion in Snow's own words of major topics in this chapter appears in Snow (1989a, 1989b, 1992, 1994), and in Snow and Yalow (1982).

statistics, but not to everyone in our intended audience, do enter the body of the argument and the research exhibits. An appendix offers introductory statements that should provide background sufficient for following any argument where those terms appear. Readers are advised to turn to the Table of Contents at this time to see the list of topics in the appendix. Some readers will skim the appendix before going further in the present chapter; others will wait to look up a term from time to time. As a reminder, we are placing a superscript ([App]) where any of the terms is first mentioned, and sometimes when it reappears after infrequent use.

Observations pertaining to aptitudes in concrete situations are scattered through the book, to show the evidence for ideas from which theory is made. Cumulatively, the variety of those exhibits portrays the many ways in which aptitude can profitably be investigated. Any exhibit can be read as a detached anecdote. The exhibit illustrates not only nearby text, however, but often the discussion in another chapter also. The exhibit format is intended to present a modest amount of detail without interrupting the flow of the running text.

WHAT CHARACTERISTICS CONSTITUTE APTITUDES?

Innumerable characteristics influence a person's behavior. The value-laden term *aptitude* is applied to only the fraction of them that are seen as forerunners of success. Therefore an ability thought of as aptitude in one period may not be an aptitude when work conditions change or the criterion of successful performance changes. Here we clarify what we count as aptitude (following Snow), because others sometimes use this concept interchangeably with ability, or with other labels for personal qualities that enable people to succeed generally. Aptitude, said Snow, should refer to being equipped to work at a particular kind of task or in a particular kind of situation.

The concept of aptitude is especially close to that of readiness (as in "reading readiness"), suitability (for a purpose or position), susceptibility (to treatment or persuasion), proneness (as in "accident-prone"). All imply a predisposition to respond in a way that fits, or does not fit, a particular situation or class of situations. The common thread is potentiality—a latent quality that enables the development or production, given specified conditions, of some more advanced performance. (See Scheffler, 1985.) In this book we use the term *aptitude* to mean *degree of readiness to learn and to perform well in a particular situation or in a fixed domain*. That is, aptitude aids in goal attainment (whether the goal is that of the performer or that of a teacher, employer, or other leader). Aptitude may be deplorable rather than laudable; Exhibit HFG (p. 201) on torturers reminds us all that there can be aptitude for evil.

In this chapter, we review how *aptitude* has been construed at various times, making no attempt to frame old thoughts in new language. But we alert the reader to one point. Some professionals write as if aptitude and situation can be described independently. Others in the field, like Snow, have taken the position that aptitude cannot be abstracted from the situation (i.e., is not an abstracted quality like height). The two conceptions mingle in the history that follows.

Ability is a generic term referring to the power to carry out some type of undertaking. Abilities are of many kinds: reading comprehension, spatial ability, perceptual speed, knowledge of (for example) geography, and physical coordination. Each facilitates functioning in some kinds of situation. Where a characteristic limits performance, the word *inaptitude* applies. What is aptitude for one role may be inaptitude for another. For example, the adult who knows subject matter thoroughly may be a poor teacher because it is hard for him to see it through the eyes of a novice.

Although every situation draws on abilities, aptitude is not limited to ability. Aspects of personality—achievement motivation, freedom from anxiety, appropriately positive self-concept, control of impulses, and others—are aptitudes as well, contributing importantly to coping with some challenges. The opposite qualities—anxious caution or impulsiveness, for example—can also be assets (i.e., aptitude) at certain moments.

A complete theory of aptitude, then, must consider affective and conative processes as well as abilities. These terms require brief explanation even though, to quote Hilgard (1980), "For two hundred years many psychologists took for granted that the study of mind could be divided into three parts: cognition, affect, and conation" (p. 107). From about 1900, however, said Hilgard, American psychology disavowed or suppressed such language as part of its rejection of "mental faculties." *Affective* has to do with feelings or emotions. *Conative* has to do with goal setting and the will. And *cognitive* refers to analysis and interpretation. It includes reasoning, remembering, and using symbols. In reporting and extending Snow's thinking, we must refer so frequently to the extension beyond the cognitive that we have coined the term *affcon* for use where we need not separate affect from conation.

The inclusion of affcon processes actually traces back to the origins of research on "intelligence." A key figure from the end of the 19th century was Alfred Binet. Binet, who lived in that pivotal time when the prescientific was giving way to the empirical in psychology, was the first to investigate higher mental processes intensively. Binet's thinking (see Wolf, 1973) inspired many of those who contributed to innovations in practice and theory throughout the century, including Terman, Piaget, Vygotsky, and Brown—all of whom reappear in our story.

The core of Binet's thinking is revealed in the title of his foundational paper "Attention et Adaptation" (Binet, 1899). That choice of words expresses Binet's conviction that intelligence consists of regulatory processes of judgment and choice. He did not identify it with well-learned associations and procedures, and notably did not equate intelligence with vocabulary size. Intelligence, for Binet, was not fixed. He wrote eloquently of the "harvest" to be expected if methods were in time devised for cultivating the abilities of children who seemed unready for school learning; his wish to adapt instruction was ignored by those successors who saw heredity as the main source of intellectual differences among young children.

Binet summed up his investigations in a famous description of intelligence: "the tendency to take and maintain a definite direction; the capacity to make adaptations for the purpose of attaining a desired end; and the power of auto-criticism" (translation by Terman, 1916, p. 45). All three of these phrases refer at least as much to conative processes and attitudes as to reasoning powers. Binet's concept of intelligence was much like Snow's concept of aptitude, save that Binet thought in terms of general readiness and had little concern for situational specificity. Also, Binet had more hope of separating the biological aspect of readiness clearly from the experiential than today's scholars would.

The series of test tasks that Binet published in Paris in 1905 set the pattern for individual mental testing around the world. It lost its dominant position only after 1944 when David Wechsler published a mental test for adults (followed in time by versions for children). Wechsler was even more insistent than Binet that intellectual functioning, in or out of the test situation, is a product of feelings, attitudes, and self-control as much as it is of abilities narrowly defined.

In the preceding pages our language has switched between *aptitude* and *aptitudes*. Both forms are appropriate. The singular *aptitude* is a generic reference to the topic. Awareness that aptitudes are plural has important social implications, because it denies that people can be placed in a single rank order of talent. Cognitive aptitudes are diverse. Much evidence does support the idea of a central system of skills and styles for handling information that can be called "intelligence" or "general ability." This ability is continually at work, but it is not all-powerful. It works together with other aptitudes (some of which also apply widely and some of which are situation-specific) to bring about success.

HISTORICAL CONCEPTIONS

In the 20th century, after the launching of psychology as a research-based profession, the desire to identify the persons most (least) likely to succeed shaped aptitude research. Sometime after 1950, the research agenda changed toward a greater concern for explaining performance in terms of underlying processes, and the agenda are continuing to change as new complexities are brought to light. The remainder of this chapter traces the history, sketchily at first, more completely as we move closer to Snow's concerns.

The tale is not one of orderly progression in time. What Lohman and Rocklin (1995) said in introducing their history of modern research on intelligence applies:

> [It] reads more like a convoluted Russian novel than a tidy American short story. There are general themes, to be sure, but also diverse subplots that crop up—some unexpectedly, others at regular intervals. Sometimes a new cast of characters, in mute testimony to Santayana's epigram for those unable to remember the past, unwittingly repeat controversies played out earlier. Others play a variation on this theme and foist old constructs with new names on a generation of psychologists lost in the present. (p. 448)

Snow began collecting data on aptitudes in the early 1960s. In the next decades, his research moved from the study of relations between pretests and outcomes in controlled instructional situations to the study of information processing, and ultimately to the study of situational and social processes. Many other investigators followed a similar path, so this chapter tells the story of aptitude research with both local and general experience in mind.

Our story departs from chronological order at times, to juxtapose similar views voiced in different eras.

The Broad View

Ancient Origins.   As early as 2357 BC the Chinese used competitive tests, basically tests of intelligence and educational achievement, to select civil servants. Confucius (ca. 500 BC) had much to say about the nature of intelligence, advising teachers and parents to recognize aptitudes for learning. "The success of education depends on adapting teaching to individual differences among learners" is a thesis discussed by Yue-Zheng in some detail in a Chinese treatise of the fourth century BC.

The Hebrew *Haggadah* tells the reader how to teach the meaning of Passover to four kinds of child—one wise, one wicked, one simple-minded, and one who asks no questions.

Among the Greeks, Socrates adapted his teaching to individual differences. Isocrates emphasized direct training of broad mental faculties through a gymnastics of mind. Plato distinguished two aspects of the soul: the emotional, dynamic, energizing function, represented by the chariot horses, and the intellective, cybernetic, control function, which he likened to the charioteer. Plato identified specialized aptitudes for various occupations in his Republic, and suggested behavioral tests of them. He was especially concerned with the military aptitudes his Guardians needed, stressing not only memory and physical prowess but also resistance to deception, timidity, and the seductions of pleasure. Aristotle went on to distinguish a person's concrete activity (observable) from the capacity (hypothetical) on which it depends. Distinguishing theoretical *constructs*[App] from observables remains an important intellectual tool to this day.

In the Roman period, the most important formulation came from Quintilian. Advising teachers of rhetoric in his *Institutio Oratoria* about 90 AD, Quintilian discussed adaptation of instruction to the individual:

> It is usually and rightly esteemed an excellent thing in a teacher that he should be careful to mark diversity of gifts in those whose education he has undertaken, and to know in what direction nature inclines each one most. For in this respect there is an unbelievable variety, and types of mind are not less numerous than types of body ....

> Accordingly, most teachers have thought it expedient to train each pupil in such a way as to foster by sound instruction his peculiar gifts, and so to develop varied endowments most effectively in the direction of their natural bent. Thus, as an expert in wrestling, entering a gymnasium full of boys, tests them in all sorts of ways, both in body and in mind, and then decides for which type of contest each one is to be trained, so it is thought right that the teacher of eloquence, after shrewdly observing which are the pupils whose natures take most delight in the closely knit polished style of speaking and which prefer the rapier stroke, the weighty manner, the sweet, the bitter, the shining, the sophisticated, should so adapt himself to individual cases that each may be brought on in the style in which he excels ....

> But the pupil who is destined for a career as a public speaker will have to work, not at some one part only, but at every part of his subject, even if

some of them appear more difficult to master; for training would be quite superfluous if natural endowment were sufficient in itself.

Thus, to take examples, if a pupil comes into our hands who is by nature faulty in taste and turgid in style ... , shall we suffer him to go on in his own way? Where we find that which is dry and barren, shall we not nourish and, as it were, clothe it? (Smail, 1938, pp. 101–103; numbers at the start of Smail's paragraphs removed)

Note, in Quintilian's remarks about stylistic preferences, the prominence of noncognitive qualities.

Quintilian's recommendations are as relevant to educational practice today as they were in first-century Rome:

Identify apparent aptitudes and inaptitudes of each learner.

Guide learners in choosing courses according to their aptitudes.

Seek to develop all aptitudes relevant to the end-goal of instruction, even if some are weak at the start; adapt alternative instructional designs to the individual's aptitude pattern, so as to remove defects and to build up needed strengths.

Do not teach in a way that runs counter to the individual's aptitudes; that may weaken those aptitudes.

Dictionary Usages.   *Apt, intelligence, capacity,* and *aptitude*— all four terms entered English from Latin via Old French, but *aptitude* entered last. The oldest reference for *aptitude* in the *Oxford English Dictionary* (OED; 1971) is dated 1548. The OED defines aptitude in these ways:

The quality of being fit for a purpose or position, suited to general requirements; fitness, suitableness, appropriateness.

Natural tendency, propensity, or disposition.

Natural capacity, endowment, or ability; talent for any pursuit ... esp. ... intelligence, quick-wittedness, readiness. (p. 420)

The historical quotations that illustrate the alternatives, with their dates, suggest that aptitude was associated with intelligence almost immediately upon entry into English in 1548. Only much later was it interpreted as capacity for *any* pursuit.

In its original, broad definition—and even today in many English dictionaries for general use—*aptitude* means aptness, fitness, inclination, tendency, propensity, or suitability to perform well in some future situation. Readiness for a situation is implied in all these terms; and *aptitude* likewise implies a fit between person and situation. Modern French dictionaries maintain the situational connection, associating aptitude with *apropos.* German dictionaries start their definitions with "apt, appropriate, and suitable" (*Geeignetheit*), working down through several levels of specialization before reaching "ability and talent" (*Befähigung*).

The historic concept was remarkably close to the technical term *readiness* that came into psychology, as we can see from this definition of readiness in a psychological dictionary (English & English, 1958): "[P]reparedness to respond. [A] state or condition of the person that makes it possible ... to engage profitably in a given learning activity. [I]t is a composite of many personal qualities and conditions and differs from one learning task to another" (p. 441). In particular, readiness for reading is:

> [t]he totality of personal factors conductive [sic] to satisfactory progress in learning to read *under given conditions of instruction.* ... The relevant factors may be intellectual, emotional and motivational, or physiological. Both general maturation and effective specific previous experiences play a part. *A child may be ready for one kind of reading method and not for another.* (p. 441; emphasis added)

This is close to the meaning of aptitude developed in this book. The definition clearly refers to properties, qualities, or states of persons that combine to enable profitable learning or development under specific conditions. That is, different composites are relevant to different situations.

Many psychologists, before World War II, included conation and affect in the concept of aptitude; witness the following from Walter Bingham's well-regarded *Aptitudes and Aptitude Testing* (1937). Bingham spoke of wanting "an instrument to measure desire" (p. 69) and continued:

> Without the capacity to achieve a genuine interest in a branch of learning or in a field of occupation, without the likelihood that its pursuit will furnish the inward satisfactions of enjoyment, the capacity to acquire the necessary proficiency is but a cold and steely asset. Interest, then, is not only a symptom, it is of the very essence, of aptitude. (p. 69)

This thought is reinforced by the recent research of Csikszentmihalyi in particular (see Exh. Csk, p. 47).

The Vision is Narrowed

The Enlightenment brought hereditary power and privilege into question. When Jefferson wrote that "all men are created equal," he was denying that anyone could or should gain influence by being "well-born."

Jefferson was mindful of individual differences, as is manifest in his proposals to select able young people for special training (Jefferson, 1787/1955, pp. 146–147). His thesis is even clearer in his 1813 correspondence with John Adams (Cappon, 1959, Vol. 2, pp. 387–392): "I agree with you that there is a natural aristocracy among men. The grounds of this are virtue and talents. … There is also an artificial aristocracy founded on wealth and birth, without either virtue or talents" (p. 388). The selection into advanced education would prepare those of worth and genius "for defeating the competition of wealth and birth for public trusts" (p. 390). The same urge to cut back on privilege motivated the liberals in British efforts at electoral reform in the mid-1800s. At one point John Stuart Mill even proposed giving a mental test to voters to determine how many votes each should have. (The practical outcome was that every graduate of Oxford and Cambridge was given a second vote, a privilege that endured for nearly a century.)

Charles Darwin, a contemporary of Mill, centered his theory of evolution on the role of the match between individual and ecology. Birds and animals in the Galapagos that were fitted to cope with their local weather, flora, and fauna had a superior survival rate and passed their adaptive powers on to future generations; the genes (biologists would now say) of those who adapted poorly died out.

Misinterpretation of Darwin's theory greatly accelerated the movement toward meritocracy. The powerful writer Herbert Spencer converted Darwin's message into a theory of social progress. The "fittest" were expected to adapt best to any environment. Intelligence was a general quality—no need to speak of situation-specific aptitudes. From this point of view, social progress called for identifying those with the greatest ability, then giving them opportunity and responsibility. It was in this climate that Francis Galton, initiator of psychological measurement in Britain, wrote *Hereditary Genius* (1869); his theme was the great number of distinguished achievers found in many high-ranking British families. From 1872 on, a conservative sociologist, William Graham Sumner, popularized "survival of the fittest" in America.

Competition for places in a fixed ecology was the essence of Nature's plan, according to this first "Social Darwinism." Therefore, policy should seek out for preferment the "best" individuals, often by means of competitive examination, and give them special opportunities for training and leadership. It was not until the 1920s that psychologists' tests, viewed as measures of talent rather than of educational accomplishment, began to exert an influence. That influence increased in England until in the 1950s the "11-plus" mental test was determining the fates of most children. That test screened a fraction of British preadolescents into high-grade secondary schools and opened the doors toward the university and positions of power. This type of preferment was devastated by a satire on elitism, *The Rise of the Meritocracy, 1870–2033* (Young, 1958), which gave stature to the antagonism of anxious parents. The system soon collapsed.

There was an alternative Social Darwinism. In books from 1883 on, the American sociologist Lester Ward framed an environmentalist reinterpretation of Darwin; in time, John Dewey helped spread the message. In this view, the effects on people's qualifications of alternative environments or social systems can be ranked from most positive to most negative. The aim should be to find or design the best educational and other *treatments*[App]. The policymaker was told to devise and arrange the best situations, in the general image of efficient American management. (That fixation too invited satire; see Callahan's *The Cult of Efficiency*, 1962.) Dewey and his allies in the Progressive movement did much to foster experimentation in education. Although highly conscious of students' individuality and the wisdom of cultivating it, they did not warm to the testing movement; Dewey feared that it could have antidemocratic consequences.

This Social Darwinism, like the first, ignored Darwin's basic principle that tied fitness to harmony between organism and ecology. For an extended account of the two movements, see Hofstadter (1955).

EVOLVING THEMES OF RESEARCH

Measures of General Ability and Their Application

The scientific psychology of the new century undertook quantitative, objective, statistical studies. Experimental psychologists devised formal comparisons of treatments. They treated differences among persons as sources of random error, hence of *uncertainty*[App] in results. It was to be controlled by equalizing groups and by attending only to averages.

Differential psychologists turned primarily to research using group-administered tests, which could collect data on large samples. With few exceptions, their investigations prior to 1930 were inspired by and elaborated on the theme of a single rank order of merit, passed on from Spencer and Galton. Those research agenda were incomplete, but important. For all the subtleties that have amended claims for "intelligence" in recent decades, general ability remains a central and useful *construct*. Later chapters repeatedly document the explanatory power of such an ability. Although Binet's individually administered test—especially in the revision by L. M. Terman—played a significant part in research on child development, group tests were the main resource for large-scale research and for educational decisions about individuals (except in special education).

Shortly after 1900, Charles Spearman in England developed group tests to study his conceptualization of general ability. Once he had developed a number of tests, he invented a systematic method—*factor analysis*[App]—to extract conclusions from patterns of *correlations*[App] among tests. Spearman concluded that a single property of the mind accounted for the tendency of the tasks he studied to rank people similarly. This thesis provided considerable support for the commitment of measurement psychologists to the construct "intelligence." They retreated from Binet's inclusive characterization to an emphasis on the cognitive, seeing abstract reasoning as the crux.

Spearman's ideas inspired the Raven matrix tests, illustrated in Fig. 1.1. Left-to-right changes follow one rule; top-to-bottom changes follow another. The examinee who infers these rules is to combine them, then is to decide which answer-option completes the pattern. Much research considered later examined performance on matrix items. (More difficult matrix tasks can be seen in Fig. 5.1.)

Small trials of group tests in the United States gave way to mass testing when the Army Alpha test was widely applied during World War I. It

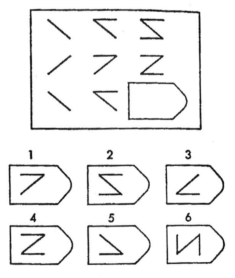

FIG. 1.1.   Matrix item like those in the Raven test. From Cronbach (1960). Copyright 1960 by Allyn and Bacon. Reprinted by permission.

stimulated a proliferation of group tests for schoolchildren—and, to a lesser extent, for job applicants. Most American tests emphasized verbal and numerical exercises. Terman indeed concluded that the best single indication of level of general intelligence was size of vocabulary.

Innumerable investigators have ranked some group of pupils or college students or graduates entering professional schools on a measure of aptitude, then compared those rankings with standings at the end of the school year or at the end of the training. An essentially consistent picture emerges (see pp. 99–104). Comprehensive measures—intelligence tests, or measures of the key skills of reading and mathematical reasoning—have substantial predictive power. So do some homogeneous tests that assess intellectual efficiency, the Raven test being a prominent example. For the present, we can speak of measures of general ability without considering the variation among tests.

With the growth of the testing technology, applied psychologists increasingly ignored the substantive roots of the concept of aptitude. *Aptitude* became nothing more than ability tested for practical purposes. Scholastic aptitude became synonymous with verbal and quantitative ability. Beyond this, some special abilities pertinent to certain school subjects or vocations were singled out. For example, predictors were sought for success in graphic art, and mechanical or clerical work. But these were atheoretical, and drew interest only for possible practical use.

Rankings from earlier to later tests were found to be highly consistent, although predictive accuracy declined gradually over longer intervals. The result fostered belief in the "constancy of the IQ," and also encouraged the belief that measured abilities represented inherited talent. Correlations of IQ with indices of family background were only moderate, which assured the measurers of that time that the tests recognized talent among the less advantaged.

A few formal studies were conducted in the 1930s to support the claim that attendance at nursery school would raise IQs of schoolchildren who started in the normal range, but such claims encountered bitter opposition—in part because they challenged hereditarian beliefs, in part because some of the data analysis was unsound. These intervention studies, like the studies relating pretests to educational outcomes, were black-box studies. The numbers summarizing pretests and posttests provided the basis for conclusions; it was rare for an investigator to look into the intermediate processes that generated superior or inferior performance.

How individuals adapted to situations was rarely studied before 1950, but we note three exceptions:

Processes underlying good or poor test performance (including affective processes) were examined in clinical casework.

Observations of problem solving, notably by Gestalt psychologists, could have influenced thinking about ability and its development, but did not.

Piaget made detailed analyses of the child's intellectual development.

Somewhat more needs to be said about Piaget's work, as it did eventually influence thinking about aptitudes.

Exhibit Pgt. Children Learn to Shift Viewpoints

Binet asked children to say what is wrong with an absurd statement like this: "I have three brothers: Paul, Ernest, and myself."[3] Only 30% of 9- to 12-year-olds could say what was wrong in that statement. There are three brothers in the family (count of a class), but a member has only two brothers (relationship). Piaget (1928/1969) saw confusion between the concepts as evidence of trouble in thinking about relations, and conducted structured interviews at several ages to trace the development of this element in intelligence.

Piaget started with questions about the child's own family and continued:

There are three brothers in a family: Auguste, Alfred, and Raymond. How many brothers has Auguste? And Alfred? And Raymond?

Are you a brother? What is a brother?

Ernest has three brothers, Paul, Henry, and Charles. How many brothers has Paul? And Henry? And Charles?

How many brothers are there in this family? (p. 98)

Consider: "What is a brother?" Before age 7, responses were at Stage 1—"A boy is a brother"—or Stage 2—"The second boy that came is called 'brother.'" About 60% of 7-year-olds reached Stage 3, speaking of a relationship between two persons. At age 9, 75% achieved this level.

Another series of probes showed similar stages in grasping "right" and "left" as relations:

---

[3]In this exhibit, we show male forms of questions, but parallel questions in female form (where appropriate) gave the same results. Also, to avoid numerous "him/her" constructions, we use female pronouns for respondents.

Stage 1 (seen at age 5 to 8). The child can hold up whichever hand is called for, but does not correctly point to the left hand of the interviewer facing her. "Right" and "left" are defined by the child's viewpoint.

Stage 2. The child now can "put herself in the examiner's position" and chooses the left hand. With objects A, B, and C set in a row before her, she has no trouble seeing A as "left." But she cannot grasp that B is both to the left (from the standpoint of C) and to the right (from the standpoint of A).

Stage 3 (usual at age 11 to 12). The child succeeds on the A-B-C questions and others that require seeing relations from various viewpoints.

In Piaget's interpretation, the child starts out "egocentric," seeing the world as organized with herself as center. Only gradually, through social interaction, does she perceive that others' worlds have their own centers. This enables her to "decenter," to consider a relationship from one standpoint after another.

This research is presented in *Judgment and Reasoning in the Child* (Piaget, 1928/1969, pp. 98–111 passim.). For related discussion in other places, see p. 62, 129.

Piaget saw intellectual operations as numerous and separable. Piaget, trained by Binet's former colleagues, began in the 1920s by analyzing how young children coped with some of Binet's judgment and reasoning tasks. He then developed tasks proofing a single concept, forming a series that scaled from simple to complex. On each task at each age, he examined how children described what they saw and did. In three books published in English between 1926 and 1929, Piaget suggested that children progress through stages, successively mastering intellectual controls. Exhibit Pgt illustrates his technique in this work: intensive interviews of children ranging considerably in age, identification of stages of development, and explanation in terms of an internal intellectual structure of which every child gradually constructs his own version. Binet's emphasis on self-regulation reappears in Piaget. But intelligence, instead of being an amorphous whole, was now seen as a repertoire of intellectual tools. Piaget's intensive studies were appreciated by American psychologists when they appeared, but they were rarely imitated. And, as they produced no scores, they did not influence how mental tests were interpreted. Only after 1955 did that change, as thought processes came to the fore in new curricula and in cognitive psychology, and as professional opinion turned away from hereditarian ideas of fixed ability.

Differential Prediction and Choice Among Treatments

Multiple Abilities.   Despite the variety of tests invented, the only usual division of general ability before 1930 distinguished verbal from quantitative reasoning. On the whole, the two kinds of ability varied together, but a large fraction of students and job applicants ranked notably higher in one than the other. Professionals concerned with employee selection and vocational guidance believed that there must be more than two significant, measurable abilities, and that a profile of scores would suggest what work a person is best fitted for.

The most influential figure in the movement to develop such profiles was L. Thurstone. Thurstone altered Spearman's factorial techniques so that, when applied to correlations within a varied collection of tests, they would identify distinct types of ability—spatial, perceptual, and so on.

Thurstone's group, and others, produced a number of test batteries—collections of tests yielding multiple scores—some of them for application to schoolchildren and (for career guidance) to adolescents. Rather few differences within the score profile had demonstrable predictive significance, however. A profile peak in mathematical ability sometimes permits "differential prediction"—prediction, for example, that a student will rank higher in a physics course than in general biology. But combining diverse scores into a prediction formula increased the power to predict grade average and other broad indices of success over the predictive power of a full-length "general" test by only a discouragingly small amount.

The ability constructs brought to prominence by Thurstone and by others who used his techniques are presented in chapter 3. Here we say only that this body of research is an important legacy for use in aptitude theory. The work of the Thurstone school of psychologists was not truly process oriented or theory oriented, yet Carroll (1976) considered them to have been the first cognitive psychologists. Theirs was again black-box research, asking how scores related to other scores rather than how each level of criterion performance was attained. The first step in the work, however, the designing of aptitude tests, required task analysis. In Carroll's words (1974):

> The tasks chosen for the ... tests were those which were regarded as having process structures similar to, or even identical with, the process structures exemplified in actual learning tasks. ... The tests were therefore measures of the individual's ability to perform the psychological functions embedded in ... or ... the information processing ... characteristic of the criterion learning tasks. The theoretical basis for assuming

similarities between aptitude tasks and criterion tasks might be of the vaguest intuitive sort; what mattered was the empirical confirmation of one's intuitions by standard test validation procedures. (p. 294)

Thurstone did not see factor analysis as sufficient. Its results were to be only an initial mapping of the cognitive terrain. It would "enable us to proceed beyond the exploratory factorial stage to the more direct forms of psychological experimentation in the laboratory" (Thurstone, 1947, p. 56). The topic of how aptitudes work Snow saw as a wilderness, one that should have been surveyed much earlier by "the cavalry" of correlational psychology. "Lee and his army could actually count on substantial help from Stuart's cavalry reports, but when most needed, the correlational cavalry was off somewhere sharpening its factor analytic swords" (Snow, 1980b, p. 27). Thurstone's impetus toward a differential psychology of cognitive processes was sidetracked in favor of exploiting the factor-analytic method.

Perhaps the high point of sophisticated application of measures of multiple aptitudes was the Aviation Psychology Program. During World War II, officer-pilots were needed in great numbers, and failures in training were frequent and costly. Psychologists from many backgrounds were recruited to refine or invent the widest possible variety of ability

---

Exhibit Dbs. Aptitude Tests Reduce Failure in Pilot Training

Early in World War II, a collection of aptitude tests was developed to select among men in the Army who applied for pilot training. Tryouts showed which tests helped predict who would graduate from training. Those tests were combined and the summary score reported on a 1–9 scale—a scale designed to have an average of 5 (and SD^{App} 2) in the full range of applicants.

As successive waves of applicants moved through the selection and training, tabulations from personnel records showed that the predictors worked remarkably well. DuBois (1947) combined data from a 2-year period late in the war. Of the 166,507 men in the cohort, 22% failed to graduate. Men above 6 in the prescreened group had superior prospects of graduating. For men scoring 3 or less, the risk of failure was more than twice the norm. There was a steep increase in graduation rates with aptitude level: 29% at Level 1, 58% at 3, 71% at 5, 83% at 7, and 96% at 9.

For related discussion in other parts of the book, see pp. 99, 107, and 238.

tests. Those that seemed most promising went into an aircrew selection battery. A few pages of biographical questions, keyed for interests and experience related at least indirectly to flying, brought in noncognitive characteristics. The summary score used for pilot selection gave particular weight to apparatus tests (coordination, choice-reaction time), technical vocabulary, and spatial ability (DuBois, 1947). Adding reading and mathematics tests to the composite failed to improve the correlation with graduation from pilot training, so these were not considered in selecting pilots. The data summarized in Exhibit Dbs implied a correlation of .45. This is impressively high, because only those admitted to pilot training were included. The correlation reached .65 when, in one wave of candidates, persons having poor test scores were not screened out before the training.

This research was a triumph for the multiple-aptitude concept. Twenty-two tests were given a systematic tryout, others having been dropped after limited screening. The formula that combined 13 of the scores and ignored the others was entirely atheoretical; it was just whatever weighted composite had given the best predictions during tryouts. The formula seemed to show clearly that learning to fly requires a complex mixture of qualities. (This result and the ones reported next may or may not conflict with recent prediction studies in the military, where information on diverse abilities added little predictive power to a reliable general-ability score [see Ree & Earles, 1997]. The tests in the battery of the 1940s were far more diverse than today's operational tests.)

Classification and Placement Decisions.   Selection of trainees merges into decisions about assignment to training. The aircrew research program formed two further combinations of scores from the test battery described previously, to predict success in navigator and bombardier training. The navigator composite counted chiefly mathematics, dial and table reading, and spatial ability. The bombardier composite consisted mostly of scores from apparatus tests. As neither was like the pilot composite, the finding was a large-scale demonstration that the makeup of aptitude differs with the task. Graduation was predicted with correlations of around .45 in navigator training and .30 in bombardier training (DuBois, 1947).

Distributing incoming candidates over the three types of training obviously called for classification decisions, not for in/out decisions in the manner of college admissions. (Only a modest fraction of the candidates who had passed a preliminary aircrew-admission test failed on all three composites and were deselected.)

After the war, Brogden (1957) formalized the logic of validation. He pointed out that, whereas a large correlation between aptitude and outcome is sufficient technical justification for a selection test, valid classification requires differential prediction. That is, one wants the formula predicting for Job A to do that well, and not to predict well in the others. With equally specific formulas fitting Job B and Job C, one has a valid set of tools for classifying.

Cronbach and Gleser (1957) noted that the same logic applies to tests used for placement in education. The general term *treatment* applies to instructional plans as well as to job assignment. Many a college obtains a writing sample from each entering freshman, and sends all those falling below a certain cut score to a remedial course rather than the standard English course. This policy is reasonable only if the remedial course makes low scorers more capable writers than the regular course would. Appropriate evidence would be obtained by a trial that randomly divides those who score below the cut score X^*, sends one fraction to the regular course and others to the remedial course, and at the end of the term collects writing samples. The analyst would plot end-of-term scores against pretest scores, in the remedial and regular groups; see Fig. 1.2, where the broken line summarizes possible results in the remedial class. Trend lines of this type are called *regression*[App] lines. When the two lines intersect as shown in the figure, the result supports the policy and the chosen cut score. Any other pattern would challenge the policy. Nonparallel trend lines are evidence of Aptitude × Treatment *interaction*[App].

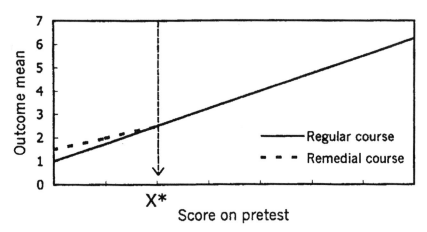

FIG. 1.2. Hypothetical comparison of outcomes for low scorers assigned to remedial English and the regular course. X^* is the cut score for selecting students into the remedial course.

Note that if the expected outcome for low scorers is not better after the remedial course, this challenges the validity, not of the test, but of the treatment in combination with the test. The appropriate response may be to modify the remedial course rather than to seek a better placement test. Thus, although a placement test is designed for sorting, it can enrich program evaluation. It would be an important contribution to theory of instruction to find out why the remedial writing courses in some colleges show the desired pattern of regressions, but those in other colleges do not.

Where a college requires that low scorers take the regular English class following the remedial course, a year-long study is suitable. In one design, students allowed into the regular class (including a sample of those who scored low on the placement test) took the posttest at the end of the first semester. Low scorers who completed the remedial-plus-regular sequence took the test after the second semester (Aiken, West, Schwalm, Carroll, & Hsiung, 1998). Again, two regression lines were compared, but crossover was not to be expected. At any level of the pretest, the remedial group ought to get better final scores than those of the same initial ability who took only one course. The policy question then is whether the benefit from the additional instruction is sufficient to warrant its cost. Aiken et al. saw mixed results in the colleges they compiled data for.

Individual Differences in Response to Instruction

Snow's Early Research at Stanford. The research design appropriate for placement studies combines experimental comparison of treatments with analysis of accuracy of prediction. Cronbach (1957, 1967a) argued that this design would provide better information on many scientific issues than conducting the two kinds of study separately, as had been the tradition. Cronbach went on to address the educational problem of adapting teaching to individual differences, by designing instruction to fit aptitude patterns. This approach would require:

> ... a new psychological theory of aptitude. An aptitude, in this context, is a complex of personal characteristics that accounts for an individual's end state after a particular educational treatment. ... [It] includes whatever promotes ... survival in a particular educational environment, and it may have as much to do with styles of thought and personality variables as with the abilities covered in conventional tests. ... Such a theory deals with aptitude-treatment interactions. (Cronbach, 1967a, pp. 23–24, 30, paragraphing altered)

That last phrase was soon compressed to "ATI." Exhibit Psc and the study by Aiken et al. (1998) provide examples of interactions. Note that a plot of the numbers presented in the exhibit would show crossing regression lines, like those in Fig. 1.2 but covering the whole range. Regression lines with unequal slopes indicate presence of interaction. The effect can have theoretical significance even when the lines do not cross within the range of the data. Results in small studies, however, must be viewed with caution (pp. 247–249).

Snow, who had completed an ATI study as a doctoral dissertation (see p. 110 ff), joined Cronbach at Stanford in 1966. Although their group carried out some empirical research from 1966 to 1969, the primary initial commitment was to review the numerous but scattered studies that had collected data on which a statistical check for interactions was possible. The initial grant period ended in 1969 and a book-length review was ready for publication about 1972. Because of an early wave of mergers and acquisitions in the book industry, the *Handbook for Research on Interactions* (Cronbach & Snow, 1977) was much delayed. Cronbach and Snow did report considerable evidence of interactions. But they found so many shortcomings in the experimental designs and analyses previously used that the book gave at least equal emphasis to what they had learned about research method.

Snow continued the line of research in the 1970s and 1980s, most of it under the flag of "The Stanford Aptitude Research Project."

Unfortunately, through the 1980s, the complexity of the problem and the failure of investigators to heed the methodological advice of Cronbach and Snow led (or misled) many educational psychologists to ignore or reject the ATI phenomenon. It should be clear to anyone who studies the literature that the ATI phenomenon is no fad. ATI are easily found, though the results on any one hypothesis are often inconsistent. Pascarella's firm replication is unusual, and that fact is instructive. "The same treatment" often changes its effects with change in the context of its delivery; such failure to replicate identifies a deeper issue for research. Educational researchers continue to make good use of ATI-style research in large-scale educational evaluations (see, e.g., Corno, 1988; Peterson, 1988). Aptitude research via the ATI paradigm is hardly dead.

Both Cronbach and Snow became dissatisfied with the basic ATI research design. Like traditional prediction studies, ATI studies were black-box inquiries. They reported little or nothing on the events occurring between pretest and posttest, hence lacked explanatory power. Moreover, treatment periods were often brief. Two weeks or less did not give students time to become familiar with a new instructional

Exhibit Psc. Instructional Support in College Calculus

Research prior to 1978 had suggested that students weak in readiness for instruction would achieve more if provided with "support." Pascarella (1978) set out to test this idea, identifying support with Keller's personalized system of instruction (PSI). Sixty students beginning calculus chose to sign up for a PSI section, which had these features:

Allowed for student self-pacing.

Provided a detailed study guide for each unit of material.

Offered scheduled tutorials for individual help and testing.

Provided optional lecture/problem-solving sessions.

Required complete mastery of each unit before moving on to new material.

Unit mastery was demonstrated by means of a unit test; students could attempt the test whenever they felt sufficiently prepared. Students failing the unit test were typically given a remedial assignment, and then could take further tests covering the same material until they demonstrated mastery. The 188 students who did not opt for PSI were taught by a lecture-demonstration method, with about 24 students per section.

A pretest on mathematical competence had been given at the start of the term; and the outcome measure was an achievement test at the end of the semester. Pascarella put pretest scores on a scale where 0 represents the mean of all students. Roughly two thirds of the students fell between −1 and +1 (1 unit equaling 1 SD^{App}). Here are smoothed mean outcome scores at five levels of the pretest:

Pretest Level	PSI Group	Lecture Group	Difference
2	105.2	103.2	2.0
1	102.3	93.0	9.3
0	99.5	82.9	16.6
−1	96.7	72.7	24.0
−2	93.8	62.6	31.2

The listing gives not the actual outcome means at each pretest level, but an estimate of what would be expected in a large sample;

that is to say, the fluctuations in the actual data are ironed out. The points indicate the positions of the two *regression lines*[APP].

The within-groups *SD* is 21, the treatment effect is large except at Level 2. The change in *effect size*[APP] from one level of pretest to another is even more striking. Pascarella confirmed this Aptitude × Treatment interaction in a second sample of students.

With PSI support, students weak in initial performance finished not much behind those strong at the outset. The regression line for the more supportive treatment was nearly flat. The correlation of pretest and posttest was only .22 in the PSI group, compared with .43 in the lecture group.

PSI support did little to improve the final performance of the students who were superior at intake; indeed, at the extreme upper end of the pretest range—around 2.5, say—the outcome difference vanished.

Notes: The contrasting treatment groups were not formed randomly, but they had similar score distributions on the placement test. Because those in the PSI group had opted for PSI, the groups surely differed in motivation.

The evidence for the greater effectiveness of PSI with students poorly prepared for calculus does not establish a generalization about supportive instruction. That can come only from studies ranging over courses, types of students, and types of support. Although PSI produced a higher overall mean than conventional instruction when all students were considered, PSI placed greater demands on instructor and students and therefore, in the setting Pascarella studied, would best be reserved for the students most likely to profit from it.

For related discussion in other parts of the book, see pp. 91, 98, 209, and 246.

method and adapt to it; yet instructional theory has to address the long-run consequences of installing an unfamiliar treatment plan. Adaptations to the instructional method, occurring over a period of months, can reverse effects seen in the first weeks. Observations of Wijnen and Snow on innovative medical education (Exh. WS) illustrate the point.

But the studies of the future should not focus on student classification. They should aim toward understanding why some kinds of persons are served well and some poorly by a style of instruction, or toward redesigning instruction to serve those students who do not prosper in the current course.

Early explanations were offered by J. Atkinson (see Exh. Atk, p. 44). In 1965 Snow had an opportunity to work with Atkinson, and with Heckhausen (who was pursuing a similar line and who is a major resource for chap. 6), in a postdoctoral summer institute at Stanford. Atkinson's theoretical proposals are reviewed in chapter 2. Here it adds perspective to mention that his research program was concerned with motivation, and sometimes with effects of motivation and ability in combination. Snow developed similar interests, as Exhibit WS testifies.

Exhibit WS. Medical Students Learn a Way of Learning

A Dutch medical faculty designed an innovative program to be taught mainly through small-group, problem-centered exercises. This departed markedly from students' previous instruction. An evaluation (Wijnen & Snow, 1975) projected student performance on periodic examinations against initial ability and stylistic aspects of personality. The aim was to describe the aptitudes characterizing students who did well (or poorly) in this new situation.

By the end of the first month, some of the highly able students were doing less well than expected, and some of average ability performed exceptionally. A *regression*[APP] line was imposed on the plot for the first midterm examination to mark the overall trend of outcomes relative to a Verbal Analogies pretest. This became the basis for defining regions in the plot.[4] Boldface, Roman, and italic type are used here to denote groups above, balanced around, and below the first midterm trend line. The rows refer to ranges on the verbal pretest.

Relative Outcome	Above Trend Line	Balanced Around Trend Line	Below Par
Ability: Low		C	
Low average	**B**		*D*
Above average	**A**		*E*
Very high			*F*

The underperformance of the small *F* group was striking.

Disproportionately, *E*s and *F*s described their work styles as independent and driven by motivation to achieve. They, and the **A**s, appeared to be less altruistic, less interpersonally oriented, and more task oriented than those in regions **B**, *C*, and *D*. The *F*s had the greatest amount of facilitating anxiety and the smallest amount of debilitating anxiety. Of all subgroups, the **B**s were on average the most interpersonally oriented and the least task oriented.

Seemingly, the situation's demand for a high degree of cooperation was well suited to the **B**s. In contrast, this instruction apparently conflicted at first with the independent, task-oriented style of the highly able *F*s.

By the 5th month of small-group exercises, the results for able students had reversed. The motivated, task-oriented *F*s had either adapted to the cooperative environment or found ways to learn on their own. *E*s moved similarly, to a lesser degree. Some of the less independent **A**s, in contrast, dropped markedly in rank as the work became more difficult.

The aptitude combination that went with superior performance at an early stage of instruction no longer applied. What initially appeared to be an aptitude for the new curriculum became an inaptitude later, at least for some students. Adaptation subtly changed the performance, and hence the aptitude requirement.

Admission or placement policies based on predictions from the initial data would have been ill-advised. Indeed, subsequent program revision was aimed at eliminating the differential-aptitude pattern, not at using it as a basis for classification. Finally, it is worth pointing out that the students in the *F* region resemble the high-G-low-anxiety students discussed at pages *121* ff. The report there is that in an experiment such students responded best with little teacher structuring and much student initiative.

For related discussion elsewhere in the book, see pages *19*, *115*, and *168*.

---

[4]The formal rules used to define regions are not fully laid out in the publications available (Snow, 1978a, pp. 87–88; Snow et al., 1996, pp. 287–288), and there are small numerical discrepancies in the reports. Our summary therefore gives the gist of the findings, without details.

Research on Processes.   In most aptitude research prior to 1960, an aptitude had been seen as something a person "has," in greater or less degree; however, Binet and Piaget (and not many others) held to a view of aptitude as a process, as something a person *does*. The rapid development of cognitive psychology in the years after 1960 made black-box research seem sterile. In contrast, intensive analysis of details within a problem-solving or learning activity could suggest how aptitude operates. Necessarily, intensive observation or measurement is limited to periods of short duration.

With Warren Seibert, Snow carried out one early study of short-term memory (Seibert & Snow, 1965). On the method and results, see Exhibit SS (p. 140). Here we mention only that laboratory equipment projected images of two stimuli in rapid succession, and controlled the time interval between stimuli precisely. Ability to report the first stimulus (a letter) changed with the interval; and different aptitudes seemed to matter, depending on the interval.

Around 1975, the Aptitude Research Project began to investigate aptitude processes. At the outset the research concentrated on cognitive processes, but it ultimately brought conation and affect explicitly into the picture. Most of the topics mentioned in this summary are covered at greater length in chapter 5 or 6.

Snow and his group were especially interested in variations of performance within persons. Going from one task to another of the same kind, the person might execute component steps in different sequences, or might change the steps themselves. That is, the person's approach would be likely to change from task to task or with experience.

We can illustrate the notion of approach—often labeled *strategy* in technical writing—with the aid of the matrix item in Fig. 1.1:

> John carefully puts the left-to-right rule of the matrix into words: "Add a line at the bottom." Next, he puts into words the flip-over rule for downward change and, combining the two rules, constructs in his head the needed configuration ("inverted Z"), and finds that image among the choices.

> Sara looks at the answers, then at the matrix. She perceives quickly that all figures in a column are similar, and concludes that 2 or 4 is the answer. Now she picks one of them impulsively and moves to the next item.

> Stephanie gets to the "2 or 4" conclusion and makes a careful check, imagining (let us say) "Z" in the empty space. At once, she perceives that rows 2 and 3 should not be the same. By elimination, 2 is the answer. If cautious, Stephanie might verbalize the flip-over rule as a check.

These distinctive response sequences bespeak preferred work styles as well as ability.

Most important, the Snow group thought, would be the person's facility in assembling component sequences and routes into a plan of attack, and in reassembling or adapting the assembled information as the work proceeds. If one could understand the individual's adaptation to ability tests (i.e., learning to cope), that should be the key to understanding similar differences during school learning. Adopting a phrase from H. Simon (1976), the group referred to the adaptive functions as assembly processes and control processes (Snow, 1978b, 1981; Snow & Lohman, 1984). We can illustrate by noting that Sara used insightful if unsystematic assembly, and did not exercise control in her final step. Stephanie did examine the soundness of her choice, and adapted to bad news with further assembly. John's every step of rule formation and combination was an act of assembly. Control entered, in his careful choice of words.

In short, the hypothesis is that aptitude for learning appears in the person's adaptations to within-task demands and opportunities, which change continually as fresh information is perceived or generated. Learners construct their performances by drawing on their resources and assembling, reassembling, and controlling interpretations as, at any moment, they perceive requirements and possibilities. Snow's group was able to investigate assembly and control by recording eye movements—John's and Sara's would have been quite different—and by an experimental breakdown of tasks in the manner of Sternberg (see p. 148). The group came to think that task complexity can be too great (or too little) for rapid learning; the appropriate level would vary with the person and type of task. Simple information-processing models are often adequate to characterize the routine performance of people doing work they find familiar and easy. A challenging task requires flexible assembly and control; no single model of information-processing steps will describe how everyone performs.

Snow's group aspired to integrate an information-processing account of aptitude for learning with factor analytic findings about abilities. They applied multidimensional scaling to old test-intercorrelation matrices, and to new ones of their own. Their aim was to represent the interrelations among ability tests in a way that could provide a more direct map of cognitive interrelations. The results were, as expected, consistent with factor analytic conclusions (see p. 65 ff). With this map in hand the group could study the degree to which information-processing models of single tasks imply a continuum of processes across multiple tasks, and could note where tasks diverged. After all, an information-processing theory of abilities has to depict similarities and differences between tasks.

Several studies at Stanford adapted Piaget's tactic of designing a series of tasks ranging from simple to complex. Typically, the fifth task in a series would require all the operations needed in the fourth task, and one additional. Lohman (1979) developed a "faceted" test of spatial reasoning by means of systematic combinations of figure merges and rotations. For a few of his items, see Fig. 5.6. The item set started with a single figural change and worked up the scale to problems that combined several transformations. (Merges and rotations are the facets of the design; analysis can check how items with m merges and n rotations, e.g., compare with items having n merges and m rotations.)

Instructive though these studies of process were, Snow came to feel that the research models remained too static. Psychologists have tended to think of applying a stimulus to which the person responds, which then leads to some consequence. Complicate this as one will by speaking of situation instead of stimulus, of the person's perceptions as shaping the response, and so on; the fact remains that psychologists have long thought of person and situation as independent variables. Snow hoped that a more adequate theory of aptitude would emerge if researchers (and practitioners) were to think of person-in-situation as a dynamic system. One catches a glimpse of these dynamics in Stephanie's performance: She responded to what was given and tested her interpretation; next, the matrix in effect spoke to her; and she then focused on a new subproblem.

In the 1980s and 1990s, the Stanford project turned to affective and conative processes. For example, Mandinach and Corno (1985) related learners' "cognitive engagement processes" to their success in a computer game that required complex reasoning. These authors, using data from Mandinach's dissertation (1984), reported how engagement processes varied with gender and ability. The process data included response patterns (errors and successes), latencies (reaction time and use of feedback), and other indicators of strategic planning and reasoning obtainable through the structure of the game. Mandinach also interviewed students about their experience, had them "teach back" their understanding of the game, and analyzed the notes they made. These data identified sets of people who seemed to engage with the game differently; the patterns ranged from passive to an active and involved gaming style.

One of the striking findings was that the more successful students spontaneously used self-regulation during learning (a sophisticated form of cognitive engagement), whenever task demands required intense engagement. The more successful students also tended to shift levels of cognitive engagement in response to feedback from the computer. Females were more likely than males to adopt one form of engagement and maintain it. Not surprisingly, success on the computer task and adaptation in cognitive engagement correlated with ability.

Later chapters amplify ideas on affect and conation voiced in many of Snow's writings (e.g., Snow, 1989b; Snow, Corno, & D. Jackson, 1996).

Learning in Groups. Prior to the 1970s, aptitude had almost invariably been thought of as aiding an individual confronting a task alone, yet students often work as a group. Group activity draws on aptitudes in a different way than individual study does, as was evident in observations Snow and a colleague made while Snow was visiting professor at a Dutch medical school. On their first encounter with instruction through group activities, students with an independent personal style had an adjustment to make. But, as Exhibit WS indicates, these bright people adapted over time to the novel demand.

N. Webb's study (1977/1978) of processes in group activity, a project study, came soon after. The policy of "ability grouping" had been debated for decades, but process-oriented studies were rare. What occurs, Webb asked, when students are placed for small-group work with others of similar ability? What occurs when the group includes all levels? She formed four-person groups of 11th graders all having high-, or low-, or midlevel mathematical ability, and other groups having one, one, and two members, respectively, from these ability strata. All groups worked on the same math exercises. The final tally of correct solutions in homogeneous groups (averaged together) was about the same as the average over all mixed groups.

Looking more closely, Webb found that members of a group created a powerful social context. Average posttest scores in mixed groups were good only when abler students took on the role of explainer, and the less able students asked for and used the help. High-ability and low-ability students did best in mixed groups. And, because most communications in mixed groups were between the high- and low-ability members, the middle-ability members did not benefit. Middle-ability students in homogeneous groups actively helped each other, and did well. In all-high-ability groups, there was little need for explanation; and in all-low-ability groups, the explanations were mostly partial or unsound.

Low-ability students did or did not benefit from opportunities available in the mixed group, depending on transactions in the group. Low mathematical ability was never an asset; but it was less handicapping in the right social environment. Able students seemed to have the aptitude needed for the lessons, but the mixed group offered them an advantage also. Those who chose to explain to their peers evidently solidified their own performance. Webb's study illustrates the value of detailed recording of instructional events (students in a working group for her; in other studies, tutor–tutee interchanges, the "thinking aloud" of problem solvers, and teach-back).

In further studies, Webb and others sought to trace causal influences in transactions within groups. Results were inconsistent from study to study when the total amount of communication was hypothesized to predict attainment. Webb extracted consistent patterns from those studies after she made a sharp distinction between giving and getting help, and another between help in the form of explanations and "help" that only supplied a correct answer or flagged a wrong answer (Webb, 1983). Giving more explanations was associated with a better outcome for the giver, at any level of ability. Giving nonexplanatory help provided no benefit to the giver, and was of limited value to the receiver.

As Webb's research program evolved, more effort was made to check results in a natural setting. In one recent study, students in 21 middle-school classes explored assemblies of batteries and resistors, individually or in three-person groups (Webb, Nemer, Chizhik, & Sugrue, 1998). Gender and ethnicity were deliberately mixed within groups, and in most groups the ability distribution was allowed to fall out naturally. The amount learned by students of low ability was greatest when the study group contained one student of high ability (a large effect), and there was some benefit to them when the ablest member was in the average range. A study of taped discussions showed their quality to be strongly related to the ability level of the ablest group member. Highly able students working individually learned somewhat more than those in wide-range groups. The adverse effect of heterogeneous grouping on the ablest, the authors judged, was enough smaller than the benefit to below-average students to justify mixing ability levels in school work groups.

THE PATH AHEAD, AND A VISION FROM SNOW IN MIDCAREER

The Topics of Later Chapters.   Chapter 2 continues our historical account, but says so much about recent frontier proposals that the term *history* barely applies. What should be evident at this point in our story is how much of the older research focused on prediction from ability tests, how much support nonetheless existed for recognizing affcon variables as part of aptitude, and how often aptitude was seen as "in the person" rather than as resident in the fit between person and situation.

Chapters 3 to 7 treat diverse aspects of aptitude. They can be read independently, there being little sequential dependency. Each can be characterized as a report on "the state of the art." Using Snow's drafts and notes, we have reviewed the relevant current thinking and summarized selected research supporting it. In many sections we point both to commendable features and to inadequacies of available research or theory, and identify dilemmas meriting attention in future work.

Chapter 3 reviews the experience of the profession in building taxonomic systems to represent aspects of aptitude. Major sections cover the cognitive and affcon domains, after which structures for conceptualizing situations are considered.

Chapter 4 deals with prediction of academic success, ranging beyond correlation of entrance tests with grade averages to consider a variety of predictors and a variety of outcome measures. A further section looks closely at a few particularly instructive ATI studies carried out by Snow or his students.

Chapter 5 reviews several approaches to tracing response processes, combining historically significant research from cognitive psychology with work of Snow's group that gave greater attention to individual differences. Throughout, the focus is on general fluid analytic ability (Gf), and what it might be. The chapter concludes with a provisional theory of Gf and a call for a broader theory that includes affect and conation.

Chapter 6 looks on affcon processes as coordinate with and working jointly with cognition. It stresses progress toward conceptualization more than methods of research. The findings included cannot be called "representative," because investigators have tended to set unique courses across this mostly uncharted sea. But the techniques reviewed do illustrate the wide range of possibilities.

Chapter 7 lays out the basis for the conviction now dominant among psychologists, that readiness to learn can be developed and that the educational programs effective for this purpose have identifiable features. The chapter is influenced by Snow's (1996a) invited contribution to a symposium on implications of research on intelligence for public policy.

Chapter 8 returns to Snow's view, expressed at the start of this chapter, that aptitude theory should be overhauled. Several of his writings indicated uncertainties and gaps in present theory, and suggested lines for new departures—but he did not set down a formulated theory. Chapter 8 is in effect a continuation of chapter 2, with its key concept of aptitude as residing in person-*and*-situation. It is our attempt to address "Where do we go from here?"—covering several subquestions more fully than Snow did.

Snow's Educational Vision.   This chapter has surveyed quickly much ground that was also covered in an invited chapter by Snow and Yalow (1982). That chapter was somewhat constrained by the request to discuss "education and intelligence," so that it could not give more than passing attention to the diversity of aptitudes or to basic psycho-

logical research. Even so, it is useful to insert here material from its final two pages, as an indication of the way Snow was thinking at that
time and of his larger vision. Nothing in his more recent writings suggests that he had changed his mind on these points, though additional
ideas entered his work both earlier and later. We begin with a summary
statement by Snow and Yalow:

> We have tried to emphasize in this chapter the importance of detailed
> process and content analyses of aptitude tests and instructional tasks,
> because this appears to be the more direct route to the construction of
> theoretically based instructional models. ... (pp. 567–568)

Snow and Yalow (1982) turned to "the advance of educational technology"—this, at a time when personal computers were just becoming
available:

> Up to the present, the advance has usually been slower than predicted,
> but it is the case that miniaturization has now broken many of the eco-
> nomic barriers. ... The hand calculator, the audiotape recorder, and the
> television receiver are already within the reach of virtually every student;
> the desk computer is close at hand for many .... Furthermore, advances
> in computer technology and in the field of artificial intelligence have been
> instrumental in the advance of cognitive psychological theory generally.
> As the computer is made more intelligent, more intelligent use can be
> made of computers. Computerized interactive instruction, computer-
> ized adaptive testing, and computerized guidance systems ... have been
> installed in some high schools and colleges. Computerized reasoning
> and problem-solving games have been placed in some elementary
> schools ....
>
> All this portends change in the medium of education. To the extent that
> intelligence is skill in this medium, changes in intelligence are also to be
> expected .... [T]he new technologies can be used to capitalize on charac-
> teristics of human aptitudes, that is, to extend and exercise aspects of in-
> telligence at new and higher levels, thereby strengthening and
> broadening the scope of intellectual skills already possessed by the indi-
> vidual. On the other hand, these technologies can also be used to ... do
> for individuals what they may not be able to do for themselves. Just as
> the writing tablet compensates for limits in human memory, the new
> technologies can be used to compensate for other information process-
> ing limitations of particular individuals or of all human beings. (pp.
> 568–569)

Snow, developing a strong interest in tutoring by computer, stimulated a number of students to analyze some piece of subject matter
closely enough to produce a tutoring program, and to test it, as in the
work of Lajoie discussed at page 199. Snow (1994), after citing other
examples, offered this conclusion:

[A]ll academic tasks are demanding in some ways—they carry certain component requirements that must be met to complete the task successfully. But academic tasks and treatments can be designed to remove demands that are unnecessary to reach instructional goals, and then to provide opportunities for persons to capitalize on their strengths and external supports and [on] prosthetic devices to compensate for their weaknesses. Of course, the design can also include auxiliary tasks aimed at removing learner weaknesses directly by training on missing or problematic components. (pp. 30–31)

Returning to Snow and Yalow (1982) we read:

We can sum up by envisioning a computer system—call it QUINTILIAN, or QUINT, for short. ... It has five component programs with which students can interact, called aptitude profile assessment, counseling and guidance, direct aptitude development, adaptive instructional treatment, and outcome profile assessment. Also, it comes in three levels, QUINT I, II, and III, for primary, secondary, and tertiary educational usage, respectively.

When a student signs on, QUINT administers an aptitude battery, using efficient adaptive testing methods to construct an aptitude profile. ... The aptitude battery includes tasks geared to provide detailed diagnoses of information processing strengths and weaknesses in various kinds of problem-solving situations, not merely ... scores on a few dimensions. It also includes sample tests to assess stylistic and strategic processes in learning and to build up provisional representations of the individual's *a priori* ... knowledge in a few broad and basic content domains. ... It informs the student about the nature of instruction in the system and why certain common goals of the instruction to come are generally valued, asking also for student opinions about these. The student enters personal perceptions, preferences and values about personal talents, life goals, various occupations, and alternative courses of study. ... The student can explore [occupational] alternatives interactively and iteratively, learning how to make educational career decisions intelligently in the process .... [C]omponents of the program work interchangeably to give instruction aimed directly at the development of relevant aptitudes and instruction adapted to fit the existing aptitude profile ....

The computer monitors knowledge and aptitude changes as the student progresses, builds up its representation of the student as it goes, and uses this to adjust its choices of succeeding items and tasks. This procession of minute-to-minute microadaptations occurs within broad alternative streams of treatment, chosen on the basis of the aptitude profile but updated month to month. There is thus both microadaptation and macroadaptation of instruction based on initial aptitude, goals, and subsequent learning history. Finally, the fifth component adds assessment of retention and transfer, provides intermediate advice and guidance, receives student suggestions and feeds back to adjust the representation of the student and various parameters of the program. Successive blocks of instruction run again through this cycle, with emphasis of different components depending on the stage and area of learning.

All this glosses over the complexities of producing such a system and the many nuances that might be built into it, but all of the components exist today in some form. (pp. 569–570; paragraphing altered)

Limited by their editor's charge, Snow and Yalow did not press the view that aptitude cannot be abstracted from the situation, which Snow emphasized in discussing theory of aptitude. Early in this chapter, we included a number of phrases from drafts for this book that stressed "a particular situation." Chapter 2 addresses the origins of that concern.

2 Conflicting Themes

THE CHALLENGE OF THE PARTICIPANT METAPHOR

Aptitude is primarily of interest where learning is taking place. Learning situations are not limited to schools and to training programs for employees; they include relations in the family, relations with health providers, relations with fellow employees, and, of course, any attempt to cope with a novel challenge. Outside the experimental-psychology laboratory, learning is taking place in group situations, embedded in an institution or in a continuing pattern of relationships with particular others. To be sure, the student doing homework may be alone; but the consequences of his or her activity will play out in tomorrow's schoolroom. In contrast, psychologists' experiments on learning have almost exclusively used settings stripped of social elements (save for the experimenter's delivering initial directions), and cognitive psychology has rarely gone beyond explaining how individuals perform in isolation.

Some recent proposals for reform of research and practice emphasize the role of person-to-person transactions in learning.[5] Sfard (1998) summarized developments to date by contrasting "the participant metaphor" (*pm*) with "the acquisition metaphor" (*am*). Put simply, *am* sees the developing person as "acquiring" knowledge, skills, habits, and so on; *pm* equates learning with becoming better able to participate in local groups and ultimately in larger communities including, for example, the scientific community. Although the *pm* reformers are engaged in empiri-

---

[5]Snow discussed major themes of this chapter in his 1992 and 1998 articles.

cal trials and have reported some conventional evidence, they are not interested in appraising person characteristics and do not look into the traditional questions about how they develop. Consequently, few *pm* writers mention aptitude, save in side remarks condemning use of tests for predicting and classifying.

Sfard ended her comparison by showing that *am* and *pm* complement each other, and together offer what might be called a three-dimensional (3-D) view of development. Resnick (1994) considered not the *am* as such but the view that biological maturation prepares the learner to acquire certain concepts at certain times. This, she argued, should be integrated with *pm* ideas. No doubt others will join Sfard, Resnick, and Snow in calls for the synthesis of these positions. After introducing aspects of the *pm* view, this chapter begins to consider in some detail how aptitude theory can incorporate ideas from the *pm* school. These ideas are revisited and developed in chapter 8.

The movement has some roots in both cultural anthropology and developmental psychology. Prominent among its inspirations are two theses of the Russian developmental psychologist Lev Vygotsky (1896–1934), who was himself influenced by non-Russian anthropologists and sociologists, as well as by Marx. One thesis is psychological: Personal intellectual development comes through interaction with others. The other is "sociohistorical": Knowledge has been created socially and will be reshaped by the learner's generation. Both theses are reflected in the label *situative,* which is often applied to reforms and theory of the *pm* type. We turn to this broader story after reviewing some work that, closer to individual development, can bridge between the *am* and *pm* schools of thought.

Intellectual Growth as a Social Process.   At the end of his report on the child's becoming able to take alternative points of view (Exh. Pgt, p. 15), Piaget stressed what later became a Vygotsky theme. Flavell's (1963) compact summary of Piaget put it this way: "In the course of his contacts (and especially his conflicts and arguments) with other children, the child increasingly finds himself forced to reexamine his own percepts and concepts in the light of those of others, and by so doing gradually rids himself of cognitive egocentrism" (p. 279). Some of Piaget's own words (1928/1969) prefigure today's *pm* writings about the teaching of mathematics: "Logical reasoning is an argument which we have with ourselves, and which reproduces internally the features of a real argument [between persons]" (p. 204). Whereas Piaget gave little thought to intervention in development, Vygotsky went on to propose that collaboration with another person is necessary for the transition from one intellectual stage to another.

Intervention efforts have used, among other tasks, matrices similar to Fig. 1.1. Elements that enter efficient performance include understanding what is wanted, focusing on how two diagrams differ, and encoding that difference (reflection, rotation, an added element, etc.). A child will perhaps solve many easy matrix tasks and then fail on harder items like Fig. 1.1. But a pattern may be observed in the inadequate performance.

Suppose that Sara's responses to many matrices appear to be haphazard choices between the correct choice and one giving the same overall impression (as do Choices 2 and 4 in Fig. 1.1). Sara is well beyond the guessing stage; only one additional control is required for consistent success. For Sara at this time, that next achievement is apparently within what Vygotsky (1978) called the "zone of proximal development" (ZPD).

A coach experienced with matrix tasks can, by carefully sequenced exercises and hints, help the learner. The mentor mediates between performer and task, showing her how to bring key elements into focus. What is learned may be a specific concept (e.g., "mirror image"), or a principle of self-regulation (e.g., Analysis is needed to confirm a gross visual impression that a figure satisfies the requirements).[6] Feuerstein developed a theoretical framework and a comprehensive intervention program that place at their center the "mediated learning experience" (Feuerstein, Klein, & Tannenbaum, 1991).

Vygotsky (1978) proposed to supplement a Binet-type mental age with a measure of the level of performance a child could reach "under adult guidance or in collaboration with more capable peers" (p. 86). The difference would dramatize the ZPD, and in many children would suggest a more favorable prognosis than the mental age does. This idea has been applied widely since about 1970—often under the name *dynamic assessment* (Grigorenko & Sternberg, 1998a, 1998b; Lidz, 1987, 1991). A. Brown, Campione, Webber, and McGilly (1992) reviewed their own work and that of other groups. It is easy to see this as a measurement-and-prediction activity, to be evaluated by calculating a traditional correlation with some outcome. And the scores on unaided individual performance, especially on transfer tasks, do seem to offer better prediction when collected after training than when collected before it. But Vygotsky was looking at absolute level of performance, not at quantitative differences between individuals. He was identifying those intellectual controls for which the learner showed promise of rapid development, that is, the instruction for which she was most ready. The performance of a low-functioning student in such an assessment (captured in a videotape, e.g.) may be used to give the

---

[6]A mentor would use simpler language in a Socratic dialogue.

regular teacher an optimistic view, but its richest yield is a short-term tutorial plan.

Many users of dynamic assessment are trying long-term programs that fuse instruction and reassessment, new plans being made week by week to fit the changing person. Treatments are of course individualized; the experimental design of ATI studies (p. 1.00) is inapplicable because there is no common "aptitude variable," and no group whose members all receive the same defined treatment. Evaluation reports have been consistently positive but generally limited to surface questions and small samples, hence unsatisfying (Snow, 1990).

Situated Cognition.   A. Brown et al. (1992), after 10 years of work with this type of training, reported dissatisfaction; performance gains did not often transfer to new tasks. Brown and her colleagues went beyond Vygotsky's proposal to use adults and qualified peers as mentors. They devised a scheme of "reciprocal teaching" among students at about the same level. Moreover, they went beyond practice in abstract reasoning to instruction on segments of the curriculum. Thus the dialogues excerpted in the discussion that follows come from lessons on related ecological themes that were as much as a year apart.

The Brown group is now carrying out studies ("design experiments"; A. Brown, 1992) that extend as long as 3 years with the same students; investigators and teachers have considerable flexibility in adjusting the curriculum and instructional practices as they observe their effects. The studies are not formal experiments with predesigned, contrasting treatments, though the participating classrooms may be compared with more conventional classrooms on end-of-year measures. The studies are trials of a generalized plan for teachers' tactical moves, a plan that is continually revised. Need for change of plan is signaled in student remarks that suggest puzzlement or misunderstanding, or from cues such as some students' inattention, or from someone's persistent failure to grasp large themes. Illustrative of Brown's analysis of class discussions is a report on the percentage of ánalogies that are truly explanatory ("Plants are food factories") rather than superficial ("Plant stems are like straws"). On tapes from one group in middle school science, the use of explanatory analogies rose from 10% to 37% as the school year progressed (A. Brown et al., 1992).

As for the more abstract situative or *pm* perspective, Resnick (1994) provided a plain-speaking account:

> The term situated cognition has come to refer to a loose collection of theories and perspectives that propose a contextualized (and, therefore,

particularist) and social view of the nature of thinking and learning. Students of situated cognition take as a starting point the *distributed* nature of cognitive activity—the fact that, under normal circumstances, mental activity involves social coordination. Getting a job done, figuring something out, are almost always done in coordination with others. ... [C]ompetence is highly situation specific. One must be good at behaving in a particular situation, with particular tools, and with particular other people. The situated cognition perspective, then, tends to lead away from a search for general structures of knowledge and toward the study of particular environments for cognitive activity and the knowledge attuned to those environments. At the same time, it stresses the social nature of cognitive activity and cognitive development. (p. 476)

In invisible ways, the history of a culture, an inherently social history, is carried into each individual act of cognition. (p. 477)

The premise is that all knowledge is socially constructed; that was a principal tenet of Dewey's pragmatism and of Vygotsky's sociohistoricism (Greeno, A. Collins, & Resnick, 1996).

A special aim of *pm* instructional programs is to make the learner an effective participant in "the community of learners and thinkers" (a phrase from A. Brown & Campione, 1990). Thus A. Brown and associates (1992) sought to instill strategies useful in grasping new subject matter.

They presented specimen transcripts of question-and-answer sessions in which one of the six group members acted as teacher, questioning the others about a brief text they have read. The children in the illustrative group were high-risk inner-city third graders. They had already learned some of the devices of "reciprocal teaching"—of probing to make sure that others are thinking clearly. During these sessions the teacher stayed in the background, occasionally praising the leader (e.g., "Good question"), rarely telling the leader how to reword a particular question, and almost never addressing other participants singly or as a class.

The student leader played the role of teacher as she had observed it.

Praising: "That's the answer I want!"

Imposing a standard: "I want the whole sentence" (following an accurate two-word response).

Probing for needs: "What's the story about? Anyone need clarifying?"

At one point she even set a soft-jawed trap. After it was agreed that lacewings eat aphids and other bugs she said, deadpan, "And they eat the farmers' crops." "No!" chorused the group; and the leader delivered a punchline about the difference between ecologically incorrect insects that eat crops and the good insects that check the bad ones.

The teaching role impels the leader to know the standards, which include relating specifics of any one story to larger themes. Moreover, as all take turns as leader, all are impelled to see teachers and learners as a single community with a shared purpose. They can apply the regulatory techniques to new topics. And they are learning norms of collegial practice, acceptable not only in the present group but in groups they will join later.

Children in Brown's program who come to appreciate the value of analogies couched in terms of underlying mechanisms have taken one step toward greater competence in developing scientific arguments. Various papers of Greeno (e.g., Greeno & the Middle School Mathematics Theory Application Project, 1998) likewise point out processes of mature mathematical work that can be identified when class members engage in a discussion, instead of applying prescribed methods to prepackaged exercises.

Criticizing the situative school, J. R. Anderson, Reder, and H. Simon (1996) saw *pm* writings as hinting that all instruction "should take place in complex, social situations" (p. 9), and found that excessive. No, they say; the designer of learning activities need not, should not commit all of an instructional program to one style. Many techniques have their uses, for example, didactic explanation (useful in teaching sexing of chicks), extensive out-of-context practice (as with violin playing), and scripting of intellectual tasks to highlight single subtasks in turn (as in writing computer programs). See also J. R. Anderson, Reder, and H. Simon (1997) and Schoenfeld (1999). In a reaction defending the situative view, Greeno (1997) seems not to disagree with this advice, but denied that the *pm* school wants to use group learning exclusively.

Sfard's picture of contrasting metaphors no doubt seems like overstatement to some adherents of each school of thought. One can read many remarks from the situative school as echoing principles long a part of the thinking of more traditional educational psychologists. Rejecting nouns such as *knowledge* in favor of verb forms such as *acting* and *recalling* dramatizes John Dewey's (1916/1966) central thesis that one validates a bit of knowledge only by using it in some context. Most writers on aptitude would reject the suggestion that they think improving ability is simply "acquiring"—a process of input received and stored. Psychologists of many types have argued convincingly that any message retained is actively transformed to mesh with preexisting cognitive structures (which are themselves transformed in the process). Piaget's books of around 1930 and Frederick Bartlett's *Remembering* (1932) made that point. The divergence between schools, then, apart from preferred rhetoric, may be no greater than that among viewpoints within schools.

For this book, the most significant point made by the situative school is that the concept of aptitude "in the person's head" should be replaced by aptitude "as a property of person-in-situation." This was the crux of Snow's effort to plot a course toward a new theory, and it would be a mistake to identify the theory primarily with learning in groups. The possibilities were dramatized for Snow at a gathering of psychologists (with experience in experimental psychology or differential psychology or both) organized in 1988 at the University of Minnesota; for the proceedings, see Kanfer, Ackerman, and Cudeck (1989).

Jenkins, in his concluding evaluation of the conference, criticized the presentations for typically paying little attention to the situation, and treating the person as separable from the situation. Jenkins noted, for example, that for decades laboratory studies of paired-associate learning had standardized conditions, not because they produced particularly typical results, but because they gave results compatible with the available theory. Hence the "laws" reported from the standard experiments were emphatically not general, even for paired-associate learning in mixed situations. Jenkins (1989) criticized work on individual differences for overreliance on artificialized tasks and for leaving cognitive processes entirely "in the head." At the end he said:

> [I]t is necessarily the case that the organism and the environment are a single interacting system, not two independent components. This is not to say that there is not a skin that separates the two, but rather that the skin is not a wall that separates two independent entities. The organism and the environment have shaped and have been shaped by each other.
>
> I hope that in 20 years ... , we will have really important things to say about psychological structures of organism-in-the-real-world. (p. 491)

As early as 1977, Snow had written forcefully on the central place specifics of the situation should have in theory about individuals' response to instruction. (Snow, 1977, p. 12.) This topic was not prominent over the next dozen years, but an article Snow (1989a, esp. p. 45) evidently had sent to press prior to the Minnesota conference shows close agreement with Jenkins. Perhaps Jenkins' talk encouraged Snow to press his subsequent theoretical agenda toward greater attention to situations.

A PRELIMINARY RECONCILIATION

The preceding sections, along with the sketch of history presented in chapter 1, show that concepts of aptitude favored at different times and in different communities of investigators have conflicted. The remainder of this chapter suggests a path toward resolution of the conflict, with the aim of redefining the topic and stating the mission of

tomorrow's aptitude theory. To develop a theory that adequately relates knowledge about aptitudes to other branches of applied and general psychology requires the creation of new terminology, and we
(following Snow) make some moves in that direction.

The *am/pm* contrast was a useful way to dramatize an important
conflict in today's literature. It was helpful also to have from Sfard and
Resnick analyses of the "participant" or "situative" positions—at odds
in some respects with traditional views. But without questioning the
potential value of an interactive classroom group as stressed by A.
Brown and by Greeno, we shift the spotlight away from the theme of
participation in order to address theoretical matters.

Tradition placed the locus of ability "in one's head." Personality
traits and motivations were likewise seen as in the person until a new
wave of thought (e.g., Magnusson & Endler, 1977) placed the emphasis
on person-in-situation. Certainly, conventional aptitude testing had as
its premise that aptitude resided in the person and went with him into
any new situation—"a-in-p." Only the work spawned by *Explorations
in Personality* (Murray, 1938)—notably in assessment for wartime co-
vert operations (OSS Assessment Staff, 1948)—had begun to acknowledge the role of the situation and placed primary emphasis on
identifying which types of stressor and other situational features a particular man or woman could be expected to cope with.

Identification of aptitude with readiness for a particular situation,
which Snow stressed in his writings of the 1990s, is fundamentally different. Whatever tomorrow's situation, the person will enter with certain characteristics. These are, if you will, in the head. But the nature of
the situation and its perception determine which of these characteristics are resources, which are liabilities, and which are irrelevant.
Therefore, a premise for tomorrow's theory is the theme that aptitude
is to be identified with person-in-situation—"a-in-p-in-s."

A theory of aptitude must deal with both concepts: aptitude as
stored within the person, and aptitude operating in the person-situa-
tion union. One of our problems is to disentangle the two. We identify
the traditional a-in-p notion with the person's unique store or repertoire of propensities. Propensities influence response to certain situations, functioning as aptitudes or inaptitudes in the p-in-s sense.

A Suggestive Theory From the 1970s

We start by recapitulating some of the theory put forward by Atkinson
and his associates in the 1970s. It addressed the core agenda of this
book, but without Snow's emphasis on cognitive processes or the
structure of situations.

Let us read Fig. 2.1 from right to left. Many important qualities of a person, at least after schooling begins, are the cumulative effects of her past performances on countless tasks. Her choice among tasks depends on her motives at that time and on the situation. (Snow adopted J. J. Gibson's term *affordances* for what the figure refers to as incentives and opportunities.) The adequacy of performance on the chosen task depends jointly on ability and strength of motivation, as described in Exhibit Atk.

The box labeled *Personality* refers to the ensemble of characteristics—a cumulative effect from the past—that the person brings to the immediate setting. (Many *am* writers would have used the label *Aptitude* for that column.) Finally, at the far left, is the conventional statement that the person is the product of nature and nurture.[7]

The Inclusive View of Aptitude. Both Atkinson's group and the Kanfer–Ackerman group (whose work we cite often) align with those writers mentioned in chapter 1 who included interests, styles of self-regulation, and other such aspects of personality within aptitude. Those writers all stretched the meaning of aptitude beyond its traditional iden-

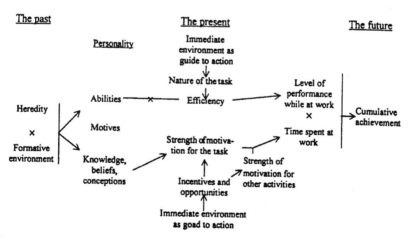

FIG. 2.1. A theory of performance and development. From Atkinson (1974). Copyright 1974 by V. H. Winston Adapted by permission. Note: The three multiplication signs link variables whose effects multiply to produce the effect seen to the right of the pair.

---

[7]This shorthand statement is useful as a placeholder. Responding to biological "nurture" is, however, an active process for which some such flow chart as Fig. 2.1 could be devised.

Exhibit Atk. How Motivation and Ability Combine

The research program of J. W. Atkinson was concerned with motivation to achieve, amplifying H. A. Murray's construct "need for achievement" or nAch. This is not ambition but rather an active interest in overcoming intellectual challenges (not necessarily academic ones). Using the "thematic apperception" technique of Murray and Morgan, Atkinson showed pictures that had deliberately been left ambiguous; the respondent was to make up a story to fit the picture. The level of nAch was inferred from the motives, concerns, and satisfactions attributed to central characters in the stories. Adolescents and adults scoring high on nAch typically make a confident effort when facing tasks.

Atkinson measured also the failure-avoidance motive, by means of an anxiety (Ax) questionnaire. Anxious persons find risk unpleasant, feeling threatened when they think an undertaking may fail.

Many lines of evidence led Atkinson and his associates to the notion of "resultant motivation." In the basic empirical work, "resultant motivation to achieve" (T_A) was represented by nAch + Ax (after appropriate scaling). Further motives may be added into T_A. Fig. 2.2 is a theoretical proposition, not a plot of particular results, but it purports to integrate a great number of observations. For reviews of the research see Atkinson and Raynor (1974) or Heckhausen, Schmalt, and Schneider (1985).

The left panel argues that an arch-shaped trend relates efficiency to motivation. At the optimum level of arousal, nAch and Ax are in balance. At the peak, eagerness to succeed is constrained by desire to avoid failure; consequently, impulsiveness is kept in check. The right panel represents the theory that forecasts production by multiplying ability by the efficiency index from the left panel. Atkinson (1974) applied this theory specifically to mental-test scores, arguing that they reflect ability and motivation jointly, not intelligence alone.

For related discussion, see pp. 113–115, and Exhibit Csk.

---

tification with cognitive abilities or with a single ability usually called intelligence.

Early in the modern period, Binet saw that successful performance in "intellectual" tasks depended on persistence and self-criticism. In his day and in more recent times, reasoning was seen to be more than "rea-

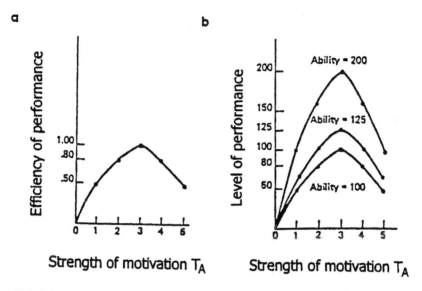

FIG. 2.2. Suggested relationships between ability, motivation, and performance. From Atkinson (1974). Copyright 1974 by V. H. Winston Reprinted by permission. Panel a: How efficiency changes with motivation. Panel b: The same effect on performance, in groups of different ability.

son" alone. And most writings on readiness gave prominence to motivational and emotional factors. Even the conservatively trained aviation psychologists of World War II (Exh. Dbs, p. 17) made a place for motivational variables via a biographical inventory. Characteristics considered in an aptitude theory should range widely, over all reasonably stable properties, cognitive or otherwise, that influence adaptation.

Snow had no quarrel with those like Thurstone who devoted years to the study of mainly cognitive abilities, or with Carroll and his sources who integrated such abilities into a structure. But he was insistent that an ability test is unlikely to be a purely intellectual measure. Binet's tasks were intellectual problems, but Binet concluded, in effect, that adroitness in using knowledge was more important than brute "brain power." Likewise, an important element in moving a child through the zone of proximal development on (say) the matrix task is training in deliberate self-monitoring—self-discipline rather than increased command of symbols. Theory of ability is in a blind alley if it cannot, in the next decades, be connected firmly with noncognitive aspects of performance. See a symposium on this topic edited by Collis and Messick (2001).

Achievements as Aptitudes.   We also propose to declare settled the conflict between achievement and aptitude as ideals, or between knowledge and analytic skill as hallmarks of intelligence. Recall that the matrix task was and is seen by many psychologists as a particularly good measure of the essence of mental ability, although it makes precious little use of "knowledge." And recall, alongside that, Terman's identification of size of vocabulary as the best single indicator of intelligence.

The only reason for the historic distinction between aptitude and achievement was the observation that some persons who had little schooling or had responded poorly to school made comparatively good scores on tests that did not require recall of material from school lessons. The wish to recognize such talent was a valid motivation. Still, lesson-based knowledge is a part of aptitude, and improved thought processes ought to be a continuing goal of schooling. These abilities are not "given."

Surely few would quarrel today with counting knowledge as part of aptitude. Courses and lessons at all levels of schooling are sequenced in recognition of the fact that the course given later relies on competence and factual knowledge acquired in the earlier course. (This is not to say that algebra must be taught before trigonometry. Rather, once the trigonometry course has been placed second, it is planned on the assumption that the students can deal with equations.)

Regarding the preferred goals of schooling, debate will probably never end. Recent years have seen battles in many communities between, for example, those who fear that basic calculation skills are being neglected and those who advocate learning-by-discovery to advance "the ability to think mathematically." Only a rarely doctrinaire advocate of "back to basics" would say "No" flatly if asked, "Should schools teach students to think?" Thus the issue reduces to questions of timing and extent. There is consensus that schools should be improving analytic processes, and it should not be hard to extend the agreement to the motivations and styles that affect thinking.

Oddly, Atkinson placed "abilities" and "knowledge" differently in Fig. 2.1, though both are placed within the box we would label *propensities*. Although we agree that knowledge can affect strength of motivation, motivation is a small part of the fruit of knowledge. Whatever ability is required by the task at hand will almost surely include particular knowledge.

Another distinction to be put aside is the identification of aptitudes (and personality) as a topic in differential psychology rather than general psychology. Measurements do display differences among individuals, but when a person confronts a task the critical question is whether her readiness is at a sufficiently high level, not her ranking in readiness.

That was one of Vygotsky's main points. To be sure, some applications of measurements in selection are intended to capitalize on individual differences. But occasions for selection are rare, compared to the number of occasions where the aim is to fit treatment to the individual (including those choices among situations she herself makes).

Emphasis on the numerical level of school achievement, and on comparison of scores with standards rather than with norms have been increasing. In the study of personality, whether the purpose is clinical or scientific, there is a long tradition of describing the individual in an integrated portrait, and emphasizing her unique perceptions of her circumstances. Although portraits differ, each person is studied in her own integrity and, where appropriate, a match to suitable situations is sought. This attempt to see the person whole, exemplified in Exhibit Csk, generates insight that cannot be attained via traditional measurements reported as comparative standings.

To give up the exclusive identification of aptitudes with individual differences does not require abandoning traditional statistical techniques of correlation and its derivatives. They have special functions; but correlation-based studies will contribute to theory, not constitute it.

The Repertoire of Propensities

We now come to the major reformulation mentioned earlier. The fundamental concepts for theoretical elaboration are (a) the person's propensities, (b) the person's transactions with a situation, and (c) the change in propensities that results. Atkinson, Lens, and O'Malley (1976) made almost exactly this distinction when they quoted two historic truisms in psychology: $P = f(H, E_F)$ and $B = f(P, E)$. At the point of entry into a situation, the person is the product of her heredity and her "formative environment"—the traditional nature–nurture distinction. And an action that takes place in a new environment depends on what the person brings and on the qualities of the situation.

Propensities is a more suitable term for what the person accumulates and brings to the situation than *aptitudes*. We develop with some care the interpretation of the term *propensity* and its relationship to the term *aptitude*. The noun is associated with the adjective *propense,* one of whose dictionary definitions is "ready." Thus, a key virtue of the new word is that it encourages us to distinguish readiness for a situation from the total repertoire. The person brings in an array of propensities. Some of these act as aptitudes or inaptitudes when brought into play by a situation. Propensities include affective and conative characteristics, whereas tradition has often identified "aptitude" with the cognitive.

We have used and continue to use the term *repertoire* (cf. Tyler, 1976, p. 24), but *repertoire* may not be the ideal word. A repertoire is usually varied, hence capable of suiting many circumstances. But the concert performer makes a conscious selection from a professional repertoire, whereas everyday response is shaped in part by propensities of which the respondent is unaware. We therefore freely substitute other collective nouns: set, array, collection, and so on.

Propensities are probabilistic. This is obviously true of a style such as proneness to check numerical results, but it is also true of abilities. Asked to recall the capitals of the 50 states, a person will recall some without hesitation (probability 1.00); in other instances will be confused between two prominent cities—is it Concord, NH? or Manchester? (probability .50)—and on some states will draw a blank (probability .10, say, over occasions). Another example is Bartlett's (1948) work on motor skills. Suppose that training for a task brings people to the point where all of them satisfy the criterion of proficiency on 100% of trials at the training center. What percentage will each person reach under distracting conditions? when fatigued? Under those circumstances, trainees who "qualified" will spread over a range of probabilities.

Any reported probability of successful performance is necessarily conditioned by the sample of situations considered; probability refers to a universe of objects or events. For example, when the teacher dominates class activities, Student X may be prone to resist with probability .05, considering a broad universe of teachers. When a certain Miss Green dominates class activities, we find Student X prone to resist with, let us say, probability .20. Probably none of the "when" clauses such as these fully represents how X's propensities are organized, but we can be sure that the activation of existing propensities is situationally conditioned. Activated propensities become aptitude to perform well or poorly in the present situation. Thus even recall of state capitals will be conditioned by whatever triggers performance anxiety in the individual.

The array of propensities is multivariate. Development consists of tuning particular qualities, increments of knowledge, refinements of skills; it is not an indefinable overall growth in one direction. Of course, development may also degrade some of the propensities by bringing confusion about a concept, or a self-doubt, or satiation with some former enthusiasm.

When we speak of propensities, we refer to tendencies that are only relatively stable. A person's response to a task is conditioned by many untraceable factors, including the unique experiences of the preceding hour or day; but until a theory gains command of regularities it cannot hope to deal with myriad temporary influences.

All the propensities save those that follow most directly from biology are achievements, the fruit of experience. To be sure, thinking of affective "achievements" does not come easily, because "achievement" has seemed to suggest intentional acquisition. Many achievements are products of implicit undirected learning.

The Developmental Picture and the Underlying Transactions

Figure 2.3 suggests how propensities develop. Propensities, their conditioning factors, and the associated probabilities evolve throughout life. The spiral, cut out of the life span for purposes of our scheme, can represent several years of development, or a month, or a single class hour. When the time scale is short, the segments represent brief events, perhaps completion of a single exercise, or even a single move in attack on a problem.

All nonbiological development arises from very brief transactions with situations. In any experience, the person's propensities are somehow altered. We have shaded one segment in Fig. 2.3 that, enlarged in Fig. 2.4, amplifies the idea of transaction.

The spiral is intended to suggest that the person repeatedly encounters situations of much the same style (but not with the regularity of the spiral). In the domain, there will be change over time in the person's fund of information, information-processing skills, self-concept, interest, and many other characteristics.

Small impacts accumulate, organize, and stabilize, and, in the long run, reshape the repertoire. They maintain aptitudes. It may be found that patterns of aptitude emerge, governed by general principles of adaptability and stability. These processes may be common to all complex dynamic systems and apply on different time or space scales. The study of dynamic systems has advanced in recent years by integrating insights from psychology, linguistics, biology, neuroscience, mathematics, and computer science (see, e.g., Kelso, 1995). The person–situation dynamic model that Snow was working on has begun to move along similar lines.

Development can be traced on coarse or fine scales. An observer may integrate the continuous stream of transactions over any preferred period. A teacher interacting directly with a student will concentrate on an immediate response, and not on the consequences for development even to the next day. The same teacher, later reflecting on the student's growth, is likely to sum up over an entire term. If the figure is taken to represent 1 class hour and each segment represents 1 minute, a spiral perhaps 100 times as high would be needed to depict a one-semester course.

Exhibit Csk. Flow as a Source of Commitment and Extended Learning

Cumulative achievement results from ability combined with optimal motivation, according to Atkinson's theory (p. 42 ff). Effort is greatest when the thrust of desire to achieve is balanced by the braking force of motivation to avoid failure.

A strikingly similar theory has been advanced by Mihaly Csikszentmihalyi and associates, and supported by a novel kind of evidence. Cumulative achievement in a sport, craft, or school subject comes from persistent, intent engagement. Commitment that generates enthusiastic participation and a feeling of "flow" builds skill; also, through cumulated pleasure, it strengthens commitment to the field. A person is most likely to experience flow when she is challenged by a task *and* feels that her abilities are sufficient to meet the challenge. Here also, a balance between perceived opportunity and perceived threat is the key. Shifting the balance to one side begets boredom; shifting the other way breeds tension.

Flow, according to Csikszentmihalyi (1975), arises in "autotelic" activities that are carried out for no tangible reward or credit. The experience itself is the main goal. The activity is its own reward because the person presses against her own limits, and that makes her keen to stay in the field and learn everything about it.

Whereas most modern research on motivation has collected scores of some kind, or interviewed people about sources of satisfaction and concern, most research on flow is based on a record of present feelings in a microsituation. Random bits of experience are sampled by "the beeper method." Each of the adolescents recruited for the typical study agrees to carry a pager at all times; when the pager signals, the student fills out a short report on the experience in progress. Files are studied both individually and statistically. The following description of Josh represents the kind of information available, but emotional tension figures larger in some lives.

A high school freshman, Josh was into sports, rock groups, and otherwise "fitting in" comfortably. An interview showed Josh to be well aware of his competence in math:

> [But] math is part of the generally uninteresting province of school, a typically boring place. ... Of the things he admits enjoying about math, competition with the school's math team stands out

> because it provides a sense that he "knows what he is doing," that he is in control of a problem. ...
>
> Compared with the guarded enthusiasm of the interview, the beeper responses showed that math provides some of the most rewarding experiences of his young life. Over 25% of his pager responses during the week ... involve mathematics in some form. Most of those instances involve computers: playing chess against a PC, reading an article about computer poetry, trying to write a program that will play a rock song, watching a program "completely blow up." (Csikszentmihalyi, Rathund, & Whalen, 1993, p. 127)
>
> The sampled reports can be rated, and the resulting numbers can be averaged over kinds of situations or groups. The numbers entering the averages reported here are something like an effect size[App], comparing a kind of activity to the average for all situations. The Csikszentmihalyi (1997) study placed beepers with some 200 teenagers identified as having an exceptional talent for athletics, art, music, math, or science. Their feelings during extracurricular activities (on a scale where 0 means indifference) reached means of 0.4–0.5 on involvement and sense of potency, and of 0.2–0.3 on sense of skill, self-esteem, and challenge. During voluntary classwork, average scores clustered around 0.2—generally positive. But obligatory classwork elicited only one strong reaction, an average of 0.4 on challenge. Means on other scales clustered around –0.1; either the classwork was unrewarding, or positive responses of some youngsters were offset by negative reactions in others (Csikszentmihalyi, 1997, pp. 180–181).
>
> For related discussion see p. 50, 169.

An adequate theory of development may be able to account for processes on all time scales. Or, as in the span from ecological biology to molecular biochemistry, alternative theories for alternative scales of analysis may be required.

The segment carried to Fig. 2.4 represents a single transaction with a situation, and the consequence. To simplify, we consider only a person reacting to and acting upon a situation by herself. At every moment she is "in a situation"; hence a variegated ribbon of situation tracks alongside the developmental spiral. For graphic purposes, an empty space separates person and situation in the figure.

When she enters situation S, a rapid act of perception occurs. The situation offers possibilities ("affordances" we call them later, p. 54),

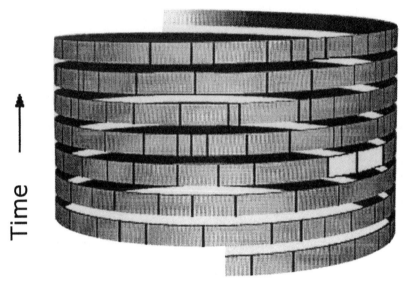

FIG. 2.3. The repertoire of propensities viewed over time. The two white cells are examined more closely in Fig. 2.4.

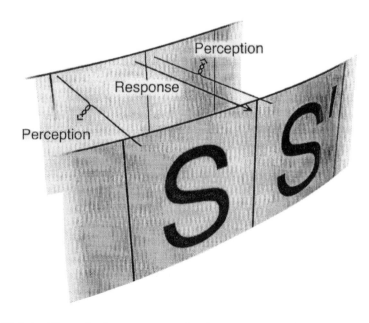

FIG. 2.4. The cycle of response to a situation.

hence an arrow comes from S. The person notes some of these; that active response is symbolized by an arrow pointing forward. The two kinds of information jointly produce the perception. It suggests to the person a response, symbolized by the right-side arrow pointing back to S. In our schema S changes to S', and a new cycle starts.

Much activity occurs between perception and response. The theory of aptitude being developed is primarily concerned with these intermediate processes. Atkinson's diagram (Fig. 2.1) shows one set of postulated actions. Our summary Fig. 6.1 sketches a more elaborate conceptualization of the internal events. To unpack any such diagram is to articulate a theory of aptitude.

An example gives body to Fig. 2.4. A woman climbs into the seat of her car (S). She perceives the familiar setting. Sensing no impending problem, her propensity is to turn the key for the starter. Whatever happens—even "nothing"—the situation changes. The perception-action-interpretation-action sequence goes on until it reaches some endpoint.

The change from S to S' may, in this case, be the audible start of the engine. Perceiving that the car has started, the driver very likely puts the car into gear. If turning the key produces no sound, the surprise brings into play other elements of her repertoire. Every reader has been in this dead-starter scenario and knows the possible range of hypotheses, emotions, and overt responses; the reader also knows that each such sequence of events does a bit to foster self-assurance, or a sense of mechanical incompetence—changes in propensities.

At the moment of feedback, when the person's trial response is confirmed or disconfirmed, the incremental effects on propensities are recorded in the nervous system. The feedback is often far more than an indication of right or wrong. In a class recitation, a student can sense much more from the experience of developing the answer, from the quality of the perceived response, and from the reactions of classmates.

Seeing aptitude as a property of the person is not incompatible with seeing aptitude as a property of person-in-situation. The former matches the concept of propensities as *potential* aptitudes. The second matches the image of transactions between person and situation. Both *am* and *pm* views have their place. The big *am* picture of Fig. 2.3 can be accepted without diminishing the significance of the myriad events on the scale of Fig. 2.4.

In an adequate formulation, person-in-situation will include the predisposition and postdisposition of the individual, being attentive to individual variation within and across situations. A concept of transfer of propensities into, through, and out of present activity is needed. Snow has used Gibson's notion of affordances to explain how propensities are activated in the situation.

The situation in a sense presents itself to the respondent. That is to say, stimulus patterns become available to the sense organs. J. J. Gibson's ecological psychology (1979/1986) and his term *affordances* (see Greeno, 1994) provide a way to think about the interchange; the person makes use of the situation and in so doing alters the situation. When Gibson, writing as a general psychologist, spoke of "the animal," he of course included humans:

> The *affordances* of the environment are what it *offers* the animal, what it *provides* or *furnishes*, either for good or ill. [The term] implies the complementarity of the animal and the environment [as in an ecological niche]. ... [A] niche is a set of affordances. (pp. 127, 128; emphasis in original)
>
> In architecture a niche is a place that is suitable for a piece of statuary, a place into which the object fits. In ecology a niche is a setting of environmental features that are suitable for an animal, into which it fits metaphorically. (p. 129)

We might speak of the menu of affordances the situation brings to a transaction, the counterpoint of the repertoire of propensities. When one of the propensities is responsive to one of the affordances, we speak of attunement.

For Gibson, affordances[8] nourish the union of observer and situation. A species is attuned to notice a subset of the affordances and to react in particular ways. Within the specie's norms, each individual has its own ways of reacting. Michaels and Carello (1981) elaborated as follows:

> To say that affordances are perceived means that information specifying these affordances is available in the stimulation and can be detected. ... To detect affordances is, quite simply, to detect meaning. (p. 42)
>
> Whether an animal flies, swims, walks, or slithers; whether it pecks, nibbles, sucks, or licks; whether it smokes, watches television, or mugs old people will "determine" the affordances it can detect. Because information specifies *behaviors* that are afforded and because different animals have different sets of [aptitudes], *affordances belong to animal-environment systems and nothing less.* [Thus] information about affordances is "personal"; it is unique to particular animal-environment units. (pp. 42–43, emphasis in original)

The ecological theory sees any of the person's characteristics as irrelevant until there is a corresponding affordance to evoke it. Similarly, the

---

[8]*Propensities* adequately replaces Gibson's companion neologism *effectivities*. Gibson was thinking about all the responses the animal is able to make as well as its preferences and inhibitions, so his term is synonymous with propensities in the broad sense. *Effectivities* came from writing about computers (von Neumann, 1966), to avoid using a word suitable for living organisms.

emerging theory of aptitude identifies aptitude with the person–situation system, in which experience in situations makes one better at recognizing affordances, because fuller perception of affordances enhances the meaning of the situation (Michaels & Carrello, 1981, esp. pp. 81, 161), and increases aptitude.

Although the ecological theory applies to a single organism, the concept extends readily to an endeavor in a human group—*our* main concern. Greeno and his followers (e.g., Greeno et al., 1998) saw learning not as acquiring a store of associations but as "the education of attention." People, they noted, provide affordances for each other, beyond those offered by material aspects of the situation. People negotiate to change the situation and the affordances available to each of them.

3 Mapping the Terrain

Early in the development of any science, some set of natural phenomena attracts attention and arouses interest. Observations of features are recorded, constructs are formulated to account for the observations, and measuring devices are invented one by one to collect relevant data. Soon come attempts to structure the growing lists of observations, measures, constructs, and relations into an orderly and parsimonious classification. As investigations continue, the form and justification of the classification system improve. A system of this kind is called a *taxonomy*.

This chapter summarizes Snow's ideas about classification systems for aptitude, treatment, and outcome after many years of studying taxonomies, including his study of principles of taxonomies that have guided biologists (see Snow, 1973).[9] Snow also considered classification of situations; we, drawing in part on his notes, consider why progress in that direction has been slow.

TAXONOMIES: DEVELOPMENT AND USES

Well-known taxonomies include the periodic table of elements in chemistry and the family-genus-species structure in biology. In these long-established sciences, the basic taxonomic work has been largely accomplished. New biological specimens are discovered each year, and in time new elements may again be added to the periodic table. But

---

[9]Snow's writings particularly relevant to this chapter are Snow (1987, 1994, 1996b), and those cited in subsections.

the novelties will most likely fit into the trusted structure, which evolved from centuries of cumulative inquiry. Although only about 70 years elapsed between Dalton's atomic theory and Mendeleev's periodic table, previous centuries of alchemy and of mineral technologies had laid the base.

In psychology and the social sciences, current taxonomies are far less orderly and less robust. To be sure, in differential psychology a great deal of research has sought to determine the kind and number of traits or abilities that should be distinguished. But with an empirical base dating back little more than a century, and relying on gradually evolving measurement instruments and inconsistent methodology, definitive findings have been elusive. Theorists are left uncertain and in no little disagreement.

The taxonomies in this chapter are provisional. Even a provisional taxonomy, however, is useful. Better taxonomies will come. New assessment methods, improved measurement models, advanced statistical techniques, new devices for recording events during learning and problem solving—all will contribute to better specified and more robust constructs and construct-systems.

Nature does not make boundaries obvious. In sorting a collection of novel insects, Scientist A might allot two specimens to distinct species whereas Scientist B calls them variants of one species. In time the community of scientists usually concurs as to which animals go together and where to place any group of them in the taxonomy, but deciding whether to call a set of related groups a family, for example, is sometimes hotly argued over a long period. Taxonomy cannot be routinized.

Similar problems arise in framing taxonomies for propensities. It was not long ago that one leading student of personality (Eysenck) considered three dimensions adequate to sum up nearly all the characteristics that self-report questions can capture, whereas another (Cattell) insisted that a minimal description would report 16 scores. Today, the majority of personality psychologists have agreed on a set of five key dimensions (see p. 86). Exchanges in the literature have convinced them not that these five exhaust variations in personality, but that as a basic framework the five scores per person are likely to suffice. (The research leading to this conclusion used a rather narrow sense of "personality"; the many dimensions of interests, e.g., were ignored. And no prestructured dimensions can depict individuality as a biographer or novelist would.)

The Form of Taxonomies.   Taxonomies take many forms. Categories can be designed to form a hierarchical or nested system, comparable to biologists' species, within genus, within family. Most objects of interest can be allocated to large categories or small ones—that is, can be given a coarse-grained or a fine-grained interpretation. Consider interests. "Interest in things" versus "Interest in people" is a coarse system that has had its uses. "Mechanical interests" is more definite, a subset of "thing" interests with many subdivisions. "Interest in working metals" is still more specific. Most established taxonomies take the hierarchical form, but there are other possibilities where the hierarchical form cannot represent the data. The chemical elements are organized in a two-way periodic table. And a three-way classification of ability constructs—with 120 cells!—was the outcome of the extensive research of Guilford (1967).

Whatever the form of the taxonomy, an investigator should judge carefully the appropriate breadth of any construct used to state a conclusion. Descriptive terms may be chosen from a high or a low level of the hierarchy. The investigator would be wise to make a preliminary judgment when designing the study. Assuming a sufficiently accurate study, not much generalization enters the conclusion "Method A was more successful than Method B in this school, for teaching solution of linear equations of the form $3x - 2 = 4$." The claim would be broader if the statement ended at "linear equations." (For example, $(3x - 2) - (3 - 2x) = 4$ would then be included.) The claim might be placed several steps up the scale by ending with "for teaching algebra." Unless the breadth of the procedure used to assess outcomes matches that of the construct invoked, the conclusion will be suspect. The broader the instrument, the less accurate will be the information it collects on a specific type of performance. The narrower the instrument, the greater the territory left unexamined. Therefore, deliberate choice of level of generality is needed in planning collection of data and in planning the analysis.

Use of Taxonomies.   Taxonomies guide the choice of constructs as starting points for research. An investigator may wish to study the causes of success or failure in some new task or educational treatment, for example. She will have developed initial hypotheses about relevant person characteristics and their relation to situational factors. The taxonomy can serve as a catalogue of constructs investigated earlier that fit into those hypotheses, assisting her in locating useful measures. The taxonomy can also suggest constructs representing counterhypotheses, perhaps worth collecting evidence on.

Second, a taxonomy helps in evaluating a newly proposed construct. An evolving science needs a functional procedure to screen new constructs, and to connect the surviving ones to an accepted structure.

Taxonomy provides the architecture. Any new low-level construct will need a place in it; and it provides tested substructures that a new higher level construct ought usually to accommodate. It is incumbent upon an investigator who advocates attention to a construct to demonstrate that the characteristic described is not adequately represented already. Sometimes, new evidence will call the accepted taxonomy into question, and suggest restructuring.

How Taxonomies Are Developed.   Taxonomies are developed in many ways. Perhaps most often, the classifier looks for similarities among objects or responses, or among their effects. Although associations can be traced by observation of qualitative correspondences and even by arguing logically, in psychological research on individual differences the most frequent and most accepted procedure is statistical correlation[App]. Ordinarily, a set of tests or observation rules is applied to many persons, and those scores that rank persons somewhat similarly are tentatively grouped under a construct label. Situations, on the other hand, are most often sorted by preparing a checklist of feature contrasts (e.g., large/small pupil–teacher ratio, much/little activity in independent work groups). Situations whose checklists match in important particulars are considered potential cell mates in the taxonomic structure.

Snow (1973, p. 103) compared four taxonomies, suggesting some correspondences between levels of learning, abilities, and educational objectives. He noted, however, that labels can be misleading; not infrequently, the same label is applied to diverse processes. Where taxonomies for an area disagree, there is a conflict to be resolved. Nonetheless, it is wise to keep in mind the words of Mayr (1982), who noted the mismatch between the taxonomic method—which assumes clean and unambiguous parsings—and many phenomena whose sorting would depend on the aspect emphasized.

CURRENT CATEGORIES FOR PROPENSITIES

For present purposes, constructs describing propensities can be sorted into nine categories, in four groups:

    Group A. Physical and psychomotor
      1. Physical abilities
      2. Psychomotor abilities
      3. Sensory-perceptual abilities

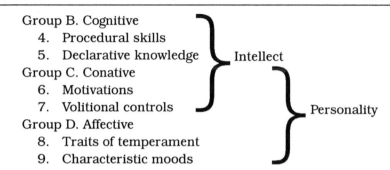

Group B. Cognitive
    4. Procedural skills
    5. Declarative knowledge   Intellect
Group C. Conative
    6. Motivations
    7. Volitional controls   Personality
Group D. Affective
    8. Traits of temperament
    9. Characteristic moods

As is common in behavioral taxonomies, the categories and subgroupings are not sharply distinct. Perceiving that two low tones differ, for example, is close to the sensory level, but perceiving whether two musical phrases differ requires reliance on memory and perhaps requires conscious encoding of a tune.

Where concepts and analysis come into play, the ability is generally labeled *cognitive*. Conative processes—which maintain goal-oriented effort—are an aspect not only of personality but also of intellectual functioning. That is the message of the brackets at the right of the list, a message that harks back to Binet's definition of intelligence. And personality clearly embraces "conscientiousness" (conative) and "excitable" (affective). Our term *affcon* for Groups C and D is a synonym for *personality* only if the latter is defined broadly to include attitudes, goals, and styles of work.

The listing just presented displays the wide range of the propensities for which improved theory is wanted. As the theory develops, it will not only provide a more systematic picture of constructs within each category but will link categories now separate (Messick, 1992). The remainder of this chapter discusses the listed constructs. We barely touch on Group A, and emphasize propensities clearly relevant to success in education, training, and higher level jobs. Interested readers can find discussion of psychomotor and sensory-perceptual taxonomies in Fleishman and Reilly (1992).

COGNITIVE ABILITIES: SKILLS AND KNOWLEDGE

The term *cognition* spans a vast range of performances: a child's first recognition of words, a toddler's ability to pile blocks to match an examiner's three-block model, an adult's ability to develop a logical argument, an expert's store of facts about the Cretaceous or his "reading" of a fossil in its site.

We did not split abilities between aptitudes and achievements, nor did we separate psychological variables from educational ones. As Snow wrote in many places, generalized mental abilities can be developed through school lessons, and facts from lessons are potential aptitudes as much as is ability to reason abstractly. Thus, the aptitude/achievement split primarily distinguishes forward-looking from backward-looking interpretations of test scores. This chapter nonetheless discusses psychological and educational tests separately, because the two have been studied separately in most research to date. As Messick (1992) said, "None of the [recognized] theories of intelligence ... deals very systematically or very well with the role of knowledge in intellectual functioning or with the role of abilities in concept learning" (p. 380). Present taxonomies of knowledge and of analytic abilities tend to describe performance at noncomparable levels of generality. Table 3.1 is designed to portray Snow's view that abilities from either the aptitude or the achievement tradition can be conceived at the same level(s) of generality.

Some taxonomies for cognition are logical whereas others are primarily empirical. To be sure, the logical taxonomies make use of experience, whether encoded as research findings or handed down in a cultural tradition. And the empirical taxonomies designed to organize research findings are constrained by logic.

TABLE 3.1
Subdivision of Cognitive Variables

Level of Generality	Procedural Skills	Declarative Knowledge
1. Most nonroutine activities	Reading, numeracy, memorizing, visualizing movement in three dimensions	Everyday assumptions about the world
2. Diverse situations within a domain (biology as example)	Domain skills (keeping a laboratory log, critiquing an experiment, analyzing an ecology)	Domain knowledge (relation of structure to function, classification of species, adaptive mechanisms)
3. Applicable to situations of a limited type	Recalling dates, solving anagrams, adjusting a microscope, using a protractor	Topical information (growing conditions for lilacs, field marks of birds, explanation of astigmatism)

Taxonomies Based on Logical Analysis

The Procedural/Declarative Contrast. The categories "Procedural Skills" and "Declarative Knowledge" (see Table 3.1) promise to be a stable basis for a useful taxonomy. The dichotomy derives from the British philosopher Gilbert Ryle, who wished to distinguish "knowing how" from "knowing that."

The categories, which evolved during the past 20 years, are now commonplace in discussions of information processing. Roughly speaking, declarative knowledge corresponds to associations that can be recalled from storage, whereas procedures are program steps capable of transforming information. (See p. 134.)

The procedural/declarative contrast has played little part in differential psychologists' discussions of abilities. The tasks of "aptitude" or "intelligence" tests are mostly procedural. Thus the mathematical parts of the SAT require analysis of novel configurations of well-known facts or concepts; they challenge procedural skills and ingenuity. Likewise, the vocabulary section of the Stanford–Binet is satisfied by recall. In contrast, the close comparison of synonyms and near-synonyms required in the SAT is weighted toward the procedural, the analytic. The procedural/declarative relationship is pertinent in educators' analyses of what is and should be learned. In this book, it is pertinent as a warning against psychologists' tendency to identify "aptitude" narrowly with procedural skills.

Levels of Generality. Table 3.1 suggests three levels of category breadth, but it should be obvious that a layout with three tiers makes arbitrary cuts in a continuous gradation.

The variables in the first row—the most general level—are applicable in a large fraction of a person's life. The first cell under "Procedural Skills" refers to broad categories of performance: reading, storing in memory, self-regulation. Under "Declarative Knowledge," the first cell refers to ideas broad enough to use every day. "I think" or "You think, and perhaps disagree with me" are statements that reflect declarative knowledge. The concept of "reciprocity" described by Piaget as the outcome of successful decentering (p. 15) is generalized declarative knowledge, as is the idea that not all antecedents of an event are causes. Concepts like these, which pervade a culture, have been studied developmentally and in cross-cultural comparisons; but they have played little or no part in modern tests of mental ability or in planning and evaluation of curricula. General knowledge of self accrued through self-observation does enter prominently into self-report inventories.

For millennia, it has been a commonplace of educational theory that rhetoric, geometry, and other branches of study have distinct contributions to make, each having its own system of questions, procedures, and answers. Psychologists have for the most part, however, studied learning as a general process, so independent of "subject matter" that laws are sought that could apply to both a pigeon's associating food with a green light and an adolescent's learning of algebra.

One of Piaget's advances beyond Binet was to trace the separate intellectual processes used to deal with numbers, language, and spatial configurations. Later psychologists and anthropologists found that the learning and use of language requires multiple processes specific to that domain. Command of language is far more than having a large vocabulary plus knowledge of grammatical rules. Hirschfeld and Gelman (1994), judging that psychological research on abilities has emphasized the general to the point of overlooking second-tier abilities, produced a book in which more than two dozen chapter authors argued that "much of human cognition is domain-specific." The second tier of Table 3.1 lists skills and knowledge at the domain level. These abilities apply to a wide range of topics the domain is concerned with.

Learned in one set of experiences, the ability can be helpful in mastering a new topic (not always in the same field). Consider keeping a laboratory log. The standards for it embody some of the main ideas of the domain. Thus, because of the premium on objectivity, adjectives such as *beautiful* are taboo. Also, moves by the investigator that seemed to make no difference are to be recorded, because explanation must account for absence of change as well as for change. Keeping this kind of log is specific to work in science, in school, and in an industrial laboratory.

The psychological skills listed in the top tier have second-tier subdivisions. A skilled reader asks different questions in reading law than in reading fiction. On the whole, however, the second-level divisions psychologists have noticed (see Table 3.2) are not specified in terms of domains of learning—unfinished business!

In the third tier come entries that may or may not be related to a domain (though our examples are so related). Adjusting a microscope is used in a variety of investigations, but the skill does not depend significantly on other aspects of botany or gemology.

Process Taxonomies Based on Logical Distinctions.   Items for traditional achievement tests have been assembled by means of specification tables; these distinguish among content categories and assign proportionate emphases to them. In the domain of biology, the categories might include structures of plants, structures of animals, and ecology. Attempts to make process distinctions as firm as such content distinctions have not taken root. Items or tasks are assigned judgmentally to a category such as recall, understanding, or problem solving. Attempts at empirical validation of such distinctions have been rare.

The best known and most used of the logical taxonomies is the *Taxonomy of Educational Objectives* (Bloom, 1956). It was originally designed to facilitate communication of specialists in examination development with college instructors and with each other. The taxonomy lists types of responses that might be elicited by assignments or examination tasks, covering both declarative and procedural knowledge. A new version (L. Anderson & Krathwohl, 2001) makes important changes. Our account is based on personal communication from Krathwohl (February 23, October 22, and November 25, 1998).

The new version is intended to assist in curriculum planning and instruction as well as assessment, and has teachers at all grade levels as a primary audience. The taxonomy is now a row-by-column table.

The rows refer to factual, conceptual, procedural, and metacognitive knowledge. Factual and conceptual knowledge are subdivisions of what was referred to earlier as declarative knowledge. *Metacognition,* a term that has become popular in the last 10 years, refers to the person's conscious awareness of what he knows and of his intended goal and plan of work. It is task-related self-awareness plus the ability to generate such knowledge through self-monitoring. This idea reappears in our discussions of self-regulation as a conative process.

The columns of the table lay out six intellectual activities, starting with the simplest:

Remember Understand Apply Analyze Evaluate Create

Verbs have replaced nouns, in line with the recent emphasis in psychology on information processing (e.g., "Create" replaces the 1956 "Synthesis"). All columns have subcategories; those for "Analyze," for example, are differentiating, organizing, and attributing.

To form a meaningful objective, the teacher must add topics to the empty frame. If one topic is *perspective,* the frame suggests the possibility of analyzing the cues to perspective in a photograph (or in an Escher drawing—a much different objective!). The large number of cells challenges teachers to broaden the curriculum and to set priorities. Activities planned for lessons can be slotted into the taxonomy.

Passing mention suffices for the companion taxonomy of affective objectives (Krathwohl, Bloom, & Masia, 1964). It has five levels, with "Attentive" at Level 1 and "Characterization by a value" at Level 5. The scheme was not much used. Imposing the model of the first taxonomy on affcon processes very likely led to a degree of intellectualization that lost from sight the humanizing, character-building goals that transcend subject fields. See Martin and Reigeluth (1999) for discussion of this and more recent affective taxonomies.

Empirical Taxonomies

Older Factor Analyses. Hierarchical models of cognitive functions, in various forms, have been popular since at least the late 19th century. As noted earlier, Spencer believed in a general, inherited "fitness," an aptitude to thrive whatever the situation. Spearman saw this fundamental capacity as differentiating into a hierarchy of specialized abilities, manifested developmentally in sensory, perceptual, associative, and (toward maturity) relational functions. In his view, this differentiation operated through evolutionary time, and also within the growth of the individual. Galton thought similarly. Spearman's *factor analyses*[App] of test intercorrelations tended to support the notion empirically; a single general dimension did seem to account for most of his test intercorrelations. Spearman labeled the dimension *g*. Others in England built on and modified Spearman's view. (For a summary, see Gustafsson, 1988, p. 38.)

Vernon (1950) suggested that a three-tier structure would best organize findings to that date. The so-called "first order" factors grouped to tests of much the same type (e.g., numerical-reasoning). Many of these factors were sufficiently related to warrant grouping them into "second order" factors. Vernon proposed two of these: "verbal-educational" (*v:ed*) and "practical-mechanical" (labeled *k:m*). Numerical and most other reasoning would enter *v:ed*. Tasks originating in vocational selection and guidance (mechanical assembly, mechanical comprehension) entered the second. But it embraced reasoning also, for example, a spatial first-order factor. The peak of the structure was a Spearman-like *g*. Vernon's view of ability organization was accepted by most British investigators and by some Americans.

Most Americans in the same period adopted Thurstone's one-level structure of "primary mental abilities" (Thurstone, 1938; Thurstone & Thurstone, 1941). The list of primaries changed from time to time; the six primaries of the early years were R (reasoning), V (word meaning), M (associative memory), S (spatial transformation), W (word fluency), and N (facility in simple number operations). In the period 1940–1950, Thurstonians regarded the primary abilities as largely independent, fundamental unities, out of which more complex performance is constructed.

The contrast between Vernon's hierarchy and Thurstone's flat list of primaries reflects the type of system each sought, rather than disagreement over facts. By 1947 Thurstone was acknowledging that his primaries were intercorrelated, hence he could not dispute the idea of a general ability. Guilford—who extended Thurstone's list—came also to acknowledge (1981, 1985) that his constructs nested within broad abilities, though he did not accept a full-span general factor. A hierarchy easily accommodates narrow abilities as specializations of broader abilities.

As is typical of correlational research on cognition by psychologists, the tests entering Thurstone's analyses (see Fig. 3.1) are overwhelmingly procedural rather than declarative, and so are the factors. The exception in the list of primaries is V, which in Thurstone's work did refer essentially to associative knowledge. Procedural emphasis was present also in the British work from Spearman onward, and in the work that Carroll synthesized (see next subsection). This means that the domain represented by psychological tests neglects "content" variables. Where content constructs do enter a psychologist's system, they are likely to refer to stimulus characteristics of tasks (e.g., Guilford's figural, semantic, and symbolic rubrics, which he crossed with procedural constructs).

Popular writers who dismissed factor analysis were judged by Snow to be wrongheaded. Stephen Gould had little sympathy with mental testing or with research on intelligence (1981, 1994), and rejected factor analysis because in his view its conclusions were artifacts of the method, not dictated by the observations. To quote from Snow's manuscript on aptitude theory: "Unfortunately, the press and some social scientists seem to have accepted Gould's critique uncritically. It has no merit. Carroll (1995) showed point by point the many errors, confusions, and misconceptions beneath Gould's argument." Snow considered his team's scaling studies (p. 69) a refutation of Gould's charge of "artifact," because the assumptions were not those of factor analysis.

Snow also resisted highly realistic interpretations of factors, as in this from his manuscript:

> It is important ... to realize what the hierarchical model of human ability organization is and is not. It is a taxonomy of ability intercorrelations designed to provide a structural model of ability constructs and their proximities to one another. The taxonomy supports intelligent evaluation and choice of ability constructs. ... The hierarchy is not a proposed model of the neuropsychological structure of cognition or of cognitive process organization within it.

Carroll's Synthesis. Carroll (1993) factored afresh most of the past century's evidence on cognitive-test intercorrelations to reach by far the best summary to date. Although most of the data came from persons of school age and beyond, Carroll found data on young children consistent with his structure.

Carroll's monumental recomputation supports a hierarchical structure: a general cognitive ability factor common to nearly all tests, and two subordinate levels ("strata"). This is today's ruling conception. A test of reading comprehension (RC), for example, customarily reflects crystallized intelligence (Gc) and a more specialized reading ability.

Table 3.2, following Snow's manuscript, shows only three specimen abilities within each second-stratum factor; Carroll had more. Snow changed the designation of several Stratum-II factors, usually employing symbols and names more traditional than Carroll's. Both Carroll and Snow used the symbol G for "general" rather than g, steering clear of historic interpretations of Spearman's *g*. The order of factors in Stratum II reflects Carroll's conclusion as to their closeness to G. Gf has the largest correlation with G.

Relatively narrow factors appear in Stratum I—Memory Span, Associative Memory, and Recall Memory, for example. A still lower level might list narrower factors such as Recall of Historical Dates. Carroll (1996) considered three strata sufficient because he had not found a fourth necessary in the tests devised for psychologists' research on abilities; but, although psychologists would not care about memory for dates as such, it might interest neuropsychologists and some educators.

Stratum II includes eight comparatively general factors that provide "nests" for tests tapping rather similar processes. Among the eight, Fluid-Analytic Reasoning receives particular attention from psychologists (and in this book). Few complex tasks, even those placed in other second-level nests, can be handled without analysis, comparison, reorganization, and other components of reasoning.

In Carroll's formulation, the factor G influences all the others. All the second-stratum factors correlate appreciably with a broad measure of general ability. This implies that the processes identified with G enter into almost any kind of intellectual performance beyond recall of familiar information.

Memory, for example, is not so general as Fluid-Analytic Reasoning, but it is general in the sense that it transcends domains and types of stimulus. In the course of a day, a person stores or retrieves memories in contexts of many kinds. One plausible hypothesis is that the person's memory will work about equally well across the board, after allowances

TABLE 3.2

The Hierarchical Factor Model of Cognitive Abilities

Stratum III	Stratum II	Stratum I	Factor Name
G	Gf		**FLUID-ANALYTIC REASONING**
		LR	Logical Reasoning
		IR	Inductive Reasoning
		QR	Quantitative Reasoning
	Gc		**CRYSTALLIZED-SCHOLASTIC ACHIEVEMENT**
		VC	Verbal Comprehension
		RC	Reading Comprehension
		PC	Phonetic Coding
	Gm		**MEMORY**
		MS	Memory Span
		MA	Associative Memory
		MR	Recall Memory
	Gv		**VISUAL-SPATIAL-MECHANICAL**
		VZ	Visualization
		SR	Spatial Relations
		IM	Imagery
	Ga		**AUDITORY DISCRIMINATION**
		MD	Musical Discrimination
		SD	Speech Discrimination
		SS	Sound Sensitivity
	Gi		**IDEA PRODUCTION**
		OI	Originality of Ideas
		FI	Ideational Fluency
		FX	Flexibility
	Gs		**SPEEDINESS**
		PS	Perceptual Speed
		NS	Numerical Facility
		TS	Test-Taking Speed
	Gt		**REACTION TIME**
		RT	Choice Reaction Time
		RS	Semantic-Processing Speed
		CS	Comparison Speed

Note. From Carroll (1993). Copyright 1993 by Cambridge University Press. Adapted by permission.

are made for expertise. But some activities call only on commonplace, much-used memories; everyone in a group can meet the demands. In such activities, although memory is used, it is not a significant source of individual differences. Some other tasks are, in the usual jargon, "heavily loaded on memory"—that is, memory generates individual differences in scores.

Some tests rank examinees primarily according to their general ability. Most instruments intended as "general-ability tests" have diverse items that require adaptive information processing, at a level challenging to the intended examinees. Coping with difficult material—"power"—is usually demanded, more than speed. "Special-ability tests," in contrast, are usually rather homogeneous. Items may or may not require analytic work. There is little scope for analysis in recalling randomly ordered digits within a limited time. A specialized test of one factor is expected not to correlate much with performance on a test assigned to another such factor.

More remains to be said about G, Gf, and Gc; but first let us consider other taxonomic analyses.

Multidimensional Scaling; General Ability in the Bull's-Eye.

The hierarchical model and the prominence of general ability do not depend on assumptions or conventions of factor analysis. Snow's group turned, late in the 1970s, to nonmetric scaling—a numerical procedure unlike factor analysis—to elicit patterns from test intercorrelations. Matrices of ability correlations, if based on reasonably representative samples of tests and persons, can be summarized in a two-dimensional plot of the sort Guttman called a radex (Snow, Kyllonen, & Marshalek, 1984).

Scaling lets points in n-dimensional space represent objects, and locates whatever geometric configuration in two (or occasionally more) dimensions best matches distances between points to the similarities of the objects. The smaller the distance between two points, the more similar the objects they represent. Because the scaling is based on the rank orders of correlations, it avoids some debatable assumptions of factor analysis. Guttman (1954) demonstrated the value of the approach for studying tests.

Guttman correctly suggested at that time that tests of ability within a narrow content area would scale as a straight-line array, with the tests ordered from simple to complex. Tests at the same level of complexity from different content areas would map as a more-or-less circular array of points. A battery of tests varying in content and complexity would form a radex, a spread of points on a disk in two-dimensional space (or within a sphere in three dimensions). One would expect to see pie-shaped regions (or cones) occupied by tests of similar content.

Before he devised a way to produce such plots, Guttman had expected simple tests to fall in the center of the radex, with increasingly complex tests radiating toward the periphery. Once he had a scaling procedure, the results (Guttman, 1965) showed just the opposite. So did those of the Snow project.

Snow's interpretation of the hierarchical organization of abilities led him to expect the following patterning:

> Complex tests with high loadings on G appear near the center.
>
> Simple tests reflecting mainly specialized factors are located near the edge.
>
> Tests of intermediate complexity (strongly influenced by factors in Carroll's Stratum II) fall in the intermediate region.
>
> Tests within a content area fall in approximately the same radial direction.

The project's test battery applied to high-school students showed this pattern (Snow et al., 1984), as did reanalyses of Thurstone's data (Fig. 3.1). Tests having large G loadings scaled in or near the center; lines radiating from the center traced out complex-to-simple continua.

The tests represented in Fig. 3.1 are typical of the sets used by Thurstone in establishing his list of primary mental abilities. Each test has many items requiring a single kind of analysis or recall. Complex tasks are found in the center of the radex, simpler tasks toward the periphery. G loadings are low at the edge, high in the center.

Content wedges are clearly discernible. The bull's-eye is occupied exclusively by reasoning tests. Tests such as Arithmetical Reasoning and Figure Classification are pulled somewhat away from the center, thanks to content influence. Near the left edge is a cluster of arithmetic skills; these much-practiced tasks demand little intellectual processing. At the bottom edge of the radex are perceptual comparisons, again simple.

Chapter 5 examines in detail the psychological processes employed with tasks of greater and less complexity. Figure 5.6 (p. 157) illustrates how items can be designed to have controlled levels of complexity. A complete test could be made up at each of these levels, and the tests would scale on a complexity continuum along a single ray of the radex. Exhibit CJS (p. 136), together with Fig. 5.1, shows how the complexity of matrix items can vary.

In another radex (see Marshalek, Lohman, & Snow, 1983, p. 121), the test battery included subtests of the Wechsler scale. A central constellation is easily identified as measuring Gf; it includes Matrices, Let-

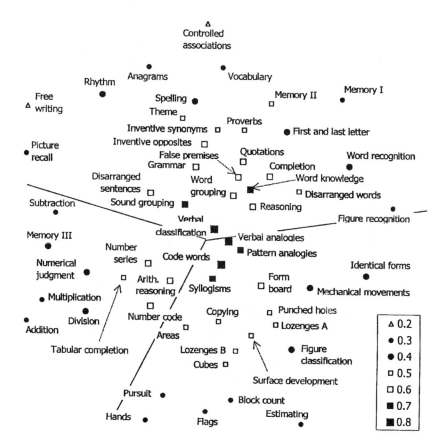

FIG. 3.1. Nonmetric scaling of ability test intercorrelations. Data from L. L. Thurstone (1938). Plot coordinates from Snow, Kyllonen, and Marshalek (1984). Copyright 1984 by Lawrence Erlbaum Associates. Adapted by permission. The symbols indicate the correlation of the test with the general factor, as decoded in the legend.

ter Series, and Guilford's Necessary Arithmetic Operations (which requires a plan for calculation but no calculation). Halfway between center and edge are five subtests of Wechsler's Verbal Scale. This is clearly a Gc cluster that includes Arithmetic as well as purely verbal tests. (The Thurstone data behind Fig. 3.1 included few achievement measures. One might say that the radex shows no Gc grouping, or that it shows two crystallized groupings, a verbal one at the top and a numerical one to the left.) In the radex of Marshalek et al., a Gv (visualization)

tion) cluster also shows clearly, located about where Surface Development appears in Fig. 3.1, toward the bottom right; the pertinent Wechsler tests are Object Assembly and Block Design. For details on the preceding analyses, and discussion of scaling as an alternative to factor analysis, see Marshalek et al. (1983) and Snow et al. (1984).

Analyses of Measures of Learning Rate. Psychologists have frequently studied the course of learning by presenting the same task repeatedly and scoring each trial (considering speed and/or errors). The successive scores of a person form a learning curve. The curve is described in terms of its slope (simple learning rate) and curvature (essentially, rate on early trials minus rate on late trials). Such scores from the psychological laboratory can be correlated from one task to another, and correlated with scores from mental tests. The radex model applies to such correlations.

Snow et al. (1984) scaled Allison's (1960) correlations, whereas Allison had applied factor analysis. As before, the most complex tests scaled near in the center of each radex. The simplest tasks did not correlate substantially with one another or with ability tests, and thus scaled toward the periphery. The several learning rates tended to distribute around the content-knowledge regions of the test-score radex, implying that each was connected to a major content factor.

The radexes had a sprawling form (Snow et al., 1984), so we present only illustrative correlations of simple learning rates with a Gf composite based on tests:

Rotary Pursuit	−.01
Breech Block Assembly	.00
Spatial Concept Formation I	.14
Knob Code	.19
Verbal Concept Formation I	.26
Meccano Assembly	.38
Spatial Concept Formation II	.40
Verbal Concept Formation II	.41
Combat Information Center Plotting	.55

A simple-to-complex ordering of the tasks is obvious. Tests that put substantial weight on information processing have comparatively large correlations. The correlations with Gc were much the same as those for Gf. With the visualization factor Gv, correlations for only a few learning rates (from spatial tasks) rose above .30.

A scaling of similar data from Stake (1961)—reported in detail in Snow et al. (1984, pp. 83–85)—again showed a gradient of complexity shared by tests and learning measures. Rather more clearly than in the Allison data, the Gc factor from tests correlated strongly with verbal learning. A Gf-Gv factor (the two could not be distinguished in Stake's data) had its highest correlations with learning rates on nonverbal and fluid analytic tasks.

Some Empirical Distinctions in Mathematics and Science. A hierarchical view of achievement suggests questions about how performance within a subject domain is organized. Another study by Snow and his colleagues shows some possibilities of empirical rather than logical analysis of achievement.

The National Educational Longitudinal Study of 1988 tested some 25,000 representative eighth graders. Questionnaires describing students, parents, teachers, and schools were also compiled. Follow-up studies in Grades 10 and 12 tested achievement at higher levels.

In the main data, factor analysis of item intercorrelations within mathematics and within science yielded psychologically meaningful subscores. In mathematics two factors appeared: conceptual knowledge plus computation, and reasoning. In science there were three factors: spatial-mechanical reasoning, quantitative tasks, and basic concepts and reasoning. Each factor had its own pattern of correlations with the background variables. Correlations linking those variables to overall scores in math and science did not bring out such information (Hamilton, Nussbaum, Kupermintz, Kerkhoven, & Snow, 1995; Kupermintz, Ennis, Hamilton, Talbert, & Snow, 1995).

In side studies, items from the same tests were administered to a smaller pool of local high school students, using interview and think-aloud techniques (Hamilton, Nussbaum, & Snow, 1994). The purpose was to examine the processing strategies and knowledge that students employed with items from different subsets.

Snow acknowledged that much more work with varied assessment instruments would be needed before placing the dimensions uncovered into a taxonomy. But this approach represents a start toward mapping psychological structure in a content domain. Not a trivial matter: If spatial-mechanical reasoning, for example, is a component of achievement in some walks of science, then educators and program evaluators should be giving it direct attention.

Issues Surrounding G

The construct of an overarching general ability is widely accepted. Jensen (1992) reported that correlations among the 120 or so measures of general ability listed in the Mental Measurement Yearbooks range from about .60 to .90, with the average near .75. Factor analyses of subtests within an intelligence test tell a similar story. Gustafsson and Undheim (1996) reported a general factor among scores from the WISC–III (Wechsler Intelligence Scale for Children, 3rd ed.), along with second-level factors. Their review of much other literature supports the conclusion that a hierarchical model emphasizing G, with several categories of more-specialized subordinate abilities, fits the accumulated evidence.

Are G and Gf Distinguishable? Gustafsson and Undheim suggested also, however, that G is not distinguishable from fluid-analytic intelligence Gf, which in turn is a close match to the inductive-reasoning factor in Carroll's Stratum I. Essentially, in other words, G = Gf = IR. Not all psychologists agree. Notably Carroll (1993), placing G above all other cognitive abilities, hypothesized (1996) that measures of Gf call upon reasoning skills not present in other G measures.

Gustafsson (2001) returned to the topic, defending the G-Gf identity and attributing the dispute to discordant analytic methods. Traditional factor analysis is exploratory. Hypotheses influence the choice of tests to be intercorrelated, but the structure is derived empirically. Mathematical constraints built into the analysis—notably, an attempt to keep the structure "simple" (by assigning each test zero correlations with most factors)—strongly influence the outcome. Carroll preferred this exploratory style.

In the contrasting confirmatory style, which Gustafsson preferred for later stages of a program of inquiry, the investigator describes in advance a structure that seems reasonable in the light of previous work, and calculates how well the correlations fit that hypothesis. Gustafsson pointed out that the long-ago analyses of Spearman and his coworker Holzinger were confirmatory in style, though lacking modern statistical tests. Vernon's synthesis (p. 65) had similar origins. Consistently, these workers and others in Great Britain found a general factor, but no reasoning or Gf factor. Once G has been put into the model, Gustafsson said, no variance[App] is left over for a Gf factor. Then how could Gf call on significant skills or processes G does not call on, or vice versa?

The argument cannot be resolved within the confines of factor-analytic research. It is best addressed within a general consideration of the nature of mental ability, especially through analyses of cognitive process. That topic reappears as this book continues.

From some perspectives, crystallized ability Gc is as general and important as Gf. Carroll's table, however, makes Gc the label for a verbal factor. For many years after the fluid–crystallized distinction was introduced, Gc referred to a broad mix that included mathematical skills.

The Gf/Gc distinction received some consideration in the 1940s, but it became prominent when Horn and Cattell (1966) showed how well it summarized the fact that some tests (fluid) show declines with aging whereas others (crystallized) hold steady or increase. Analytic problem solving, which declines, is interpreted as a manifestation of Gf, whereas recall of information and word meanings is "crystallized." Crystallized abilities have been consolidated through extensive practice, starting in school. Competence of this sort tends to hold up in later adulthood when flexibility and analytic functions weaken. Horn and Noll (1994) updated the evidence on these changes.

Horn and coworkers examined just which processes within problem solving and learning become less dependable with advancing age (Horn, Donaldson, & Engstrom, 1981). Among these are:

Forming hypotheses about likely answers.

Holding many items in mind at once.

Not devoting further attention to what has been found irrelevant.

Encoding new information so that it can be easily recalled.

Making comparisons and inspections rapidly.

On the whole, these seem to imply declines in the efficiency of performance processes such as Snow speaks of in the quotation that follows, and which is considered further in chapter 5.

Snow (1980b) characterized Gf and Gc as follows:

> ... Gc represents the long-term accumulation of knowledge and skills, organized into functional cognitive systems by prior learning, that are ... units for use in future learning. ... [T]ransfer relations between past and future learning are assured. The transfer need not be primarily of specific knowledge but rather of organized academic learning skills. Thus Gc may represent prior assemblies of performance processes retrieved as a system and applied anew in instructional situations not unlike those experienced in the past, whereas Gf may represent new assemblies of performance processes needed in more extreme adaptations to novel situations. The distinction, then, is between *long-term* assembly for transfer to *familiar* new situations versus *short-term* assembly for transfer to *unfamiliar* new situations. (p. 37; italics in original, but we have altered the style of Gf and Gc to match our text)

Gc gains its practical importance from the fact that measures of it are superior predictors of school and college performance. Measures dominated by Gf usually predict summary indices of success less well; but Gf plays a special role when a task is unfamiliar and must be "figured out" (cf. Ackerman, 1989). Chapter 4 provides much further information on academic prediction.

Gf and Gc were not the only broad factors reported by Horn and Cattell, but Cattell considered the others distant from intelligence. For some time Horn and Cattell favored a two-headed hierarchy, with Gf and Gc as equals in the top rank. Some tests would clearly fall in one of the two families, whereas others would connect with both. More recently Horn (1989) advocated a structure with many broad factors, and no G or Gf at the top. Horn's factors are similar to Carroll's second stratum.

Gardner's Challenge to the Idea of General Ability.   A list of "multiple intelligences" put forward by Howard Gardner (1983) has impressed classroom teachers. The seven intelligences are Linguistic, Musical, Logical-mathematical, Spatial, Bodily-kinaesthetic, Interpersonal, and Intrapersonal (clarity regarding one's own feelings). Gardner originally said that he would be prepared to list additional varieties—but in the years since 1983 there has been only one vague addition, a "naturalist" talent (Kleckley, 1997).

Gardner (1983) stressed that the seven intelligences are separate—"relatively autonomous" (p. 8). The form of the list, but not much of the content, is reminiscent of Thurstone's "primaries." Gardner thought of strength in any one of these abilities as arising from superiority in certain parts of the brain, and developed through cumulative experience with particular types of stimuli and symbol systems. The seven sequences of development within the person have few interconnections, and proceed at their own rates to generate an evolving profile of areas of expertise.

The popularity of Gardner's proposal arises from its message that, with multiple lines of development, every child is likely to have one or more areas of superiority. He implied that the intelligences have equal social worth. Although Gardner's emphasis on biological bases carries hereditarian suggestions, he placed equal stress on the need for intensive, cumulative experience with a symbol system to make the relevant ability fully useful. Gardner's writings speak optimistically about students who do not show promise in verbal and numerical tasks, and encourages schools to use several alternative modalities in teaching any branch of knowledge. For descriptions of school programs inspired by Gardner's thesis, see Potter (1996) and J. Collins (1998).

Gardner based his scheme particularly on evidence of specialized excellence and deficiency. Prodigies or at least stellar performers are readily identified in most of the areas, and their life histories say much about how expertise can be built up. Patients with performance deficiencies, often arising from injury or surgery, provide much evidence on localization of brain function. Beyond these case studies, Gardner looked to experimental psychology and cognitive psychology for evidence of distinctive processes associated with handling of a symbol system. (Gardner discounted the conceptions, popular among cognitive psychologists, of a central executive function and a central working memory.)

Interpersonal or "social" intelligence, which was essentially absent from the data Carroll reevaluated, requires particular comment in a chapter on taxonomy. For a long period, proposed constructs of this type were rejected by the psychometric community because supposed cognitive measures in the area were statistically indistinguishable from measures of verbal ability. Now, data from measures of social adaptability based on behavior and not verbal questions and answers support the idea (Ford & Tisak, 1983; N. Frederiksen, Carlson, & Ward, 1984). Perhaps the construct should in time be added into Carroll's system (see Goleman, 1995). Still, it appears likely that social intelligence consists of a collection of abilities and styles that are not strongly intercorrelated—hence not a unified "intelligence."

Snow's notes in the margins of Gardner's (1983) *Frames of Mind* and in the outlines for this book show that he was highly skeptical regarding Gardner's argument, but recognized Gardner's contribution in broadening educators' efforts to develop aptitude. Apparently Snow stayed with the view he expressed when *Frames of Mind* appeared:

> The book teems with valuable hypotheses about brain organization and about culture, in relation to human abilities, but only the expert can tell which statement is probable fact, which is bold hypothesis, and which is in the vast range between. (Snow, 1985, p. 110)

Snow thought well of Messick's (1992) closely argued review. Messick complained that Gardner chose not to assemble a rigorous argument for his position and did not relate it to the findings of past research:[10]

> [T]he descriptions do not derive from any consistent set of empirical data and can be tied to data only in piecemeal fashion, thereby being constantly threatened by the perverse human tendency to highlight results that are consonant with the theory's logic over findings that are dissonant. (p. 368)

---

[10]Gardner did eventually publish correlations purporting to show that his abilities are uncorrelated, and not correlated with the Stanford–Binet (1993, chap. 6). The evidence carried no weight with technically minded reviewers, because faults in the design and analysis "essentially guaranteed" low correlations (Lubinsky & Benbow, 1995, p. 937).

Messick argued that Gardner's profiles would serve equally well if he acknowledged cross-connecting general processes and was not antagonistic to factorial hierarchy. Gardner (1999) was aware of the evidence for G but set no store by it; it comes from "short-answer tests," and—he surmised—would not be found if, instead, correlations among performance tests in the same domains were examined. Because performance tests are notoriously unreliable, the conjecture would have to be checked out by means of a multitrait–multimethod[App] design, taking adequate measurements on samples of 100 persons or more, of just two or three of Carroll's second-level factors at a time.

Messick's case against Gardner becomes much stronger in the light of recent neuropsychological evidence for central processing machinery. MRI imaging was used to record brain activity of adults facing matrix tasks that called for much, or for rather little, analytic reasoning (Prabhakaran, Smith, Desmond, Glover, & Gabrieli, 1997). The more analytic tasks appeared "to activate many, if not all, domain-dependent and domain-independent working memory systems" (p. 60). Finding domain-independent systems that assist in reasoning gives physical testimony to the reality of one aspect of general ability. Evidence that certain regions are domain-independent comes from Baker et al. (1996), from Quartz and Sejnowski (1997), and from other articles cited by Prabhakaran et al.

Gardner's proposal seems to favor concentrating much of a child's experience in those subdomains where she shows the most promise; this has obvious potential value. Some kinds of development, however, could be shortchanged when this is done. Society should not prefer high school graduates who are verbally proficient yet tone deaf in mathematics and music, nor Olympics-ready gymnasts whose literacy is rudimentary. And, if planned experience can develop the "cross-connecting" processes of learning and problem solving (Snow, 1996a), a curriculum concentrating on specific domains will miss the opportunity to develop intelligence in the large.

Sternberg's Triarchic Proposals.   Another system of thought that challenges the centrality of G or Gf comes from Sternberg. In 1985 he presented a three-pronged or triarchic conception. At that time, Sternberg spoke of three subtheories—contextual, experiential, and componential. These, even when he elaborated, seemed more like points of view or aspects to be investigated than like theories (cf. Humphreys, 1984).

The "contextual" question asks what a culture would consider intelligent. One culture may value navigation skills highly as a marker of intelligence whereas another places its premium on hunting skills. Sternberg saw the present-day United States as principally valuing analytic or fluid abilities, knowledge-based or crystallized abilities, and social-practical abilities.

The "experiential" viewpoint asks to what extent the person has had opportunity to automatize the needed responses. Whereas most of those proposing to measure intelligence have deliberately devised somewhat novel tasks, Sternberg is unique in suggesting that the ability to automatize processing is itself a good indicator of intelligence.

"Componential" inquiry seeks to tease out the cognitive structures and processes underlying intelligent behavior. This inquiry is a principal topic in chapter 5, and need not be explained here. (See particularly Exh. Strn., p. 150)

Although these points of view remain important for Sternberg, his work in the 1990s has emphasized a different "triarchy." He has distinguished three types of presumably general intellectual competence:

Analytical abilities, the abilities used to analyze, judge, evaluate, compare or contrast.

Creative abilities, the abilities used to create, invent, discover, imagine, or suppose.

Practical abilities, the abilities used to apply, put into practice, implement, or use. (Sternberg, 1998, p. 3; italics removed.)

Sternberg (1996) is a vigorous advocate of matching instructional methods to aptitude patterns, and has developed instructional materials for presenting the same course in each of the three modes.

The analytic approach assesses ability by means of traditional tests of reasoning, including Number Series and Matrices; and the corresponding instruction stresses problem solving. The creative tests call for working in unfamiliar intellectual contexts—for example, performing arithmetic using a freshly defined operation along with the common ones. Practical intelligence requires identifying significant aspects of a problematic situation, and balancing pros and cons of possible solutions. Sternberg has often used questionnaires rather than performance samples to assess this type of acuteness in managing oneself, others, and a career. And these have shown moderate correlations with various objective criteria of success (Sternberg & Wagner, 1986).

No issues arise regarding the analytic subdivision.

The separation of creative from analytic activities is not controversial; Carroll's Gi factor (Table 3.2) recapitulates a common finding. However, Guilford, the strongest proponent of the concept, considered his category to be a collection of distinct abilities to deal with particular contents. Sternberg considered creative ability to be sufficiently general that the undifferentiated construct can guide instruction. Low task-to-task correlations make reliable measurement of the variable difficult. The question remains whether creative tasks show appreciable coherence over and above the positive correlation attributable to their shared Gf.

If Sternberg's approach to practical intelligence proves valid, it will have addressed the long-standing criticism that mental tests have overemphasized scholastic aptitudes. Sternberg asked examinees to propose policies for effecting some change in a group or institution. But no one is likely to be consistently superior or inferior across a set of problems. Therefore, essentially the same questions of unity and distinctiveness arise about practical intelligence as about the creative subdivision.[11]

To be sure, even if creative and practical applications of intellect are much less general than G, they merit investigation. If the practical ability of, say, a marriage counselor to reconcile couples can be reliably measured, and differences among trained counselors is not accounted for by G plus task-specific knowledge, a socially important and scientifically interesting variable has been brought to light. Clarifying even that small sector would be a large job, however.

Competing Interpretations of G.   One can gain an impression of what G (or Gf, or the Gf-Gc compound) is from the tests that have strong loadings on the factor. One can gain information of a different kind by turning to studies of brain activation. But neither of these really characterizes the construct for which the name *intelligence* has so long been used. A detailed characterization of it has proved elusive.

The emotional baggage carried by the term *intelligence* distorts the picture. No one will admit to being low in intelligence, or low in any performance likely to be interpreted as indicating intelligence. Many a person is tempted to define intelligence so as to emphasize her own strengths and ignore areas of weakness. There are deeper fault lines

---

[11]Detailed correlations from the most complete study to date (Sternberg, Grigorenko, Ferrari, & Clinkenbeard, 2000) have not been published, but we have some from personal communication (E. Grigorenko to L. Cronbach, June 2, 1998). A correlation of 0.57 between multiple-choice measures of analytic and creative ability, set alongside internal-consistency reliabilities just above .60, suggests that very little of the creative score is attributable to a general factor independent of Gf. The data set includes a correlation of .51 between analytic and practical scores (multiple-choice), along with a reliability of .45 for the practical score. Again, great overlapping of the constructs is implied.

also—for example, the conflict between those who see intelligence as inherited potential and those who see it as achieved competence.

To reduce misunderstanding, it is becoming commonplace to refer to the psychological construct represented by IQ tests and similarly complex tasks with the symbol G. By that symbol we mean "relatively general phenotypic mental ability developed up to the time of testing." *Phenotype* refers to characteristics of the person here and now. (The contrasting term *genotype* refers to the range of phenotypes the person's DNA at conception would favor.) One characterization of G does not deny genetic influences, but it clearly asserts that everyone deals with characteristics of the person at a stated time. As of now, there is no way to assess the genotype.

To develop a sense of what general ability is, each theorist has pursued one of three suggestions:

1.   An aggregate of lesser abilities? Intelligence is, for some, the aggregate of all abilities such as Table 3.2 encompasses. Some go further. Humphreys (1971, 1979) went so far as to include:

the entire repertoire of acquired skills, knowledge, learning sets, and generalization tendencies considered intellectual in nature that are available [to the person] at any one period of time. An intelligence test contains items that sample the totality of such acquisitions. Intelligence so defined is not an entity such as Spearman's "mental energy." Instead the definition suggests the Thomson "multiple-bonds" approach .... (1971, p. 32)

Thomson's (1916) hypothesis offered an early alternative interpretation of Spearman's *g*, based on the idea that mental tests sample the multiple stimulus-response connections already accumulated through the person's learning history. Each test calls up its own sample. The overlap of two tests' samples determines their correlation. Thus, *g* simply reflects large overlap in the samples of connections. The best tests for *g* would be those that call forth the most representative samples. Humphreys added in the possibility of generalizing from a lesson, so that one need not store a specific response for each stimulus.

2.   An integration of processes? Whereas View 1 sees intelligence as a library or storehouse, View 2 emphasizes adaptive assembly of what is stored. Intelligence then refers to a smoothly operating system for coping. Theorists of this school start by recognizing that any complex mental performance is the product of interwoven mental processes and contents, followed by executive, managerial, coordi-

nating actions. Cronbach's (1990) factory analogy captures the flavor of these definitions:

> To say that one person is more intelligent than another can only mean that he or she uses information more efficiently to serve his or her purposes. The efficiency of a factory is not to be located in this or that part of the operation. Rather, the purchasing division, the mechanics, the operators, the inspectors, and the shippers do their tasks with few errors and little lost time. Efficiency is a summary statement of what they accomplish as a team. Knowledge, motivation, self-questioning, and so on team up to produce intelligent behavior. (p. 230)

> "[A]bility" is like "efficiency"; such terms refer to multiple coordinated processes. It is appropriate to assess general ability "as a whole" and also to identify processes within good or poor performance. Maturing consists of more or less simultaneous small advances along a broad front, accompanied by gains in an "executive" or "managerial" skill that ties together these resources. This statement and indeed almost all the facts and conclusions [about ability tests] also apply with equal force to achievement tests. (p. 275)

3.   A unitary essence? A third alternative, the unitary view, seeks to identify the essential component of intelligence. Spearman's explanations (e.g., "mental energy") put him in this class. Not all unitary theories focus on the same "essence." Within cognitive theory, inferential reasoning is the key for some. Others, however, see working-memory capacity (or the closely associated process of allocating attention) as closest to intelligence (see pp. 143). No one doubts that all the enabling repertoire of contents and processes is carried in the nervous system, and some think of an "essence" at that level. They may speak of the biological integrity of the neural system, or of accuracy and speed of neural transmission.

Despite extensive research in the cognitive domain, a strong taxonomic architecture is still lacking; but we do have a provisional foundation that provides a sound basis for continuing research. (Snow would have perhaps spoken of a "firm" foundation.) Much is said about cognition in chapter 5. Now, though, we turn to taxonomies in the affective and conative domains.

SUBDIVISIONS OF AFFECT AND CONATION

Controlled analysis of affect and conation has a comparatively short history. Thought about the conative and the affective shows no such orderly progress as was made in the ability field from Spearman to Carroll. Rather, each investigator has invented a terminology. We offer one example from the personality domain. Four prominent personality inventories applied notably different descriptive terms to scores within the area of sociability.[12] We find the following trait labels:

Among 13 scores of GZ: Friendliness, Good personal relations, Sociability.

Among 16 scores of 16PF: Group-tied versus Self-sufficient, Trusting versus Suspicious.

Among 22 scores of PRF: Affiliation, Aggression, Succorance.

Among 19 scores of CPI: Social presence, Sociability.

The inconsistency across systems and the proliferation of terminology filled the research literature with findings that defied integration. Fortunately, as we see, recent work has brought five constructs to the fore.

Apart from this, there has been little taxonomic effort in the affcon domain, apart from the factorial approach. As Gardner (1985) pointed out in his history of cognitive science, the behaviorists effectively drove out of psychological theory references to "such topics as minds, thinking, or imagination, and such concepts as plans, desires, and intentions" (pp. 11–12). Terms such as *purpose, will,* and *need* were, at best, long-range inferences from what could be observed, too vague to be taken seriously by theorists of 1910–1950 (with distinguished exceptions such as Tolman and Lewin).

Even the extensive work on cognition after 1950 has generated nothing like an ordered categorization of processes. Many constructs have been studied sufficiently to serve in serious theory, but they are studied in dissimilar experiments and little information on their interrelations is yet at hand. Not surprisingly, then, affcon concepts are not systematic. It is not clear how profitable it is even to distinguish affect from conation. Summarizing discussants' views at an international conference on the research of 20 years ago, editors of the report said:

There is a handful of constructs that clearly are crucial for contributors: excitation, inhibition, strength, mobility, arousal, activation, regulation, reactivity, optimum arousal, anxiety, sensation seeking, dynamism, and energy exchange. It is surely clear that if the works presented here are to progress as an integrated endeavor, then there must first be a thoroughgoing theoretical evaluation of these constructs, their logical limits, and

---

[12]The tests and principal sources on them are:
GZ: Temperament Survey (Guilford & Zimmerman, 1949).
16PF: 16 Personality Factor Questionnaire (Cattell, Eber, & Tatsuoka, 1970).
PRF: Personality Research Form (D. N. Jackson, 1984).
CPI: California Psychological Inventory (Gough, 1987).

their degree of dependence or independence. ... The investigation of this communality of constructs must be conducted at the theoretical level before much more empirical work is done; otherwise, the work will diverge ... , and an opportunity for synthesis will be lost. (Gale, Strelau, & Farley, 1986, p. 19)

The opportunity was not seized, and the disorder has increased, as will be apparent by the end of chapter 6.

Despite the incoherence of affcon theory, Snow et al. (1996) ventured a provisional taxonomy. The constructs are prime candidates for use in a theoretical network. Snow et al. emphasized relatively stable characteristics causally related to performance for at least some persons, and not variables merely correlated with successful coping. Almost without exception, ability affects a performance positively (if at all). An affcon characteristic, however, may play a highly constructive role in learning or performance, yet may be counterproductive at another time.

The organization we present in Tables 3.3 and 3.4, and in the list on p. 59 ff, derives from versions in Snow (1996b), Snow et al. (1996), and Snow and D. Jackson (1997). We have reconciled minor differences between versions and made some editorial changes. As in the cognitive domain, categories overlap. For example, because motivation is at the heart of goal setting, Snow placed it firmly in the conative domain. This of course does not deny that interests, attitudes, and values generate emotional (affective) reactions. Redundancies remain in the lists simply because these constructs are not a tidy set.

Affective Variables

Initially we recognized two broad types of affective variables, traits of temperament and characteristic moods. The first and third columns of Table 3.3 subdivide these, and show how they connect with the Big Five personality traits listed in the center. Our brief discussion here is amplified in chapter 6. We first consider the left and right columns in turn. But the chart is structured to draw attention to the sideways connections of constructs.

Temperament.   Start at the left. Temperament is a concept dating back to ancient Greece; it refers to constitutional, biologically based styles of reaction. Allport (1961) defined temperament generally: "the characteristic phenomena of an individual's emotional nature, including ... susceptibility to emotional stimulation ... customary strength and speed of response ... prevailing mood, and all the peculiarities of fluctuation and intensity in mood" (p. 34). Buss and Plomin (1984)

TABLE 3.3
Affective Constructs

Traits of Temperament	Personality Factors ("Big Five")	Characteristic Moods

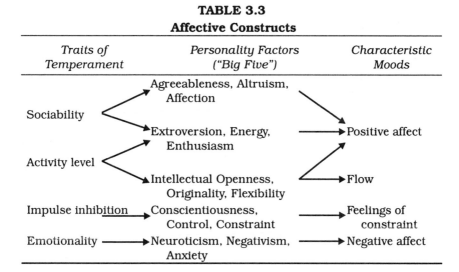

Note. From Snow, Corno, and D. Jackson (1996). Copyright 1996 by Macmillian. Adapted by permission.

narrowed the definition, referring to those "inherited personality traits present in early childhood" (p. 84), including strength and speed, mobility, and balance of the nervous system as a function of biological evolution. Thus traits of temperament are aspects of personality heavily rooted in biology, highly heritable, and little influenced by personal learning history.

The four traits of normal temperament listed at the left of Table 3.3 were separated in the empirical work of Buss and Plomin (1975, 1984). The mechanisms underlying these variables have not been pinned down; to justify these constructs, Buss and Plomin relied mostly on statistical evidence of heritability.

Some infants are highly active and alert, aroused by small amounts of stimulation. Others have high thresholds—it takes strong stimuli to evoke a reaction. These differences tend to persist over many years, and Pavlov argued that this "reactivity" is an important property of individuals' nervous systems. Observers of babies recognize sociability; it can be seen as behavioral energy that reflects the need for social interaction and for shared rather than solitary activities. Emotionality refers to intensity or frequency of physiological arousal associated with the emotions of distress, anger, or fear. As Buss and Plomin noted, impulsivity may best be regarded as a resultant of more basic variables, including, for example, quick decision time and poor impulse inhibition.

Mood. Under "Characteristic moods" are affects sometimes thought of as fleeting. However, most persons have considerable day-to-day consistency in their feelings. Characteristic moods (Tellegen, 1985) are broad emotional states, frequent in the person's life (e.g., the regular exhibition of cheerfulness). Positive affect implies an on-the-average readiness to respond positively to many kinds of experiences; negative affect implies the opposite. School regularly elicits positive moods in some students and negative moods in others. "Feelings of constraint" refers to a cautious, wait-and-see attitude, that is, to an anxious person on the alert for threats. Finally, "flow" is the term used by Csikszentmihalyi (Exh. Csk, p. 47). It describes the state of a person absorbed by a commitment (whether to work or to play or to support a friend) and relishing the engagement. Some people are chronic seekers after situations that absorb them in this way.

Links to Personality. Numerous personality variables have been mapped into the five superdimensions referred to earlier, the "Big Five." The center column of Table 3.3, "Personality Factors," summarizes this mapping; see Digman (1990) and John (1990) for its history.

The center column lists some labels that offer a partial characterization of each dimension. Although Table 3.3 connects personality to affect, there is a conative aspect to conscientiousness, and a cognitive aspect to openness. Of the five dimensions, intellectual openness is perhaps the least familiar and the one most likely to be misunderstood. The "open" person is curious, intellectually adventurous, and playful, and has broad interests. Although such people tend to score above average on general mental ability, openness should not be confused with G. Many people who do well in school and display intellectual flexibility show little openness. Speculation, fantasy, and intellectual investment for the fun of it are not their style.

Many personality psychologists accept the Big Five list. To be sure, some wish to probe deeper into an area such as extroversion and bring in additional constructs (e.g., energy, enthusiasm, ambition). Moreover, some work has treated personality in a hierarchical manner akin to that used with ability. Ackerman and Heggestad (1997), for example, proposed a three-stratum hierarchy with many factor labels at the lowest level and few at the top. A structured taxonomy for personality has yet to be produced, however (see Hofstee, DeRadd, & Goldberg, 1992).

Sharp criticisms of the Big Five have been voiced (Block, 1995; Pervin, 1994). A fundamental complaint has to do with the neglect of situational influences (a neglect that can be seen in all three columns of Table 3.3). Some people can be described as characteristically agreeable (to take the first term in the Big Five as an example); some, as characteristically disagreeable. But most people are in a middle range. A careful record of a typical day for a typical person might tally agreeableness in 30% of all dealings with others, 10% disagreeableness, and 60% neutral (i.e., devoid of sociable or unsociable overtones). Even probabilistic information about the response tendency is a poor description, however, because we do not begin to know the person until we know what kinds of situation elicit an agreeable or disagreeable response. Shoda and associates (Mischel & Shoda, 1995; Shoda, Mischel, & Wright, 1994) spoke of the need for "if–then" profiles linking probability, in each of several categories of situations (the "if"), of making, for example, a disagreeable response (the "then").

At this time, all three columns of Table 3.3 are cast in terms of a kind of statistical average of responses over all situations. This is a limitation but not a fatal flaw. To move toward an "if–then" mapping, one would need categories for "then" events; the listing in Table 3.3 may be of considerable use for that purpose.

Each Big Five dimension has links to aspects of temperament and characteristic mood. The links in Table 3.3 are suggested by connections seen in past research; many of the links were discussed in detail by Snow et al. (1996). For example, measures of positive mood correlate with agreeableness and extroversion. Measures of negative affect are associated with neuroticism, and its aspects of negativism and worry (Hepburn & Eysenck, 1989). Activity level and impulse inhibition are traits of temperament that relate fairly clearly to extroversion and conscientiousness. And a person who readily experiences flow tends also to be open intellectually, that is, sensitive to circumstances that invite such work. (See Csikszentmihalyi et al., 1993; and Perkins, Jay, & Tishman, 1993.) Another obvious link is between conscientiousness or self-discipline and feelings of constraint in the right column.

Conative Variables

Table 3.4 elaborates the conative section of the taxonomy. A crescendo of commitment runs from wishing to wanting to intending to acting (see Corno, 1993; see also p. 175). Motivation and volition are distinguished within conation, a distinction that traces back to Wundt, James, and Ach (Heckhausen, 1991). Motivation covers the internal

TABLE 3.4
Provisional Taxonomy of Conative Constructs

Motivation	Volition
Motivational orientations	Self-regulation
Achievement motivation	Action orientation
Intrinsic motivation	Action controls
Learning orientation	Mindful effort investment
	Self-regulation in learning
Achievement-related attitudes and interests	Conative styles
Value and career orientations	Learning styles
Subject-matter interests	Defensive styles
Attitudes	Motivational and work styles
Beliefs about self	
Self-concept	
Sense of efficacy	
Beliefs about self-development	

Note. From Snow (1996b). Copyright 1996 by Pergamon. Adapted by permission.

Exhibit Msch. Self-Regulation as an Enduring Attribute

Mischel and colleagues studied children's self-control—specifically, their willingness to delay gratification (Shoda, Mischel, & Peake, 1990). This work is a rare inquiry that followed the same persons longitudinally, relating impulse control at an early age to conative controls at later ages.

In an experimental setup, preschool children tested individually were encouraged to delay gratification. Each was invited to say whether he or she would prefer to receive one or two marshmallows (for example). The child had already been shown that when the experimenter left the room the child could bring him back at once, by ringing a bell. In the delay test, the child was told that if she did not ring the bell before a scheduled interval elapsed, she would get the award she preferred. If the child rang the bell to shorten the wait for a reward, she would get the lesser reward. These rules were fully explained to the children.

The most self-controlled children, it was found, used mental devices to ward off impatience: "obscuring temptations" (looking away), "generating diversions" (singing a song aloud, playing with hands), and "self-instructing" (e.g., saying aloud, "I'll wait so I can get two marshmallows instead of one").

For roughly half the children the rewards were left in sight; for the others they were put away. Both these groups were split, half being advised to think thoughts such as the one quoted previously. The other half were left to "spontaneous ideation," which might or might not have similar content. The average delay time in the spontaneous, reward-exposed (SE) condition was only 60% of the average in the other groups (pooled here as NSE). Waiting was harder for SE children, who had maximum temptation and no advice on coping. The investigators called that the "diagnostic condition." SE was demanding enough to expose weak self-regulation.

Some subjects were tracked down in late adolescence, and SAT scores were obtained for 94 of them. Their delay times at an early age correlated about .50 with SAT; that is, superior ability to delay gratification at an early age forecast superior intellectual growth. Within-subgroup analysis of NSEs generated correlations in the range −.20 to −.30. The authors noted the need for caution, given the sample size.

Parents rated the coping behavior of 41 SE adolescents and 91 NSEs; caution is again in order. Among NSEs, correlations of delay times with later parent ratings were mostly in the −.20 to +.20 range. Among SEs, 5 of 14 correlations were in the .50–.60 range (positive or negative) and 7 more were between .30 and .40. In adolescence, those who had delayed under stress as children now resisted temptation and exhibited self-control.

On another instrument returned by somewhat more parents (48 and 117, respectively) there was again not much relation among NSEs of ratings to preschool delay scores. There was a modest tendency ($r = .30$ to $.40$) for SEs who had delayed successfully to be rated in adolescence as unflurried under stress, open to reason, and planful.

No doubt we are seeing here not just consistency of traits in a child but consistency in the parental style that generates a self-controlling youngster.

For related discussion in another part of the book, see pp. 178, 204.

states that precede a commitment to action. Volition connects conceptually with conscientiousness; it refers to a person's state in planning
for and during the action, and the controls used to sustain the intention (Gollwitzer, 1996). This concept connects to early research on
character and intelligence by E. Webb (1915; see Spearman, 1927), as
well as to Ach's (1910) psychology of will. Apart from the British investigator Aveling, subsequent research on volition was confined to conti-
nental Europe until recently (Heckhausen, 1991).

Motivation enhances orientations such as willingness to master
tasks; goals, interests, and attitudes; and various beliefs about oneself. Each of these fosters investment of effort or task avoidance. For
example, a strong interest and a learning orientation result in effort
and engagement. The person desiring to avoid failure, or having a low
sense of efficacy for a task, is likely to engage gingerly or not at all.

Aspects of self-regulation are the principal elements in volition. Persons classified as "action-oriented" by the indicators described at p.
177 make appropriate plans. Action controls and mindfulness direct
effort and maintain it, as do the specialized controls of self-regulated
learning. Such controls are seen in the behavior of preschoolers described in Exhibit Msch. Finally, conative workstyles reflect characteristic ways of investing effort in tasks.

The criticism made of Table 3.3, that its response categories ignore
the influence of situations, applies at only a few points in Table 3.4. Intrinsic motivation, for example, manifestly describes the reaction to a
category of activities; no one is attracted to all types of activity. As a second example, sense of efficacy interacts with the situation; a generally
secure and confident person will be well aware of what she does well,
and less well. Those entries that seem to reflect characteristic motivations also have situational links. Thus the theory developed around
achievement motivation is concerned with how persons high or low on
that trait respond to challenges.

TAXONOMY FOR SITUATIONS

Movement toward taxonomies of situations is clearly needed to coordinate with taxonomies of propensities, even if in the short term only a
start is possible. Information from studies of learning can be systematically compiled only if sets of "similar" situations can be identified.
Identifying tentative classes of situations, one after another, is a necessary first step. Within education, groupings based on curriculum and
instructional method will be pertinent for most lines of investigation
related to questions about aptitude, but additional variables should be

considered: for example, demographic mix in a class, teacher qualifications, and parent support. Whether it will be possible to sort such sets into a taxonomic system, or to locate them in a multivariate space, cannot be foreseen.

It is important to note that these educational examples refer to a continuing but far-from-constant situation, perhaps of a semester's duration, which increases the difficulty of arriving at any simple system. But, as chapter 2 suggested, research on person-in-situation will observe momentary and evolving situations. Each scale of analysis will probably require a different taxonomy.

Ambiguity in Treatment Labels

In ATI research, "we have measured aptitudes with micrometers and treatments with divining rods." That appraisal comes from Berliner (1983). Until recently, the "T" (treatment) in ATI research has stood for a complex combination of task, teacher, subject matter, and instructional method. (School and community contexts are usually ignored.) Educational treatments, however much planned, are often loosely named. Among treatments given the same label, such as cooperative learning, one finds many variations. Indeed, even when one teacher uses the same plan with two classes, the treatments may differ meaningfully. Another complication: Treatments named differently are sometimes functionally equivalent (e.g., teacher centered and "direct" instruction).

The Problem as Seen in a Meta-Analysis[App]. It is easy to underestimate the difficulty of categorizing situations. Some writers (e.g., Kulik, 1981) have urged meta-analysis as the way to bring seemingly dissonant findings on aptitude–treatment interactions into harmony. But meta-analysis can process only studies that have been selected judgmentally as addressing the same question. Statistical formalities are worthless if the initial informal judgment is undependable.

Whitener's (1989) meta-analysis is a case in point. Whitener found in the literature suggestions that performance on a pretest interacted with "instructional support." Perhaps increased support gave an additional advantage to abler students; or perhaps it gave a boost to low-ability students while doing nothing for able ones (or boring them). What would the evidence show, she asked, when studies were compiled? Whitener proposed to contrast two kinds of treatment:

> "individually focused, learner controlled, and self-paced"—little support;

"group oriented, structured and organized"—greater support. (p. 67)

From her analysis, Whitener concluded that greater support had produced larger differences in outcome between high-pretest and low-pretest subgroups than little support did.[13] The source of difficulty in the examples that follow, and others that might be drawn from the Whitener study, is her definitions. In each of the two definitions, she mingled features that need not contribute similarly to support.

Eleven studies entered the meta-analysis. One that illustrates the hazards of misclassification is by Ross and Rakow (1981), who varied the teaching of mathematical rules. Whitener classed the "program control" (PC) treatment as giving much support and the "learner control" (LC) treatment as giving little. (No question arises about the LC classification.)

Whitener's text and the conventions in the field would lead the reader to think that the PC treatment gave strong support to everyone. The point of the Ross–Rakov study, however, was to assess effects of individually prescribed, nonuniform support. PC subjects were supplied as many as seven examples (exercises) per rule or as few as two, the greater number being given to those with very low pretest scores. The added support ultimately brought persons low at pretest nearly up to the level of those high at pretest; the *regression slope*[App] was about half the slope in the three other treatments.

Three other treatments? Yes. Whitener considered it necessary to force all studies into a standard mode for meta-analysis. If any study compared more than two treatments, she selected two and ignored the others. If there were two or more initial measures, or two or more outcome measures, she selected one of each and discarded data on the others. The nonadaptive treatments of Ross and Rakov (coded NA and L) gave five examples per rule to everyone. LC was adaptive, supplying two examples and allowing the learner to call up as many as five more. The regression lines in these three treatments were nearly identical; the low-pretest subjects had very poor outcomes in all of them. As Ross and Rakov had no treatment that provided strong support to everyone, they did not address Whitener's question.

A more dramatic example of the hazards returns us to Exhibit Psc. (p. 21) Two of Whitener's 11 studies came from the single paper of Pascarella (1978). His abstract identified his treatments thus: "high instructional support (Personalized System of Instruction) and low instructional support (Lecture)" (p. 275). Whitener inverted this, identify-

---

[13]The following discussion draws on an extended file of comments prepared by Shindong Lee, working with Snow.

ing Pascarella's lecture as high support and PSI as low support! The reason apparently is that self-pacing—an element in Whitener's "low-support" concept—was a feature of PSI, along with tutoring and three additional procedures. We need not pause to debate which categorization is soundest; the conflict as it stands documents the difficulty of characterizing situations. (Recall from the exhibit that PSI conferred a considerable benefit on students low at pretest.)

Pertinent Taxonomic Methods

Instruction can be seen as a particular sequence of learning activity, embedded in particular classroom or school contexts. For example, one third-grade teacher in a suburban public school designed a 4-week unit on historic China that included: a Chinese banquet; student reports on Chinese traditions, customs, and language; Chinese craft projects; and Chinese mathematical games played in small groups. Situation variables could be defined at the level of the activity or the classroom or the school—or spanning them. But as of now there are no structures for organizing such variables.

In some limited domains, situation dimensions might be identified using a factor analytic approach paralleling that used for propensities. (See references cited in Murtha, Kanfer, & Ackerman, 1996, to the literature on personality.) Variations among teacher styles (Gage, 1985) and college-campus cultures (Pace & Stern, 1958) have been studied by means of correlations.

In most situation-oriented quantitative research, however, only one or two situation variables have been measured or manipulated at a time; many more are readily recognized in a natural setting. When task, treatment, and context variables are all given attention, finding higher order interactions is usual (Cronbach, 1975, 1982). Correlations among situation variables as they occur in the field often cannot be disentangled (Brunswik, 1956; Snow, 1974). And it is impossible to study all relevant levels and kinds of situation simultaneously, just as it is impossible to study all relevant person variables at once.

Mischel and Shoda would describe propensities in "if–then" terms, and we also called for that in chapter 2. But even low-level, atheoretic summaries of observations will require grouping similar situations and grouping similar responses to provide, respectively, the terms that could follow "if" and "then." Philip Converse (1986), a political scientist committed to the view that behavior is conditioned by institutional structures (situations), saw little promise in the development of hierarchical taxonomies of situations for wide application. Rather, he advised social scientists to abstract, from the innumerable ways situations differ, a handful of features likely to affect the responses of immediate interest. If "likely" is an inference from accumulated experience, so much the better.

Before looking at attempted solutions in the literature, we recall that response is shaped by perception. Taxonomy might follow either of two styles. One style would classify on the basis of objective features of the situation; the other would classify situations-as-perceived. The incentives and opportunities referred to in Fig. 2.1 lie in the situation-as-perceived. In the causal chain, the perception is much closer than the objective reality to acts of learning or problem solving. Abilities, in the usual sense, come into play subsequent to perception. But some propensities—for example, to perceive threats in ambiguous situations—determine the perception.

Theory of Educational Situations: A Short History

The study of psychological properties of educational situations dates back at least to the 1960s and the ecological psychology of Barker and Gump (1964). These pioneers conducted detailed analyses of the structural and functional properties of classrooms and schools. "Behavior settings" that they identified in the school included, for example, the spatial arrangements of objects that convey information about function. An enclosed space with books and forward-facing desks suggests academic business whereas certain other structures suggest play. Some recurrent activity (or task) structures such as classroom recitations consist of repeated sequences of teacher statement, question, student response, and teacher reaction, suggesting appropriateness of participation. Any student's life space, however, encompasses many and varied situations, in and out of classrooms. The Barker group's descriptive theory illustrated the diverse challenges and supports that students find in moving from setting to setting during the school day.

In the 1970s, prescriptive theories of instructional design tried to categorize learning tasks and processes (e.g., Gagné, Briggs, & Wagner, 1988). Instructional objectives from Bloom's taxonomy were paired with types of "instructional events." Questions demanding recall were said to give information on recognition learning, whereas higher order questions called for analysis and synthesis. Unfortunately, higher order questions resulted in higher order learning only when students perceived the questions as higher order and teachers explicitly prompted them to think in that way (e.g., Clark et al., 1979). Theories of instructional design have evolved and become less prescriptive—compare, for example, Reigeluth (1983) with Reigeluth (1999). Some (e.g., Case & Bereiter, 1984) have explored the relation of propensities to elements of instruction in careful detail. In addition, theories of classroom climates (Moos, 1979; Walberg, 1977) and the structural characteristics of a curriculum (Bossert, 1978) contributed to modern ideas about situations.

In 1983, Berliner advised psychologists to record salient features of situations, suggested by ecological, behavioral, and cognitive psychology. Berliner's 11 categories of classroom activity structures included reading circle, seatwork, two-way presentations, media presentations such as films, construction, and play. He illustrated what can be done with close attention to classroom activities, and even elaborated a taxonomy suitable for his own research.

Another approach characterized instruction by its content. Kyllonen and Shute (1989) listed the following categories, some declarative, some procedural: proposition, schema, rule, general rule, skill, general skill, automatic skill, and mental model. Kyllonen and Shute thought of arraying courses, topics, or jobs in a multidimensional subject-matter space, and then linking the two systems. Each academic task, then, is designed to promote learning of a bit of subject matter using a planned method to reach an intended outcome (e.g., Newton's Second Law, by means of analogy, leading to competence in schema induction). Particular styles of teaching may have a natural fit with a domain—for example, hands-on experiments in science, text analysis in history or humanities, role playing in social studies, one-on-one tutoring in art, and so on. Information-processing analyses of such pairings can demonstrate the validity of the presumption of fit.

Pointing in another direction is the observation that instructional treatments differ in their demand for information processing. Some treatments demand much learner activity, much appropriately invested mental effort (Salomon, 1983). The teacher regulates the demands—perhaps eliciting the higher order thinking that then results in better performance on tests designed to measure such thinking. For example, a teacher can use discovery scenarios to entrap students and bring errors in reasoning to their attention. That technique would be expected to serve able learners best. On the other hand, some instruction should try to offset low ability and inefficient self-regulation. The Vygotskian treatments mentioned in chapter 2 are designed for this, not just for putting across small lessons.

A taxonomy of food-producing plants intended to bring out the similarities and differences that concern a farmer—demands for rainfall, sunlight, and nutrients, for instance—will have little in common with a taxonomy that serves a nutrition specialist; and neither would much resemble the botanist's taxonomy. In applied work, taxonomy very likely should be purpose-driven.

SNOW'S CHALLENGE, AND A NEW TERRAIN

In framing requirements for aptitude theory, Snow referred often to "boundary conditions," expanding like this:

> (... the set of situations) within which a particular ability construct serves as an aptitude for learning. ... ATI appears when a situation variable spans such a boundary and thus demarcates the limits of that ability construct as aptitude. In other words, the boundary defines a class of treatments within which the ability serves as aptitude for learning. (Snow, 1998, p. 97)

From this point of view, some distinctions between abilities in Carroll's Stratum II can be ignored, unless and until they are connected with differential response to learning situations. Some Stratum III distinctions will no doubt rise in prominence if Snow's question is pursued. Likewise in the affcon domain; recall the Mischel–Shoda emphasis on "if–then" sentences.

Exhibit MKA. Taxonomy of Persons-in-Situations— A First Step

The Big Five traits (Table 3.3) provide descriptions of the person in the abstract—of behavior averaged, as it were, over situations. For two of the traits, Agreeableness and Conscientiousness, situation-focused self-report questions were devised by Murtha, Kanfer, and Ackerman (1996). They also administered a general personality inventory to college students, collected ratings on them from acquaintances, and made a few behavioral observations.

Correlations among items did support the appropriateness of general trait measures; behavioral style was moderately consistent across situations. Items related to similar situations, however, formed clusters; a much fuller picture was captured by distinguishing at least four situation-focused factors. The situations clustered somewhat differently within Agreeableness than within Conscientiousness, but the two structures were similar.

We give some details regarding Conscientiousness only. One type of item had been written specifically around conscientious

---

acts or feelings—in work, school, or home, or with regard to belongings. Another type started with a narrative describing a likely situation vividly, and then asked for agreement or disagreement with, for example, "I think things over before coming to a decision in this type of situation." The same statements were applied to each of the situations in turn.

Of the factors detected, the first referred to situations having definite rules or norms. The people most likely to obey the rules were not, in general, unusually strong on conscientiousness in other situations. This trait did not correlate with general Conscientiousness (self-report or peer report), but it did correlate with behavior—specifically, with on-time arrival for the research sessions.

Another distinction was between situations involving things and those involving people. Persons who said that they were conscientious in handling things also appeared to have an orderly lifestyle (compared with those concerned about people and not so much about things).

Whether a person reported conscientiousness in dealings with close friends had next to no correlation with the general score on Conscientiousness. Finally, conscientiousness in cooperative group work was noted in some persons.

This patterning of conscientious behavior has important implications. Correlations between kinds of behavior are likely to vary from one type of situation to another, and a general Conscientiousness score will not do a good job of predicting behavior in several important types of situations.

A recent development that moves in this direction is the research outlined in Exhibit MKA. Murtha et al. found support for traditional variables (e.g., agreeableness) that describe behavior on the average across varying situations. But then they showed that among people with middling general agreeableness, some may be unruffled in unpleasant situations and some may be nasty, the nastiness being offset in the total by enthusiastic sociability in pleasant circumstances. The research demonstrates the potential value of limiting an individual-difference variable to a narrow range of situations. Murtha et al. took steps toward, not a taxonomy of situation-free propensities, or of person-free situations, but of situation-response combinations. More of this type of work will advance taxonomy of situations appreciably in the future. Surely techniques departing in various ways from those of Murtha et al. will appear in the next 10 years and advance the work.

4 Antecedents of Success in Learning

The previous chapter included a review of current conclusions, extracted from correlations among ability tests, about a suitable conceptual structure for abilities. In the history of psychology, studies of intercorrelations were far outnumbered by studies of the predictive power of ability tests, and we move now to a summary of current conclusions on prediction. The conclusions were largely consolidated before Snow entered the field, and he rarely did such research. Snow did much, however, to locate evidence that affcon variables have causal and predictive power, as the term *aptitude* implies. Research in that vein has led only to scattered (but suggestive) conclusions; this chapter presents some current ideas about practical prediction. The sophisticated prediction studies to which Snow devoted nearly 20 years are the final topic of the chapter.[14] Aptitude-treatment interaction (ATI) studies in education hypothesize that a student is likely to have greater readiness for one type of instruction than another; recall the example in Exhibit Psc. The extensive empirical research on ATI has raised many conceptual questions, but conclusions from statistical comparisons across experimental treatments are, by themselves, too specific to generate theory. The last parts of the chapter illustrate the style and rationale of ATI studies Snow directed; these laid the ground for the studies of process to which he turned following the appearance in 1977 of the Cronbach–Snow book on ATI.

---

[14]Relevant publications by Snow include Snow (1978a, 1989a) and Snow and Lohman (1984).

98

FORECASTING EDUCATIONAL OUTCOMES

Abilities as Predictors

Ability measures have undeniable predictive value. An achievement test in a school subject predicts standing in the same subject a year and more later. For mental tests also, year-to-year correlations are large over short intervals, and taper off over time (Cronbach, 1967b.) Between 1935 and 1970, a number of eminent psychologists argued that intelligence tests, in particular, do not indicate ability to learn, but that their predictive powers derive solely from the overlap of the knowledge they assess with the content of future lessons. Fallacious statistical reasoning underlay that contention (Cronbach & Snow, 1977).

As Exhibit Dbs (p. 17) illustrates, ability tests can effectively reduce failure rates in expensive training. The set of tests used to select for roles in an aircrew was developed according to the multiple-factor ideas of Thurstone and Guilford. Prediction of navigator success was indeed improved by giving extra weight to mathematical abilities, and for bombardiers by weighting psychomotor abilities such as reaction time. Still, the dominant predictive variable for these roles (as for pilots) was a combination of Gf and Gc. The more specialized abilities served the purpose of classification.

Selection of applicants likely to do well in a program has a clear justification, so long as the number of places available is limited. Pure "meritocratic" selection came into question, however, from the early days of testing. As columnists for *The New Republic* in the 1920s, John Dewey and Walter Lippmann asked whether identification and encouragement of the talented might generate an elite and so threaten democracy (Cronbach, 1975). Today's practices in building for a selective university a student body or, in a business, a cadre of trainees typically reject applicants unlikely to succeed—but selection officers do consider qualifications other than high rank in ability.

When an instructional program seeks to serve nearly all comers, as is true in American public education up through the community college, diversifying instruction to accommodate many levels of ability appears to be logical. Thus, younger students are grouped into "slow" and "fast" sections. Some ninth-grade math classes are designed to repair computational skills whereas others to move up the scale into introductory concepts from calculus. Teachers of literature, knowing the range of proficiency in an incoming class, may raise or lower the level of assigned reading material to provide a fitting challenge. Students who know their junior-year PSAT scores look up reports on recent freshman classes of the colleges they might apply to, note each college's score distribution, and then choose a comfortable level of challenge.

Multitrack instruction has faced continual criticism. Classes for children with low test scores have been challenged in court as being noneducational ("basket weaving"), hence a violation of the children's rights. Judges have often agreed. Assignment to a slow section has often implied an interminable sentence to substandard curricula, rather than a focused remediation that could, in principle, bring many lagging students up to speed, as Binet and Vygotsky envisioned.

Whether the "ability-grouping" schemes typically adopted in schools produce consistently better long-run results than wide-range classes is in doubt. Research has not pinned down the features likely to make ability grouping superior to mixed classes (Gustafsson & Undheim, 1996). One reason is that outcomes emphasized in courses for students whose abilities are high, low, and mixed differ qualitatively and quantitatively—as they must in differentiated instruction. Consequently, no measurement can adequately compare them. Test tasks that could reflect the enriched curriculum of an able class would not be meaningful for below-average students (Cronbach & Snow, 1977). Tests that cover only the common ground cannot recognize the benefits of enrichment. More fundamentally, too little research has examined *how* to adapt regular-class instruction to ability levels. In the absence of inspired evaluations, the adaptations teachers have made intuitively are of unknown value.

Some questions about the predictive power of ability tests are primarily practical, and some of primarily theoretical interest. The practical questions interest those who set policy regarding selection, or differentiation of instruction: What kinds of tests predict educational outcomes, and how well? The theoretical questions are: Do tests of mental ability predict the rate at which people learn? If so, which tests? How well? And, down the road, why?

Accounting for rate of learning. Allison (see p. 72) attempted to predict learning on tasks where everyone started with no directly relevant experience. Predictive correlations of learning rate reached the .40–.50 level for only a few of the tasks. Because measures of learning in a brief experiment are unreliable and therefore hard to predict, the correlations of .40 are impressive. All but one of the predictable performances required inductive reasoning. The exception (a physical-construction task called Meccano Assembly) required analysis but not abstract reasoning.

Gc and Gf predicted equally well—surprising, because the tasks gave no advantage to persons with superior knowledge. The finding does fit with the view that Gc reflects a history of efficiency in learning, hence an efficient learning style. Prediction (from Gf *or* Gc) was reasonably successful when the task required organizing new information. Prediction was quite poor when a code or other set of arbitrary associations, not capable of systematization, was to be learned.

On the tasks that required processing of information, persons high on Gc and Gf got off to a faster start than others. Their learning curves looked like the left half of an arch. These abler persons tended to "get a handle on" the novel tasks fairly quickly, perceiving what information to attend to and how to interpret it. That done, their refinements on later trials led to only small changes in score. The curves for learners low in ability were nearer to straight lines; they grasped the fundamentals only gradually.

Ackerman (1988) used the radex analysis by Snow's group of the Allison learning tasks and predictors (p. 72) to support his theory of the role of tested abilities in learning. According to the theory, demands for analysis of new information—a load on attention—is usually great at the outset. Just as the learner must try to sort out what is relevant and irrelevant, so must the person taking a test of general ability. Therefore, the correlation of performance on the new task with G is high on early trials and then declines. Perceptual speed, on the other hand, is expected to help the learner progress after the main intellectual work is done. And, on late trials, psychomotor speed will contribute most to further improvement. Ackerman confirmed these expectations in several laboratory tasks that were more complex and joblike than Allison's.

Ackerman warned, however, that another generalization holds when tasks are "inconsistent." A consistent task, in his sense, is one where the signals retain similar importance and significance over all sessions. That would be true, for example, in plotting combat information in the command center of a battleship. The coordinates for targets that are called in to the plotter by observers always have the same bearing-and-range structure no matter how the combat episode is configured, and are handled the same way. Once the rules are mastered, improvement comes through quicker response. An example of an inconsistent task would be playing poker. The rules stay the same, but in every hand the information in the exposed cards and bets requires analysis; and further interpretation is required when the would-be expert has to "read" the style of new players. On an inconsistent task, the correlation of learning with G is expected to decline very little as the task becomes familiar, because reasoning never ends.

Exhibit RLM. "Perfecting" Prediction of College Success

The tabulations and calculations ordinarily used to judge how well success can be predicted from tests or past histories do not report "the whole truth." Practical measures of success are, first of all, influenced by vagaries of judgment of those who rate the performance. Variation that does not reflect students' merits enters when some select harder courses than others and so are graded lower. Fortuitous events such as illness and variables such as amount of part-time work also limit the meaning of the outcome measure. And the correlation between personal qualities is biased downward when the calculation is made on a preselected *group*[App].

Ramist, Lewis, and McCamley-Jenkins (1994; see also Ramist, Lewis, & McCamley, 1990) set out to estimate what the correlation would be if much of this distortion could be eliminated. They made two statistical adjustments. First, a long-accepted formula estimated what the correlation of a predictor with freshman grade-point average (FGPA) would have been, within a college, if the entering class had been unselected (more precisely, if the class had matched the entire national population of persons who took the SAT, there being neither self-selection by applicants nor selection among them). Second, they adjusted for *unreliability*[App], that is, for the fortuitous variation indicated by the typical less-than-perfect correlation of first- and second-semester marks in a course sequence.

Before these adjustments, FGPA correlated .30 with SAT verbal scores, .31 with SAT mathematical scores, and .39 with high school grade record (HSR); with all these combined, .48. The adjustments raised the values to .50, .53, .61, and .68 respectively (Ramist et al., 1994). (Forty-five colleges were pooled in the analysis.)

The group invented a new way of summarizing grade records to replace the traditional FGPA in research on prediction. Students having SAT scores above the average for their college tend to select courses where grading standards are high (science, e.g.). Grade averages are thereby lowered. To recognize this, the new analysis predicted grades for one course at a time. Approximately eight predictions for a student in freshman-year courses could be averaged into a "predicted FGPA" that took severity of grading into account. When the prediction was made in this manner from SAT-M, SAT-V, and HSR together (Ramist et al., 1994), the correlations with actual FGPA were .60 (uncorrected) and .76 (adjusted for selection and unreliability). Recognizing variable grading standards thus brought an impressive increase. The increase was equally notable for predictors considered singly.

These idealized values do indicate the relevance of SAT and HSR to college success more adequately than the usual numbers. But the main value of the adjustments may be to permit valid comparisons of one student subgroup to another, with no need to make further allowance for their choice of colleges and courses. Ramist et al. (1994) found that the SAT was a better predictor than HSR for students for whom English is a second language (.61 vs. .58, compared with .65 and .69 for native speakers of English). A startling, but somewhat artificial, calculation found that the fully adjusted correlation was .85 for persons in the top third of their student bodies and .65 in the lowest third.

Predicting school marks.   Though the power of ability tests to predict school grades is familiar, nuances emerge from closer looks.

We begin with a study of freshman grade point averages (FGPA) in 120 colleges and universities (Lenning, 1975). The median of within-college correlations was .48 when the ACT battery was used as a set of predictors, and .60 when high school grade record was taken into account also. ACT is a comprehensive measure of skill and knowledge in the principal school subjects; it is closer to Gc than Gf. The correlations Lenning found are consistent with other experience.

Correlations varied a great deal from college to college. Considering ACT alone, 8% of the colleges had correlations of .60 or above. However, 19% of the colleges fell below .40 (including 5% below .30). One reason for the spread is that some colleges are highly selective whereas others are open to most high school graduates. Selection reduces the range of predictor scores and so lowers correlations. (Recall the demonstration of this in the aviation-psychology program; Exhibit Dbs., p. 17) Correlations were also lower in colleges having a highly varied curriculum. When students are held to much the same range of courses and grading standards, grade averages are comparatively predictable. When students are free to choose between demanding and undemanding courses, and when grading standards vary over courses, then the grade average becomes harder to predict.

A recent study of the SAT (a Gc-Gf compound) pursued these questions. Exhibit RLM outlines the technical features of the study. Its idealized final coefficients assume that colleges are not selective, taking in applicants at random from the population completing the SAT, and that grade average is made "perfectly reliable"—as if every student were graded on a very large number of courses. Such assumptions are unrealistic, but calculations based on them provide a reasonable basis for comparing two prediction rules or two college programs. After the predicted grade average was adjusted downward for students who took courses with strict grading, and upward for those who chose less demanding courses, the correlation rose to .65 (SAT V + M), and to .76 when high school record was added in.

A Swedish study (Gustafsson & Balke, 1993) used somewhat similar corrections, but was able to estimate the relations of purified criteria to "perfectly reliable" measures of ability. (This calculation adjusted out any difference among predictors in accuracy of measurement.)

For more than 800 students, abilities had been tested in Grade 6, and Grade 9 marks in 17 courses recorded. These are the correlations for five of the more academic courses.

English	with Gf, .59	with Gc, .75	combined, .77
Swedish	.59	.66	.70
Mathematics	.64	.16	.66
Civics	.53	.59	.63
Biology	.54	.56	.61

(In Gustafsson's system, G and Gf are indistinguishable; see p. 74.) Gc was defined primarily by measures of vocabulary and language skills.[15] The "combined" column reports the perfected correlation that would be expected using reliable Gf and Gc together as predictors.

In these academic courses, save for English and mathematics, Gc and Gf were about equally good as predictors. In English Gc was notably better. A third predictor considered was a measure of crystallized numerical skills. It predicted powerfully in mathematics but not in other subjects.

---

[15]Gustafsson and Balke (1993) reported the correlation not for Gc but for a residual variable from which the contribution of G had been removed. We reconstituted the correlation for Gc under the assumption that the correlation of G with Gc was .60. Other plausible values for the correlation would alter our conclusion only in detail.

Other Predictors

Personality Measures.   Although measures of ability have power to predict attainment, the prediction is far from perfect. In the Ramist and Gustafsson studies, heroic statistical allowances for errors that reduce correlations still left the ability-outcome correlations considerably below 1.0. It follows that students who start as equals in the intellectual sphere spread quite a bit along the scale of later attainment. It is easy to suppose that "personality" determines which students make the most of their abilities. But innumerable studies have tried to raise correlations by weighting measures of personality or motivation alongside ability in the prediction, and their hopes of improving prediction were generally disappointed.

Positive findings were scattered and inconsistent. To deserve attention, a result should be substantial and dependable. We consider the result substantial if adding information on personality increases the square of the predictive correlation for grade average by .05, when the base predictor combines previous grade average and a measure of G. Further, the finding should have been confirmed in at least one other sample. By this standard, measures of personality and interests do not predict success.

Common sense suggests that on average students with greater motivation will achieve more. Atkinson, however, questioned this presumption. The curves shown in Fig. 2.2 imply that motivation may be too strong as well as too weak. This idea of an optimum level has been suggested by observations on emotional arousal, self-criticalness, persistence, and many other affcon variables.

Whether one could predict educational success by fitting to data a curvilinear trend such as that in Fig. 2.2, rather than the usual straight-line trend, is an open question. A larger sample is required for stable results when a more complicated formula is fitted. Moreover, the optimum level of a personality trait or emotional state probably varies from task to task; if so, a particular nonlinear prediction formula will work in only a limited range of situations.

A remarkable exception to the sad story of the preceding paragraphs is the strong relation of personality scores to success in deep-sea diving (Fig. 4.1). The successful divers had generally described themselves (prior to training) as dominant, confident, and free from anxiety. They were vastly different from the divers who failed when the training became stressful. This result was obtained in a training situation, but at a stage in the training where coping with stress was paramount, rather than acquiring knowledge or skill.

Exhibit Lmbr. Success in Stressful Training Predicted From Affective Variables

Lambrechts (n.d.; see Snow, 1984) administered several personality inventories to men of the Belgian navy who volunteered for diving school. For a period of 3 years, volunteers were accepted without reference to the personality data; an ability battery and medical examination governed selection. Data were available from 80 candidates who subsequently succeeded in the training course, and 30 who subsequently failed.

Figure 4.1 displays averages on the most clearly interpretable of the personality measures used by Lambrechts. Instruments represented include the Guilford–Zimmerman, Bernreuter, and MMPI (Minnesota Multiphasic Personality Inventory) inventories. The scales are arranged here to support the interpretation that Extroversion and absence of Neuroticism account for most of the differences.

Although diver candidates were dropped from or voluntarily quit the training program at various points, a substantial number of losses occurred when training moved from pool diving to the open sea. Very likely, state anxiety as well as the complexity of the task increased at this time. Successful diver candidates appear to have been low enough in anxiety and high enough in assertiveness to cope with both complications as training progressed.

Past history.   You get to play for the Atlanta Braves only if you looked good wherever you played baseball in past seasons. Past performance is the main resource for practical prediction. High-school record predicts college marks because abilities and work habits carry forward.

The biographical inventory is a favorite means of augmenting a battery of ability tests; it was the only measure outside the ability domain that contributed to prediction for the Army Air Force (Exh. Dbs, p. 17). Such an inventory can touch on interests, skills, and style of interacting with others. It thus collects a variety of affective, conative, and cognitive information, and the typical scoring key assigns points to whatever responses are given with greater-than-average frequency by successful trainees.

A large study commissioned by the College Board (Willingham, 1985) supplements our previous account of academic prediction. This study asked freshmen accepted into 13 colleges to describe their par-

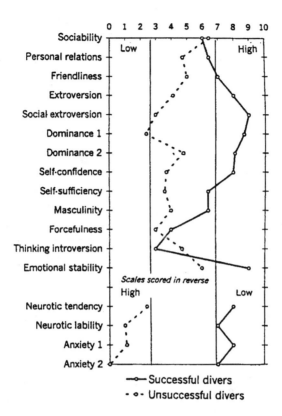

FIG. 4.1.   Personality scores distinguishing successful from unsuccessful diver trainees. Data from Lambrechts (n.d.). Figure adapted from Snow (1984).

ticipation in high school extracurricular activities. The analysis used verifiable facts from those accounts, and so the data were free from most of the biases of overstatement and undue modesty that can color inventory responses.

As usual, high school grade record (HSR) and the SAT predicted college grade averages (GPA). Also as usual, no summary variable from the personal-history file improved the prediction of college GPA by much. But colleges look beyond course marks in judging which students have been most successful. Three main nongrade criteria of college success were collected for this study:

Leadership   Elected to a student office or selected by college
                              officials for a responsible post

| Accomplishment | Named by the college as having shown notable performance, in any field: athletics, art, organizing, and so on. |
| Success | Identified by a faculty-staff committee as one of the most successful students, in the light of the college's goals. |

(The Success and Accomplishment nominations were made only for purposes of the research.)

Of the past-history predictors the study considered, a "follow-through" rating was the best predictor of the "leadership" and "accomplishment" criteria, and was second only to HSR as a predictor of the "success" criterion. The research staff rated follow-through by tracing, in the detailed accounts of high school careers, the extent of "continuous commitment and success" there in community, athletic, leadership, and creative activities (Willingham, 1985, p. 100). The following percentages of students nominated for Accomplishment are fairly typical (p. 93):

| Among all seniors | 24% |
| Among seniors scoring high on follow-through | 35% |

No doubt many causes lay behind the accomplishments in high school and college, but a strong conative component was obviously a continuing trait. This component is like the cumulative effect of the "flow" experience (Exh. Csk., p. 47).

Attitudes and Beliefs.   Whatever the predictive shortcomings of all-purpose measures of motivation, emotional stability, and the like, measures narrowly defined to tap situation-relevant beliefs and attitudes frequently show predictive power.

In a survey of high school sophomores, one question asked, "How important are good grades for your future?" O'Malley later checked which of them continued their education beyond high school. (This analysis is published only in Atkinson et al., 1976.) Among students strongly valuing grades, the percentage continuing their education was almost 20 percentage points higher than among the others. Moreover, continuing in school was especially unlikely among sophomores with low achievement motivation and high anxiety.

Most attitude measures are somewhat ambiguous. In the O'Malley study, saying that grades do not matter much may have been a defense for students who had been having little academic success, the kind of face-saving responses sometimes called "self-handicapping" (Urdan, Midgley, & Anderman, 1998). It is a good bet, also, that an adolescent's attitude toward schoolwork is likely to match that of like-gender friends (Urdan, 1997). Probably the friends do much to shape the attitude; and the attitude affects the choice (and keeping) of friends. The attitude then is an indicator of development, a propensity—but not an independent causal variable. One theorist (Wigfield, 1994) did explain in detail how valuing of achievement influences the day-to-day processes of academic work.

"Self-efficacy" and closely related beliefs about one's capabilities often are related to continuing academic performance. Students with a strong sense of efficacy describe themselves as alert to check their own progress, unthreatened in the face of difficulty, and expecting to do well. Indicators of efficacy show, in study after study, a power to predict success in learning over and above the success accounted for by conventional tests of ability. We summarize two studies to illustrate methods and findings:

- Each student entering a social-studies course in high school was asked about his or her sense of efficacy, and also asked what grade he or she expected. Both variables apparently had a causal influence. Past grades in social studies correlated only .23 with grades in this course. A combination of grades with scores from a questionnaire on perceived self-efficacy and academic goals correlated .56 with end-of-course grades (Zimmerman, Bandura, & Martinez-Pons, 1992).
- Air-traffic controllers monitor rapidly changing displays of planes, and apply rules in order to direct landings and take-offs. An inventory asked some entering trainees to estimate their usual confidence during training, study, and test taking, and asked how they reacted to difficulty (Ackerman & Kanfer, 1993). The authors referred to the instrument as an inventory of "motivational skills," but perhaps it is better described as an indirect report on past success. Outcomes of an 8-week training course (and, in another sample, of a much briefer simulation) were predicted by this measure of perceived efficacy with correlations of .3–.4. Combining information on attitude and ability predicted better than ability alone.

We postpone to chapter 6 discussion of research tracing connections between affcon variables and the processes observed during learning. There we emphasize how characteristics of the learning situation influence the relevance of various motivational variables. Our summary here has emphasized grade averages over a mix of situations as the target of prediction; such merging of situations masks the power of any situation-dependent predictor. The powerful prediction of success in diver training, on the other hand, can be interpreted as evidence of personality–situation interaction. The breakdown of performance among anxious introverts occurred when the training moved from shallow to deep water. Not many men had failed earlier.

THE APTITUDE REQUIREMENTS OF ALTERNATIVE INSTRUCTIONAL SITUATIONS

The fit between person and situation was the main theme of Snow's entire research career. Here we consider a few of the formal experiments by Snow and his colleagues on aptitude–treatment interaction. The classic design calls for:

Alternative methods of teaching the same content.

Random assignment of students to treatment.

Initial testing to measure propensities hypothesized to be more relevant to one treatment than to another.

(The illustration of this approach in Exh. Psc, p. 21, departed from ideal experimental control in allowing students a choice of treatment.) Nearly all the studies of abilities that Snow directed in this vein had been completed by 1976, and were reviewed and integrated in the Cronbach–Snow "handbook" (1977). We have nothing new to say about the Stanford studies of ability prior to Snow's shift in the 1970s to an emphasis on process; that later work is the topic of chapter 5.

This chapter, however, summarizes Snow's doctoral dissertation as a significant piece of his initial thinking and for the lessons it provides for all instructional research on interaction. Our second topic is the follow-up by Snow's group on one of the most intriguing hypotheses from the Cronbach–Snow literature review. Various investigators, notably George Domino (1968, 1971, 1974), had replicated evidence that scores on some aspects of personality interact with style of instruction. Snow's dissertation itself had provided one of the earliest demonstrations of such relations under formal experimental control. Several Snow students of the mid-1970s traced how outcomes in contrasting treatments related to selected personality variables. We deal at some length with one pair of predictors—anxiety and ability. The account illustrates the intriguing hypotheses in this area and the difficulty of pinning down conclusions.

Learning From Live and Filmed Demonstrations in Physics

When he was a graduate student, Snow served as an assistant in the Purdue University's Audio Visual Center. One assignment was to analyze results of an instructional experiment. Two members of the physics faculty had teamed with the Center to film the demonstration part of each session of the basic physics course. Presentation on film was expected to have such advantages over live demonstrations as close-ups, slow motion, the opportunity to reshoot during filming and to edit, and, for the student, a good view from any part of the room. In all, 20 films were produced, ranging in length from 4 to 33 minutes (median 9).

Once the film was made, an experimental trial was set up. One large section of the course saw films throughout the term, whereas another saw live demonstrations. In the film (F) treatment, the films were shown, with no special introductory or concluding remarks by the instructor. In the live (L) treatment, everything was the same except that the experiment was performed and narrated by the instructor; apparatus, event sequence, script, and mathematical notes (on the blackboard) matched the film.

Questions at the end of the class hour about the day's demonstration provided a measure of immediate recall. In the first year's trial, F instruction did lead to higher scores than L, on the average over daily quizzes. On questions in midterm and final examinations about principles the films had demonstrated, differences were small (Tendan, 1961; Tendan & McLeod, 1962; Tendan, McLeod, & Snow, 1962). Might it be that the films worked well with one type of student and not so well with another? Repeating the experiment the following year and checking students' success against their initial characteristics served the instructors' goals and Snow's research interests. In the second trial, the F group did only a trifle better than the L group on the quizzes, and a trifle worse on the demonstration-related questions at exam time. The average treatment effect, then, appears to have been negligible. The new analysis focused on individual differences.

Several features of this environment supported an exceptionally strong ATI study:

A term-long, professionally prepared innovative treatment.

Cooperative instructors dedicated to delivering the treatments as planned (save for unforeseeable equipment malfunctions and the like).

Instructors who saw the scientific merit of random assignment and had the power to carry it out.

Cooperation of instructors in pinpointing what should be learned from each lesson and in preparing quizzes.

Students who needed the course as preparation for engineering, hence were well motivated.

A large sample: roughly 200 students per treatment, after dropouts and after elimination of data from some with (for example) poor command of English.

For the sake of experimental control, the normal practice of allowing students to review the films during free time was suspended.

Procedure.   As initial characteristics to be measured, Snow chose variables in five categories (see Snow, 1963; Snow, Tiffin, & Seibert, 1965):

Domain knowledge: pretest on knowledge of physics.

Ability: numerical ability, verbal ability, grade-point average.

Personality: ascendancy, responsibility, emotional stability, sociability, total self-evaluation of personality.

Attitudes: toward instructional film, toward entertainment film, toward physics.

Experience: with instructional film, with entertainment film, with Purdue library films.

Prior knowledge of physics had served in the first-year trial as a control variable, to allow for the head start of some students, and it played that role in the second-year analysis also. The verbal and numerical scores came from standard tests routinely administered to Purdue freshmen. The attitude measures were six-item scales. The personality scores came from the Gordon Personal Profile (Gordon, 1953). The experience variables were self-reported frequencies. The tests showed adequate reliability; no estimate of reliability was made for the experience variable and grade average.

Each class hour having a demonstration ended with a 5-minute quiz on it, requiring multiple-choice or brief written responses. The total score on the 14 quizzes measured immediate recall. Each course examination included short-answer questions on several demonstrations. The score on those particular questions, summed over the five examinations, provided a measure of delayed recall. Snow estimated that students' rankings on immediate recall and delayed recall would have agreed closely if the delayed tests had been more reliable. Sometimes, however, subgroup averages on immediate and delayed recall told different stories.

In tabulating the data, Snow sorted students into three groups according to their prior knowledge of physics (PK). These groups were again split three ways on whichever further predictor an analysis examined. The analysis asked, Is there a statistically *significant*[APP] F – L difference in any of the nine cells? This could easily flag chance differences. We concentrate on findings that represent reasonably consistent trends across cells.

Findings.   Overall, scores had much the same distribution in each treatment. But there were interaction effects. We consider families of predictors in turn:

1. Ability. Snow had expected ability to relate more strongly to performance in the L treatment, because equipment problems at times made the L demonstration less organized, hence intellectually more demanding. The data for verbal ability and grade average did not show such a trend.

Numerical ability, however, was more strongly related to immediate recall in the L condition than in F. The effect was about as strong among those with low PK as with high PK, and absent in the middle group. This variation could well be due to small cell sizes. There was no similar interaction effect on delayed recall; the F and L regression lines within any PK level nearly coincided. Snow's interpretation of the effect on immediate recall was that live instruction may allow math-able students to "think ahead" when the instructor is developing a formula. And the weak advantage of F instruction for low-numerical students might have arisen from superior clarity in the film.

2. Personality. Of the five personality variables, two interacted with the F/L contrast in generating immediate-recall scores. Although the patterning of means was not uniform in the PK subgroups, this irregularity apparently reflected sampling fluctuations. Figure 4.2 therefore follows Snow in combining PK subgroups.[16]

Gordon (1953) spoke of high-ascendants as active, self-assured, assertive, and independent. Such students did much better in L than in F. The effect of Ascendancy, shown in Fig. 4.2a, appears to be of medium size. Students describing themselves as followers, dependent on others, observers rather than participators, and weak in self-confidence did a bit better in F than in L. These findings on immediate recall were present on delayed recall also, but much smaller in magnitude.

The L condition was superior for students low in Responsibility (Fig. 4.2b). Again, the delayed-recall analysis provides a hint of con-

---

[16]Our numbers differ slightly from those in Snow's several reports (e.g., Snow et al., 1965) Averages plotted here take into account the numbers of cases in the subgroups being pooled, whereas the older analyses treated the groups as if equal in size.

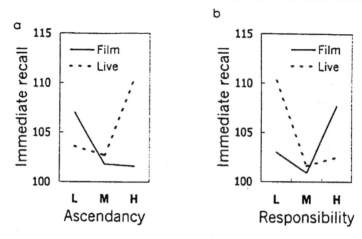

FIG. 4.2.   Mean immediate-recall scores as a function of treatment and personality. From Snow, Tiffin, and Seibert (1965). Copyright 1965 by the American Psychological Association. Adapted by permission.

firmation, the F mean being above the L mean for those high in Responsibility and the L mean higher among the lows. But the delayed-recall finding is quite weak.

Gordon (1953) described those low in Responsibility as "unable to stick to tasks that do not interest them, and in the extreme ... flighty or irresponsible" (p. 5). Snow suggested the following explanation for the result in Fig. 4.2b. In live presentations an authority figure is observing the class, and class members know it. In contrast, films shown in a darkened room provide no social pressure. Neither ascendant, sociable individuals nor those who are relatively irresponsible seem to learn as well from film as from live presentation. Showing films can foster a spectator attitude, hence less learning. Active, assertive students may be ill at ease under these constraints, whereas the spectator role is comfortable for submissive students. Similarly, less responsible students may relax when viewing a film and under no social pressure to concentrate.

3. Attitude. No consistent interaction of attitude variables with treatment appeared.

4. Experience with films. Self-reported experience with instructional and entertainment films was not related to outcomes.

Past use of library films did show an interaction pattern in the sample (Table 4.1), but the effect on immediate recall is weak and within the chance range. The effect on delayed recall is of medium

TABLE 4.1

Mean Scores in Film and Live Treatments as a Function of Past Use of Library Films

	Immediate Recall		Delayed Recall	
	Film Group	Live Group	Film Group	Live Group
High film usage	106	103	42	37
Low film usage	103	105	38	39

size, but could also be a chance effect. (The scales for the two outcome measures differed, with the SD^{App} for delayed recall being approximately half that for immediate recall.)

Snow recommended that future instructional research give attention to experience-with-method variables. Hoban and Van Ormer (1950) and Miller (1957) had drawn particular attention to instructional film in this regard, and there had been talk of "film literacy," the acquired ability to learn from film. Perhaps, Snow said, styles or strategies especially suitable for learning from film develop through experience and are available for transfer to new film instruction. (Exh. WS, p. 27, seems to show in another context such evolution from experience-with-method.)

Evaluation of the Research.   Snow pointed out that most instructional research on aptitude had assessed only one or two possible predictors. Many kinds of individual characteristics might influence response to instruction. In principle, he said, research would be more informative if such variables were considered together, in the same study. He employed 14 predictors, all having some rationale behind them and the whole set neatly calculated to require a minimum of student time.

His inclusion of noncognitive variables as predictors was, in its day, a rarity in research on instruction. Of the 14 variables, just 4 showed a pattern persuasive enough to be included in our summary of positive findings; 1 was an ability, 1 was a report on past experience, and 2 were personality scales. So the excursion into new territory was well conceived.

Snow himself, however, made this comment nearly 30 years later (1992):

This study was strong in important respects; it used a substantial amount of real instruction, clearly defined treatments, good quality measures, and a large student sample. But the methodological criticism is obvious (at least it is *today*); aptitude *complexes* should have been studied by considering all the individual variables jointly. There might well be moderating relations between [physics knowledge, quantitative ability, responsibility, and ascendancy]. There should also be patterns of relations among these variables that define profiles or categories of persons well served by one or another treatment. These are defined in a multivariate aptitude space, but they are categories of whole persons, not lists of interacting variables. (p. 14; emphasis in original)

Measuring both immediate recall and delayed recall was also a good plan but it produced puzzlement. The two variables gave fully consistent findings only on such overall effects as the predictive power of PK and the lack of any strong F/L difference. One part of the problem is measurement error. Another reason for inconsistency is that a student who did not immediately grasp a demonstration had an opportunity to study the topic before the examination that produced the delayed-recall measure. When Snow's Stanford project later collected immediate and delayed measures, inconsistency of results was a frequent source of perplexity. Perhaps a new type of inquiry will be required to trace just what competence is lost, or gained, between initial test and delayed test. Obviously, so long as findings vary with the delay interval, delayed tests should have a prominent place in instructional research.

Propensities Acting in Combination   In many places (see especially Snow, 1987), Snow spoke of "aptitude complexes." The central thought was that some pairs of propensities (or larger sets) have joint effects. That is, in some treatment the relation of outcomes to aptitude A depends on the level of a second aptitude A′ —an A × A′ interaction. Associated with this at times was the suggestion that some combinations, such as being high on Gf and on Carroll's factor Gi, might identify distinct types of intellectual functioning. A sharp difference in performance, then, might be expected between persons within the region and others who fell just modestly below "high" on one scale or the other. The contrasting conception is found in the usual prediction study whose statistical model presumes that the effects of aptitudes are additive; that is, assumes that a higher score on A can compensate for shortcomings in B.

There is commonsense support for the joint-action hypothesis. The old New York joke had it wrong; if you want to get to Carnegie Hall, "Practice!" is not a sufficient answer. Both talent and motivation are needed to sustain extended commitment. Strongly motivated practice without talent sets the person up for disappointment. The endless practice needed to raise superior talent to concert quality skill will prove dreary if the person does not find performance gratifying. Dropping out is the usual end result. A higher level of talent does not offset deficient interest, and strong interest does not compensate for a shortfall in talent.

Mathematically, an A × A′ interaction produces a curved regression surface. Thus it may be that in most of the range there is some positive relation of both ability and interest to amount of practice, the regression surface being a plane in those regions. With interaction, however, we would expect a marked increase in slope in the region where A and A′ are both high. The "twisted sheet" found in Peterson's analysis (p. 123) is an instance of such curvature. Atkinson's theory (Figs. 2.1 and 2.2) illustrates another form of A × A′ relation.

Until about 1975, studies in the Stanford aptitude project almost always considered single initial measures in turn, or additive combinations of them. Reporting that a measure did not predict, or did not interact with a treatment variable, was too easily overinterpreted as "no relationship." Bringing a second propensity into the picture and searching for joint effects might have turned some findings of no effect into positive findings. Snow led his students to carry out the several studies reviewed in the remainder of this chapter, and he saw the results as supporting the joint-action hypothesis.

Immersed as he had been in ATI research, it was natural for Snow to frame this hypothesis in ATI terms, as an A × A′ × T hypothesis—logical enough but comparatively difficult to test. If joint action of some A, A′ pair (e.g., talent and interest in the example of this section) is documented, that is of interest even if the effect varies with T or is universal over treatments.

Joint Action of Ability and Anxiety

We turn now to an instructive story about the pursuit of a particular higher order interaction. Researchers had suggested that the effects of anxiety on learning depend on the student's ability and on the style of instruction. This inspired a rare sequence of inquiries into joint properties of cognitive and affective variables.

Structure and Demand for Participation as Treatment Variables. Over many years, research findings had hinted that situational stress impairs the performance and learning of those who are anxious at the outset. Theory had suggested the idea of an optimal level of arousal, an idea often echoed and repeatedly reshaped (as in Exhs. Atk at p. 44 and Csk, p. 47, respectively). Even a mild challenge to an already anxious person may generate tension that blocks response. For those low in anxiety, however, situational pressure may bring arousal nearer to the optimum. Cronbach and Snow (1977) collated many studies that asked whether one or another treatment contrast would interact with anxiety (Ax). Strong and consistent effects were not found.

One hypothesis in this area did survive: Strongly structured instruction helps anxious learners by making clear what is expected. Dowaliby and Schumer (1973) compared two sections of college introductory psychology. One featured teacher presentations; in the other

TABLE 4.2
Partial Definition of Peterson Treatments

S+ P+ : High Structure, *High Participation*	*S+ P– : High Structure,* *Low Participation*
Teacher elicits desired goals/objectives from students by asking questions.	Teacher tells desired goals/objectives.
Teacher uses student ideas and adds verbal markers to emphasize important points.	Teacher states important points with verbal markers for emphasis.
Teacher asks many questions and uses questions and student responses to structure lesson.	Teacher asks few questions, but uses those few questions and student responses to structure lesson.
Teacher tells students they will be required to participate in class and does call on students during class.	Teacher tells students they will not be required to participate in class and does not call on students during class.
S– P+ : Low Structure, *High Participation*	*S– P– : Low Structure,* *Low Participation*
No mention of goals/objectives.	No mention of goals/objectives.
Few verbal markers of importance.	Few verbal markers of importance.
Teacher asks many questions to elicit facts, concepts, principles, and opinions but does not attempt to use them to tie the lesson together.	Teacher asks few questions and does not use those few questions to tie the lesson together.
Teacher does not explicitly tell students they will be required to participate in class, but does call on them during class.	Teacher does not mention student participation and does not call on students during class.

Note. From Peterson (1977). Copyright 1977 by the American Psychological Association. Adapted by permission.

the teacher encouraged student discussion. With strong structure, the more anxious students did better than others. Where participation was encouraged, students low in anxiety did better than anxious ones. Domino (1974) replicated the finding.

Peterson (1976, 1977) suspected that teacher direction and student participation should be seen as distinct causes rather than as opposite poles of one dimension. She defined a structure variable S and a participation variable P. Using + and – to indicate high and low degrees of each variable, this creates four treatment patterns: S+ P+, S+ P–, S+ P–, and S– P–. Peterson considered nine aspects of class activity in her experimental protocol; the four listed in Table 4.2 illustrate how each combination of S and P could produce a distinct style.

Procedure.   A single teacher taught each of four sections of a ninth-grade unit on American social problems. The reading selections, which told the stories of individuals in difficulty, seemed likely to be interesting and provocative of discussion. The teacher was trained in the four styles defined by Peterson and applied one to each section. (He explained to the group at the start of the 2-week experiment what style he was adopting with it.)

As initial measures that might interact with S and P, Peterson employed a vocabulary test (V) and a trait-anxiety score (Ax). (Two additional scores, from the California Personality Inventory, tested a hypothesis we do not discuss; see Snow, 1978a, pp. 55–67.)

Each section had 24 to 30 students. In Snow's dissertation study, even with six times as many students per treatment, statistical tests of all but the simplest relationships had been equivocal. It was therefore recognized that Peterson's study had low statistical power; but it was as large as was practical in a dissertation. Her significance tests must be discounted because she made dozens of them, and some fraction of the regression slopes would change considerably in a second sample.[17] (See *Uncertainty* in the appendix.)

In an attempt to provide an economical cross-check, all Peterson's measures were applied in seven sections of the same course taught by other teachers. The styles of those teachers were not controlled, but

---

[17]A study of an A × A′ × T hypothesis with a single treatment contrast would require fitting to the data a regression equation with eight terms. This degree of complexity would create little extra opportunity for chance to operate. Peterson's hypothesis, however, called for two predictors and a two-way treatment contrast, raising the number of fitted constants to 15. Matters got out of hand (in the analysis on which she based conclusions) when she added two further interacting predictors to test an additional set of hypotheses. This excess bespeaks the fact that hers was the first attempt at applying generalized regression to a multilayer hypothesis about aptitudes in an experimental study; it was outside the experience of three methodologists who supervised the dissertation.

observers rated each one on the features that Table 4.2 illustrates. In principle, those naturalistic data might have confirmed any finding from the experiment. In practice, it proved so difficult to match to Peterson's categories the styles observed in the uncontrolled classes that the extra data could neither affirm nor contradict the experimental findings. The principle of carrying inquiry beyond a single class or school is fundamental, but natural situations vary along so many lines that the results often do not send a clear message on the tidy contrasts a theory-driven hypothesis implies.

Peterson administered immediate and 3-week-delayed posttests on the lesson content, in both multiple-choice and essay form. (She also collected and analyzed attitude measures.) Our summary reports numbers for only the immediate multiple-choice measure. Patterns on the immediate essay were much the same. The retention tests produced a somewhat different picture, but those tests were abbreviated and unreliable.

Exhibit Ptr. How Conclusions Are Reached From Within-Treatment Regression Equations

The Peterson experiment, like many ATI studies, was designed to produce a separate regression equation for each treatment. This exhibit illustrates how such a set of equations may be "read" so as to bring conclusions to the surface.

In these equations, Y stands for the outcome. Peterson set the scale for V (verbal ability) to make the overall mean zero; the standard deviation was left at 13. For Ax (anxiety), we have amended the equations so that they apply to a scale with mean zero and SD 1; the equations (Peterson, 1976, p. 180) become:

(S+ P+)Est. $Y = 24.75 + 0.33\ V + 0.58\ Ax + 0.01\ (V)(Ax)$.
(S– P–)Est. $Y = 24.87 + 0.35\ V + 2.51\ Ax + 0.31\ (V)(Ax)$.
(S+ P–)Est. $Y = 24.64 + 0.31\ V + 0.60\ Ax + 0.13\ (V)(Ax)$.
(S– P+)Est. $Y = 22.54 + 0.22\ V + 1.10\ Ax + 0.08\ (V)(Ax)$.

The product term at the right enables the equation to describe a "twisted sheet" rather than a plane. With V or Ax fixed, the cross-section of any of the surfaces is a straight line.

Reading down the column gives some preliminary conclusions. At the mean of the groups pooled (where $V = Ax = 0$), all terms on the right save the first one vanish. This describes the mean outcome, and it is evident that the treatment means are close together save for the poorer average result in S– P+. Because the SD of Y within groups is 5.4, it will be convenient to think of a difference of 2.5 points as a medium effect—worthwhile but limited. The average in S– P+ departs from the others by almost this much.

The coefficients for V are remarkably similar, suggesting that, for students with average anxiety, ability matters equally in all treatments. A more definite interpretation is reached by setting Ax to zero, and estimating Y when V is 13 and –13. This amounts to looking at the averages in roughly the lower and upper thirds of the V distribution. The first equation, with $V = 13$, becomes $24.75 + (0.33)(13) = 29.04$ for S+ P+. A similar calculation gives 28.67 for S+ P–. We next simplify by averaging these two values, reaching 28.86 for the upper-right entry of this next table. Other tables are formed in the same way.

	Low V	High V	Net
S+	20.5	28.9	
S–	20.0	27.4	
Difference	0.5	1.5	1.0

We can read across the resulting table to see how ability relates to structure. The differences within the S+ and S- rows confirm the powerful effect of ability.

The difference labeled *Net* is an index of the interaction effect. The interaction here is negligible. But when we return to the equations and substitute +1 and –1 for Ax while setting V at zero (and average the results from the two levels of S), the table shows a strong interaction:

	Low Ax	High Ax	Net
P+	22.7	24.5	
P–	26.8	22.8	
Difference	–4.2	1.7	5.8

The anxious students learned about equally well in P+ and P–, but the Lows gained appreciably more from the nonparticipatory class.

Findings. Peterson carried out a regression analysis within each treatment, with V, Ax, and the V × Ax product as predictors. Exhibit Ptr demonstrates how conclusions are read from the resulting equations. Combining the two levels of P and setting Ax at the mean found a strong effect of ability at each level of S. Anxiety did not interact with S considered apart from P. The Ability × Structure interaction was negligible. The story is essentially the same for the P+/P– contrast, and we need not give details.

Ax had a positive weight in some equations, negative in others. In a table like that in the exhibit, but relating S to anxiety, the High/Low difference was less than 1 point, and the summary index Net (see Exh. Ptr) was only 0.4. But the values for P shown in the exhibit indicate a strong interaction; the low-anxious gained appreciably more in the nonparticipatory classes. This seems contrary to the finding of Dowaliby and Domino, but to this point the main finding is that distinguishing S and P was worthwhile.

Now we proceed to consider the treatment variables together.

Figure 4.3a displays the four trend lines for outcome as a function of Ax, among students at –13 on V. (This is not a plot for the sample of students exactly at –13; each line is a slice through a regression plane, whose location is influenced by all cases in the treatment.) This and the companion Panel b compress a great deal of information, and seem forbidding. We suggest a toe-in-the-water approach.

Note first the contrast between the a and b panels; this displays the main effect for ability. Second, note the closeness and flatness of the lines in the left panel. Low-ability students showed much the same poor performance regardless of style of instruction and level of anxiety. (The upward slope of the result for S– P– is out of line with the others, but the uncertainty of regression equations based on small samples makes the finding questionable.)

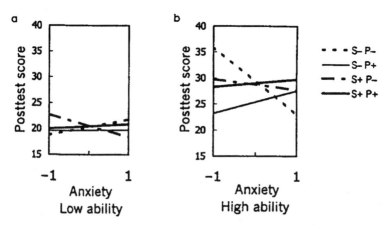

FIG. 4.3.   Joint effects of anxiety and ability under four patterns of instruction. Data from Peterson (1976).

In Panel b, striking (and at least nominally significant) interactions appeared. These are the highlights:

Anxious, able students tended to do better than the less anxious in S+ and not in S–. They also did moderately better in P+ than in P–. Both P and S, then, helped such students—a possibility the Dowaliby design could not detect.

In S– the major finding is a sharper picture of the moderating effect of P. In S– P–, the able low–Ax students outperformed all other groups by more than 1 SD. Among anxious students, the value of high ability was lost in the S– P– condition.

Among able students, the correlation of outcome and Ax in the S– P– condition was negative, and in the P+ conditions positive.

One can envision the charts pasted onto a transparent box, with Panel a at the front and Panel b at the back. Front and back points for the same treatment can be connected, and the connecting lines on the right and left would show the effects of ability at high and low anxiety levels, respectively. Thus one may think about the wall-to-wall surface for any treatment. For three treatments, this surface is close to a plane; but the S– P– surface is a twisted sheet. This twist is the hallmark of a powerful interaction, depicting an effect of V and Ax jointly and not a simple additive effect.[18]

Peterson (1977) suggested that able, anxious students were handicapped in S– P– by not being given a clear idea of "what they are supposed to be doing and being able to do it. They would be frustrated by a lack of apparent cues in the [S– P–] class and might go off on impulsive tangents" (p. 790). The able nonanxious "do not need the structuring provided by the teacher because their learning is facilitated by their own careful choice of learning cues and the reflective, deliberate application of their ability" (p. 790). Peterson (1979) later added that "they were able to remain inconspicuous, and the teacher did not put frustrating information-processing demands on them ..." (p. 532). This treatment, obviously, was the one imposing the fewest constraints and demands.

Companion Studies. Over time a number of companion studies were mounted. These were not "replications"; Snow and his group made a strategic choice to investigate the hypothesis in a variety of edu-

---

[18]Various pictures of the continuous surfaces have been published (e.g., Peterson, 1977, p. 788; Snow, 1978a, p. 59). In those charts, the range for V was –22 to 22 and the range for Ax was –2.2 to +2.2 (on our converted scale). These values represent the outer limits of scores in the data. Such charts dramatize the curvature of surfaces, but our narrower range is better designed for highlighting the well-populated part of the range.

cational situations. We do not go deeply into the procedures of these studies, but only summarize the findings as reported.

Peterson went on to apply her research design in sections of a college psychology course and reported significant ATI effects for V, Ax, and their product; four of nine such interactions reached the $p < .05$ level (see p. 247). S– P– was the best treatment for able, anxious students, and also for low-V, low-Ax students. It was the worst treatment for those at the other two corners of the V,Ax space. The finding differs strikingly from the ninth-grade results. Peterson (1979) concluded:

> [T]he results show no support for the generalizability of the ATI for ability and anxiety across high school and college settings. These results confirm Snow's [1977, p. 12] notion that general instructional theory may be impossible and that researchers should concentrate on [theories for local situations], "intended to generalize more across time in one place than across places." (pp. 532–533)

A dissertation within the Stanford project by Porteus (1976) applied the Dowaliby design in two high school courses: education and economics. In each year-long course, the teacher taught one section with a high degree of structure and one with an emphasis on student participation and choice. The predictors were essentially like those of Peterson. In this study, the data included audiotapes, teacher logs, and student reports of their perceptions, along with scores on four examinations. The study, with only two small classes of students in each course, was thus planned as a set of intensive case studies. In the tradition of Snow's laboratory, elaborate regression analyses were carried out, but Porteus and Snow recognized the study's lack of statistical power.

Snow (1978a) reported Porteus's result alongside Peterson's, saying:

> Porteus's results were remarkably similar to Peterson's ... if one is willing to equate Porteus's student-centered and Peterson's [S– P–] conditions on Test 1 and then make some allowances for student and teacher adaptations across Porteus's very long time scale. ... The student-centered treatment assumed the same twisted-sheet pattern [on the first test in Economics] as seen in [Snow's counterpart of our Fig. 4.3], while the teacher-centered treatment yielded a sloped regression plane quite similar to the planes for Peterson's other three treatments. ...
>
> In Education, there was no ATI at Test 1. After that, the same pattern as seen in the Economics data emerged across time. ... Here again, High G-Low Ax and Low G-High Ax students did best with student centering; students low on both aptitudes or high on both did best with teacher-centering. (p. 62)

Porteus explained changes in patterning from test to test in the light of the supplementary qualitative information (summarized in Snow,

1978a). In that information, Porteus and Snow saw a causal explanation for the differences between results in education and economics.

In Corno's (1979) study, no experimental structure was imposed. She collected classroom observations to record the behavior of 33 third-grade teachers, and, following Peterson's definitions, computed frequencies of teacher demand for structuring (S) and student participation (P). "Teacher focus" scores were counts of teacher actions directed to the whole class. In addition, observations on a subset of children yielded "child focus" scores describing teacher remarks directed to an individual. Early in the term, matrix, vocabulary, and reading-comprehension tests were given, along with a measure of anxiety. Gc was evaluated by a combination of reading and vocabulary, Gf by matrices. Gc and Gf were given equal weights in G. The same three tests were repeated in the spring and used as outcome measures.

Corno's study has the rare feature of a two-level analysis, considering both between-class regressions (i.e., regressions calculated from class means rather than data points for individuals) and pooled within-class (student-level) regressions. Between-class and within-class effects were confounded in nearly all prior ATI studies, including some we have reviewed earlier.

Corno's large sample (840 students) warranted separate analyses of class-level and individual-level effects.

Six between-class analyses were made, three of them on teacher-focus ratings. In one of the latter, G × S interaction accounted for 3% of the between-classes *variance*[App] in the vocabulary posttest, a weak effect not reaching the .05 significance level[App]. Snow (1978a) previously concluded that able students tend to do better when a good part of the information-processing burden is put on them; but the studies he had reviewed confounded between- and within-class effects. Corno found this pattern in one between-class analysis but not in five others.

Corno's within-class analyses used the child-focus scores as an index of the treatment received by each child. We can illustrate differences between teacher-focus behavior directed at entire classes and child-focus behavior directed at individual students by describing a few teachers. One teacher rarely developed structure in addressing her class as a group (–.77 was her *standard score*[App] on structuring); interacting with individuals, she provided or elicited an average amount of structure (standard score on structuring .38 with child-focus data). Another teacher rarely structured (–1.18 score for teacher-focus and –.35 score for child-focus). Her participation demands addressed to the class as a whole, on the other hand, were high (1.09), whereas her demands directed to individual students were low (–.49).

Within classes, Corno found one nominally significant G × S effect on the matrix posttest, an effect accounting for just 1% of the outcome variance. Here, those less able students who had been given little personal teacher direction averaged better than the ones prodded often. Among abler children, a smaller mean difference was in the same direction. If the finding of different patterns between and within classes was to be confirmed in other studies, it would pose an important question for aptitude theory.

With Peterson's finding in mind, we are primarily concerned here with the G × Ax × S and G × Ax × P interactions. Corno did not test the four-way interaction. Again, there were nine statistical checks, and none reached even the 10% level of significance. (Corno drew attention to one of the Ax × P interactions. Actually, in four of the nine analyses, this effect accounted for at least 1% of the variance. In three instances, the regression coefficient was positive, implying that high P demand improved performance of anxious students, and low P demand helped the nonanxious. But the fourth—nominally significant—relation pointed in the opposite direction.)

Evaluation.   In applying hindsight to this work from the 1970s, we note that at the time three of the seven writers of this book had a hand in some of the work. We have no intent to reproach our younger selves, or Snow's, for what was "state of the art" research. We do, however, wish to recognize that thinking about research strategy has evolved, partly with the help of these pioneering studies.

An attempt to compile consistencies and contradictions across these studies would only heighten confusion. Corno found crisscrossing regressions with G and S as predictor variables, whereas Peterson's regression lines were parallel. Peterson found a strong interaction effect of Ax × P; Corno found an echo of this in three of her nine analyses, with reversal in a fourth. A genuine causal relationship may not be powerful enough to produce significant findings in every data set. And it would be foolish to deny that circumstances may well alter relationships, as in going from the ability range in high school to the range in a selective college, or in comparing results in an education course with results in economics. Yet after-the-fact explanations are easy to dismiss as rationalizations.

Optimists and pessimists can both tell stories about a set of studies like these. It is easy to believe that personal characteristics interact in determining reaction to a situation, even in the absence of definitive evidence. After all, natural sciences have often reached simple conclusions only by bringing numerous aspects of a complex process under reproducible control. The optimist will see studies like these as an intriguing, potentially rewarding frontier for the study of propensities in situations. The pessimist will say that, if response to instruction is so complexly determined, it will never be feasible to obtain consistent results in studies like those reviewed.

Before fresh studies can hope to clarify or reject a particular A × A´ × T interaction, methodology needs to be thought through. Most of the studies reviewed in this section were unreasonably complicated for their time. When the number of significance tests is large, p values lose their meaning. Chance accounts for some proportion of the so-called "significant" findings, and one could judge which those are only in the light of auxiliary evidence or theory.

If the analyses had pointed toward the estimation of *confidence intervals*[App] for the regression surfaces and for the differences between surfaces on which interpretation rested, the reports would have had a different flavor. Where noise was swamping out signal in many of the higher order interaction terms, modern reports would have made that evident. This would have encouraged some collapsing of distinctions, and could well have shown that the finding in one study of a certain relation was much like that in another, even where $p > .05$ in one or both. If this had been attempted before 1980, it would probably have foundered, because the only calculations available would have had to rest on a sizable pyramid of questionable assumptions. Statisticians have now developed "resampling" methods that depend less on assumptions; these are worth trying in studies of higher order interaction. (A potentially valuable methodology of this type is "classification and regression trees"; see Breiman, Olshen, & Stone, 1984.)

The qualitative portion of the Porteus research suggests how to add credibility to post hoc explanations. Often in the studies reviewed here, the investigator recognized that the student's perception of the instructional situation and attitude toward it might have causal significance; but such variables were almost always depersonalized, buried as dependent variables in a regression analysis. Porteus used the qualitative material to trace how the treatments evolved over the months, and had a vivid story to tell about tensions in teacher and student that led to shifts in the treatments. (She did not trace the learning history of individuals.) We think now of the potential value, in formal statistical research, of an intensive side study of persons with markedly different initial profiles (cf. Snow, 1992), selected perhaps as near-matched sets from contrasting treatment groups.

5 Analyses of Cognitive Process

Fully interpreting scores from ability tests requires an exceptional understanding of test-taking behavior. Historically, interpretations rested on fairly superficial summaries of performance. Not much theory of intelligence went into forecasting school grades from Binet scores. To explain why some students succeed and others fail requires more evidence and larger inferences. Even a seemingly small step—from interpreting the score as a sample of behavior to interpreting it as an estimate of ability—presumes at least some understanding of process. A person displays one set of processes when acquiring knowledge and skills, others when answering test items on them. The interpreter tends to assume that, on one or both occasions, events in the test taker's head fit the label attached to test scores—that is, a reasoning test engages reasoning processes where a spatial test engages spatial processes. To interpret test scores as aptitude one must identify not only the processes producing competences that can transfer, but also which competences are evoked by this or that situation as it unfolds.[19]

Traditional ATI studies require some of this thinking. The researcher who would adapt instruction to reduce its dependence on G can justify an adaptation only by considering what G might be. If G is speed of processing, then reducing the pace of instruction makes sense. If G means ability to monitor one's efforts, then for adaptation

---

[19]Snow's major writings on this topic are Snow 1980b, 1994, and, with Lohman, 1984, 1989.

to low G it seems suitable to pair students—one attempting a solution, the other taking half the load by monitoring. Thus, one must know how situations evoke processes and how tests sample such transactions.

How can one examine such processes? The methods available prior to the emergence of cognitive psychology in the 1960s, such as self-report and introspection, were distrusted. In the heyday of behaviorism, most American investigators were unwilling to probe for thought processes using methods such as Piaget's interviews (p. 15).

The cognitive revolution revived some of these old procedures and made radically new procedures available. Self-report was resurrected as a method for inferring what transpires after stimulus presentation and before response. Other resurrected techniques included recording eye fixations, and breaking tasks into segments that yield observable responses.

The most important new method was computer simulation. Theories about how cognition worked could be incorporated into a computer program, the output of the program being compared with behavioral records of humans solving the same problems. Exhibit SK summarizes an early and influential effort of this sort (see also p. 131).

Other work made direct inferences about process from behavior in the laboratory. These more conventional experiments used the computer as a metaphor for the cognitive system. Computers take in, transform, store, and communicate information. Might human thought be described in similar language? Experience soon showed this metaphor to be much more fruitful than earlier analogies to wax tablets, hydraulic systems, and switchboards.

Among attempts to explain abilities in information-processing terms we discuss three, starting with the path through artificial intelligence (AI). The goal in AI is to develop computer programs that solve complex, intelligence-demanding tasks in ways that resemble human problem solving. Tasks range from seemingly simple perceptual problems (as in object recognition) to inductive reasoning.

An alternative is to search for basic mechanisms of thought. If the human brain can be modeled as an information-processing system, then determining the general characteristics of that system can suggest a process theory of intelligence. Candidate characteristics include speed, processing capacity, the retentiveness of long-term storage devices, and the rate and fidelity of information transfers from one part of the system to another. Analyses of this character tend to have a reductionist flavor, often moving toward neuropsychology.

A third path looks into the processes that make up performance on one or another test. The hope is that understanding how people gener-

Exhibit SK. A Computer Simulation of Performance With Letter Series

H. A. Simon and Kotovsky (1963) developed a computer program that could solve letter-series items much as humans do. Their program has two parts: a pattern generator and a sequence generator. Supplied a sequence of letters such as *cdefdefg...*, the pattern generator searches for a rule that describes the pattern. The sequence generator then uses the rule to deduce the next letters in the sequence.

The pattern generator begins by determining the period of the sequence. The sequence *abab* has a period of two; *abcabc* has a period of three. The pattern generator looks for a relation (e.g., same, next, or step back) that repeats at regular intervals. For example, in the sequence *cdcdcd*, it discovers that *c* occurs in alternating positions; likewise for *d*. Given *defgfghijijk*, it discovers that a step-back move occurs after three forward moves.

If such periodicity is not found, the program seeks a shift in pattern occurring at regular intervals. For example, in *aaabbbccc*, a break occurs at every third position. To locate shifts, each pair of successive letters is coded as same, next, and step back. The coding is stored in short-term memory. Finally, relations between corresponding elements of successive segments are examined. Consider *abcbcd*. In the *abc* substring, each move is to "next." And that is true in *bcd*. The connecting move from *c* to *b* is "back." From the stored pattern description "next-next-back" and its knowledge of the alphabet, the sequence generator will generate additional letters, with *cde* the first of them.

Simon and Kotovsky wrote four increasingly powerful variants of the pattern generator. These solved, respectively, 3, 6, 7, and 13 of 15 problems.

The performance of a program was compared with the human success rate on each item in three samples. The first two consisted of 12 adults and 67 high school students. The participants took the test under more or less standard conditions.

The third sample, 14 Carnegie-Mellon students, were allowed to view only one letter at a time. Think-aloud protocols were collected from them. In general, the computer's response times and actions corresponded fairly well to those of humans. For example, on 12 of the 15 problems, the pattern description most frequently generated by humans was also the one the program generated.

These participants made most of their errors when extending strings, not in rule induction. The key difficulty was keeping track of one's place on two or more segments. This suggested that working-memory resources may be critical in letter-series performance, a suggestion later investigators pursued.

Comparing the performance of the four variants of the computer program with all the data—especially with the verbal protocols—was itself an exercise in pattern matching, one that required considerable judgment. Participants sometimes mentioned a feature explicitly but often their solution processes had to be inferred (e.g., from a pause in punching letters).

Discrepancies between human and program turned up. People remembered the relations between letters they had observed while determining periodicity; the program did not. People thus did not exhibit a clean break between these two phases of pattern induction. Another important difference was that string length predicted the computer's solution times, but not that of humans. Most likely, this reflects the fact that people immediately recognize *pqrs* as an ordered string, whereas this computer program had to test systematically every pair of letters.

See related discussion at page 135.

ate answers to test items will enable one to understand the functions represented in scores.

We discuss these approaches in turn. Discussion of AI illustrates how general theory in cognitive psychology informs thinking about abilities. The search for basic mechanisms of thought brings us closer to identifying broad cognitive processes that are central to abilities. Third, in-depth study of ability tests shows both the need for these basic mechanisms and for other, higher-order processes not previously envisioned. Throughout we focus on general fluid analytic (Gf) ability. Following this survey, we return to the question Snow considered central to a theory of abilities. Why is Gf ability increasingly required as tasks become more complex? Embedded in our answer is both a provisional theory of Gf and a call for a broader theory that includes affect and conation.

ARTIFICIAL INTELLIGENCE

General Problem Solving and Expert Systems

Many of the early AI programs were designed to solve a wide range of problems. For example, the General Problem Solver (Newell & H. Simon,

1961) implemented a rule of thumb called means–ends analysis. The respondent using this rule examines the current state and the desired goal-state, then selects a move that will do the most to reduce the distance between them. Means–ends analysis "works backward"; the analyst starts with the goal and tries to work back to the present state.

Studies of expertise, however, demonstrated that although novices tend to work backward, experts on the topic of the problem tend to work forward (D. Simon & H. Simon, 1978). For example, experts in algebra may begin by rearranging terms without seeing clearly how the switch gets them closer to the goal. Once the terms are rearranged, the new pattern will generally suggest another move; the process repeats until an answer is accepted. Experts in other areas as diverse as chess and natural language comprehension also apply domain-specific rules in this way (Schank, 1980). Such findings led to a shift in the center of inquiry from the knowledge-lean General Problem Solver and its kin to knowledge-rich expert systems.

Knowledge-based systems have taken many forms. Nonetheless, certain structures and processes distinguish more intelligent from less intelligent artificial systems. Sternberg (1990) listed seven, each suggesting a potential source of ability differences among people:

- More intelligent systems use multiple indexing: tagging or indexing new information in many ways. This allows the person to locate it by many routes. How people recall and use information depends critically on how elaborately that information is processed at input.
- More intelligent systems make extensive use of higher order knowledge structures—that is, of scripts ("What typically happens at a wedding?") or schemas ("What does it mean to be married?"). Schemas enable the system to organize information, to determine which new information is important, and to make inferences that go beyond the information given.
- More intelligent systems display what may be called beliefs. Beliefs typically comprise very high level knowledge structures. They function as general schemas. Children have beliefs about what it means for something to be alive; scientists have beliefs about what constitutes evidence. Beliefs are often laden with emotion, and tend to persist despite contradictory evidence. The poorly structured problems of everyday life create exceptional difficulties for the brain-damaged who are unable to connect feelings with beliefs (Damasio, 1994).
- More intelligent systems more readily make good inferences. Inference is sometimes made via high-level structures such as

schemas; the system fills slots in the schema with default values. For example, the adjective *married* suggests that an individual has one spouse, that the spouses are of the opposite sex, and that there was a wedding. Any of these associations may be wrong. A more intelligent system will stop with plausible inferences, and will use *more* of the leads in the data when doing so. Further, a subsystem may be programmed to detect how far new information departs from the normal or expected. Schank (1978) argued that an intelligent system will make good use of such unusual information. By analogy, those human problem solvers who are more successful will do the same.

• More intelligent systems develop a deeper level of understanding (Schank, 1984). If working at a high level, a system justifies an action in terms of goals, alternative hypotheses, and knowledge. By analogy, then, more intelligent people are better able to explain their behavior.

• More intelligent systems profit more from feedback. At the simplest level, systems learn by adding new knowledge to an existing knowledge base, strengthening (or weakening) associations among elements in that base, and reorganizing what is stored. More sophisticated systems can learn new skills and problem-solving procedures, and can convert factual knowledge to skill. By analogy, people too differ in the learning processes they command.

• More intelligent systems are attuned to the type of problem they are expected to solve. Expert systems that assist physicians in making medical diagnoses consider hypotheses one at a time. In speech recognition, however, programs have modules that work on different aspects of the analysis at the same time. The human brain also contains modules that perform specialized functions. People differ in the facility with which they perform these operations.

Anderson's ACT System

J. R. Anderson's Adaptive Control of Thought (ACT) system has had great impact on thinking about thinking. The system is too complex to describe here, but Anderson (1993) provides a readable introduction. We list only some features of the ACT system that are especially suggestive regarding abilities.

For Anderson, all "higher cognitive processes, such as memory, language, problem-solving, imagery, deduction, and induction, are different manifestations of the same underlying system" (1983, p. 1). Even so, ACT posits special-purpose peripheral systems. These convert sensory information into distinct perception-based memory codes, such as images and temporal strings; these preserve information about configuration and temporal order, respectively. Beyond that, higher processes depend on a memory representation that preserves meaning. Indeed, Anderson argued that such abstract, meaning-preserving code dominates long-term memory, even for memories that seem to be based in perception. For example, much of what one remembers about a visual scene depends on one's interpretation of what one saw.

This multicode theory of memory has interesting analogues in research on individual differences. For example, specific learning disabilities may be caused by dysfunction in one or more peripheral systems that encode information from the environment or systems that decode the products of thinking into responses. The dominance of the meaning-based code, on the other hand, corresponds to the dominance of the general factor in individual differences on complex tasks based on unlike contents. Indeed, general ability—as typically estimated—may reflect the ability to create, transform, and retain meaning-based representations (Snow & Lohman, 1989).

A second feature of ACT that can inform theorizing about intelligence is the distinction between declarative and procedural knowledge. These categories appear in many, although certainly not all, AI theories. As we said early in chapter 3, declarative knowledge is knowing that something is the case, whereas procedural knowledge is knowing how to do something. Declarative knowledge can be thought of as a network of ideas, and procedural knowledge as a list of conditional commands of the form "If [stated] condition holds, then perform [stated] action." Thus, declarative knowledge is static; procedural is dynamic.

Procedural knowledge can be brought to bear automatically, even unconsciously, whereas declarative knowledge is often accessed slowly and consciously. New declarative knowledge can be acquired relatively quickly—often in a single trial—by connecting it to prior knowledge. Procedural knowledge is likely to be acquired slowly, and refined by practice with feedback. The declarative-procedural distinction bears on an important aspect of ability development:

- Acquisition of new cognitive skills is critical in the development of abilities. ACT models cognitive skills as procedural knowledge. Therefore, the subtheory describing conversion of declarative knowledge to procedural knowledge also describes an important aspect of ability development.
- Abilities, says the theory, gradually become differentiated. This can explain, for example, how long division can require general problem-solving skills from an inexperienced student, whereas the experienced student relies mostly on task-specific skills.

- By making the distinction between declarative and procedural knowledge, the theory implies that it is important to separate students' factual knowledge from their ability to analyze unfamiliar materials in the same domain. Assessing declarative knowledge usually samples the examinee's store of facts, schemas, and beliefs; attempts to assess procedural knowledge examine the extent to which skills have been automatized, and the range of contexts in which they can be applied.

Theories such as ACT have changed the way psychologists talk about cognition. These theories recognize the importance of general mechanisms (e.g., the General Problem Solver) and also the situation-specific skills of expert systems. The general mechanisms describe thinking in unfamiliar situations; they help explain the behavior of the novice who has little domain knowledge, but can accomplish something by hard reasoning. At the other extreme, the behavior of the expert is better explained by a system that possesses thousands of specific knowledge packets. These lessen the need for general reasoning, which frees working memory for other types of processing. For example, novice readers devote considerable attention to deciphering words. Skilled readers recognize more words automatically, so they can use attentional resources for comprehending.

Simulation of Ability Tests

As noted earlier, direct evidence on ability processes comes from simulations. We discuss two examples: a study of inductive reasoning with patterned letter series, and an extension of that work to matrix problems.

Modeling Rule Induction.   Some of the most convincing demonstrations of the power of the AI approach used ability tests as experimental tasks. Exhibit SK describes a classic study of the letter-series task that inspired much subsequent work.

As Exhibit SK showed, H. Simon and Kotovsky (1963) sought to answer the question: How do people infer the pattern in a letter string? A partial answer can be reached through a second question: How might a computer be programmed to extend the series? The key insight was that complex patterns can usually be generated from a handful of simple relations. The goal was not to develop an automaton that breezes through series problems. Rather, it was to create a system that performs like a person, stumbling and stalling at the same places, and from time to time making errors like those of humans.

A Goal Monitor as Aid to Reasoning.   Processes do not stand up and show themselves once a task is opened for inspection. Rather, processes must be inferred from scattered evidence that an interpreter sees as consistent. The analysis of Raven matrices by Carpenter, Just, and Shell (1990) combined evidence from task analysis, protocol analysis, and computer simulations, and used an equally diverse array of dependent measures: retrospective reports, eye fixations, response errors and response latencies, and success/failure of the simulations. The main steps beyond the Simon–Kotovsky work are explicit (rather than incidental) analysis of individual differences and incorporation of a goal monitor. The goal monitor performs what are sometimes called executive functions.

Exhibit CJS provides some details. As it illustrates, Carpenter et al. resolved inferencing into phases:

Exhibit CJS. A Model of Reasoning for Matrix Tasks

Matrix tests—particularly those of Raven—have long been used as a marker for Gf. Trying to understand how such tasks are performed, Carpenter, Just, and Shell (1990) began by classifying Raven items. They found that each complete pattern was generated by one of a few rules. Ordered from simple to complex, the rules were:

Identity relations. Every element is the same across all rows and columns.

Pairwise progression (cf. Fig. 1.1, p. 12). An element changes systematically from cell to cell (e.g., decreases in size across columns).

Figure addition or subtraction (Panel a of Fig. 5.1). The first two entries combine to make the last entry.

Distribution of three values. An object or attribute appears once in each row and each column.

Distribution of two values (Panel b of Fig. 5.1). An element appears in just two places in each row and each column.

Identifying the rule applying to an element is called "correspondence finding." H. Simon and Kotovsky (1963) had argued that series-completion problems require correspondence finding, pairwise comparison of adjacent elements, and induction of rules based on similarities and differences.

Carpenter et al. (1990) asked 12 participants to think aloud while they worked, and recorded their eye fixations. People in a second sample worked silently and then described the ideas lead-

---

ing to each response. "The most striking feature of the eye fixations and verbal protocols was the ... incremental nature of the processing" (p. 411). People appeared to solve problems by extracting subproblems and solving them. Ability to generate subgoals in working memory, to monitor progress toward them, and to set successive subgoals appeared to be major sources of variation.

Two simulations tested hypotheses about these response processes. FAIRAVEN scored about as well as a typical college student; BETTERAVEN scored much higher.

FAIRAVEN's limitations were these:

It could not "induce" especially complex rules.

It had no way to backtrack when a hypothesized correspondence was incorrect.

Considering many high-level goals at once overwhelmed the processing system.

For related discussion see pp. 67 ff, 136.

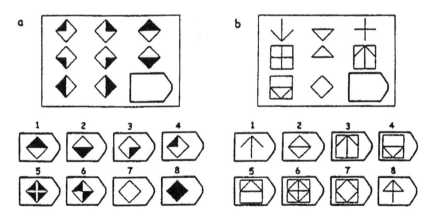

FIG. 5.1. Problems illustrating two solution rules for matrix items. Panel a illustrates a rule where combining two elements in a row (or column) produces the third element. Panel b illustrates the rule labeled "distribution of two values." In any row or column, each figure contains two or more lines. A line such as the horizontal in Row 1 appears in just two of its three figures. In the rightmost column, then, the horizontal must be part of the missing figure. Applying a similar rule down the column, the square that appears at the right of the second row must appear in the answer. Combining these two requirements reduces the choices to 4, 5, and 6; tracing one more detail identifies 5 as the correct answer. From Carpenter, Just, and Shell (1990). Copyright 1990 by the American Psychological Association. Adapted by permission.

Pairwise comparisons of elements within a row to identify a rule that applies to both the first and second pairs of columns.

Comparison down the rows to identify changes in rules from one row to the next.

Generation of missing elements in the third row by applying the rules induced in the previous two phases.

Two simulation programs were developed. The comparatively simple FAIRAVEN program had limitations that the BETTERAVEN program was designed to overcome. In particular, BETTERAVEN "knew" more abstract rules, such as the "distribution of two" rule. And BETTERAVEN also exercised some strategic control over its own processes by adding a goal monitor. The goal monitor set main goals and subgoals. It worked to ensure that higher level processes proceeded one at a time, to order candidate rules for checking, and to track the model's progress toward the goals. With these enhancements, results were good. Carpenter et al. (1990) concluded that matrix tests measure the "common ability to decompose problems into manageable segments and iterate through [subproblems], the differential ability to manage the hierarchy of goals and subgoals ..., and the differential ability to form higher level abstractions" (p. 429).

They also noted that the functions of the goal monitor are strikingly similar to the processes Snow's group suggested to explain Carpenter et al. saw their work as supporting this statement of Marshalek et al. (1983) on the Raven test's position at the center of the radex: "More complex tasks may require more involvement of executive assembly and control processes that structure and analyze the problem, assemble a strategy of attack on it, monitor the performance processes, and adapt these strategies as performance proceeds" (p. 124).

PROCESSES WITHIN COGNITIVE PERFORMANCE

Every computer system is limited by the speed and capacity of its central processor, of its temporary and long-term storage devices, and of the pathways that move information between devices. Researchers have looked for similar limitations in the brain. One type of study focuses on determining general characteristics of the nervous system, such as the speed with which information is processed or the capacity of working memory. A second type of study aims to measure the efficiency of particular operations, such as retrieving name codes from long-term memory, and to estimate the contribution of each process to broad ability constructs (e.g., verbal ability).

Speed of Processing

Simple reaction time (RT) correlates significantly with G (Jensen, 1982, 1998). The correlation increases with task complexity—moving from requiring a quick release of a button to requiring a choice among buttons. Beyond a certain degree of complexity, however, the correlation decreases. For example, Sternberg (1975) found that the time to respond with a "ready for next" signal when shown a lighted blank field correlated higher with reasoning than time to read a word. In an analogy task presented one term at a time, the correlation of time and a measure of Gf declined as more of the analogy was exposed. This surprising pattern can be explained. The more complex the task, the more room there is for individuals to proceed differently. On very difficult tasks, latency reflects persistence more than ability. On hard tasks, ability is reflected in the quality of the response, and only secondarily in its speed.

In principle, one could estimate processing speed on any task where past learning, motivation, strategy, and so on matter little. Jensen used a simple task: Move a finger when a signal light comes on. Correlations between RT and G (adjusted for measurement error) can be substantial when a group ranges widely in ability. However, the correlations do not go beyond –.4 in samples having the ranges used in most research on abilities (Roberts, 1995; see also Sternberg, 1985, and Deary & Stough, 1996).

Jensen concluded that G scores reflect fundamental differences in speed and efficiency of neural activity. Others, however, see attention control rather than speed as the more important factor in these experiments. On successive trials, a distribution of RTs builds up for each person. Individual standard deviations of RT correlate across trials with G about as strongly as mean RT does. The least able respondents tend to show greatest variability in RT. This suggests that, at least within the normal range of intelligence, the ability to maintain attention is more important to performance than speed of response.

The Search for Mental Mechanisms

Each computer operation—input, storage, or transformation—takes a measurable amount of time. By analogy, latency became the preferred measure for experimental investigations of thought processes. Most early studies examined perception, venturing only so far as initial sensory memories. They ignored individual differences.

One of the few exceptions was the large study by Seibert and Snow (1965), whose methods and results are described in Exhibit SS. Their investigation into speed of processing was in many ways ahead of its time, and notably avoided some problems that plagued later work in the area. Their group-administered film tests controlled stimulus exposure

---

Exhibit SS. Individual Differences in Short-Term Visual Memory

One of Snow's earliest attempts to investigate individual differences in elementary information processes used film tests to explore an effect called *backward masking*. The task is designed to measure how much meaningless visual information can be retained for a fraction of a second. On any trial, the person sees an array of letters; one of them (underlined) is to be held in mind and reported when the exposure ends. Averbach and Coriell (1961) discovered that the target letter was "erased"—could not be reported—if a fresh stimulus arrived at the same retinal location an instant later.

Seibert and Snow (1965) used 16mm motion-picture film to create a test that could be administered to a group. Letter strings were exposed for 31 ms. They specified alternative time intervals between termination of the letter display and the brief appearance of the masking stimulus (a small circle), and included eight trials at each interval. For 100 engineering students, the mean baseline recall score was just above 80%. That score plummeted below 40% with a delay of 94 ms (about 0.1 s), then recovered gradually, regaining approximately the original score when the delay was 400 ms or more. The longer the delay, the more likely that the letter had been stored stably in memory.

Several other film and paper–pencil tests yielded scores on reference factors. When letter recall at each delay interval was correlated with factor scores, the results were as shown in Fig. 5.2. At the peak of the masking effect, Perceptual Integration accounted for almost half of the variance. This factor, defined by several of the film tests, was thought to represent the ability to quickly integrate visual information. At intermediate delays, Verbal Comprehension had the largest correlations. And, at long delay intervals, those for Perceptual Speed were largest. These three abilities correspond nicely to an information-processing model Sperling (1960) suggested. He envisioned three processes, each a source of variation: rate of visual-memory decay (reflected in the PI factor), speed of name-code retrieval (the VC factor), and ability to retain in memory and compare randomly ordered strings of letters (PS).

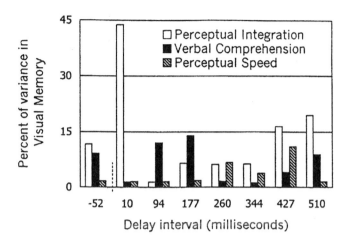

FIG. 5.2. Influence of three ability factors on retention of stimulus information at various delay intervals in the short-term-memory task. Data from Seibert and Snow (1965).

with great precision. Also, the paced film presentation controlled any tendency to work slowly for the sake of greater accuracy. Later investigators used self-paced computerized tests that lacked such a control; those investigators had trouble deciding what to do with latencies of error responses and how to adjust for speed–accuracy trade-offs. These (minor annoyances to investigators comparing means across conditions) cause headaches when individual differences become the object of inquiry, being submerged in the "error term" of the statistical comparison. Further, though the information-processing task presumed several component steps, Seibert and Snow made no attempt to estimate scores for each person on each process. Later investigators who computed component scores often saw reliable individual differences disappear (because the estimation procedure subtracted one score from another). Finally, typical of Snow's studies, a large and representative battery of ability tests was administered, which enriched the interpretation of performance on the central task.

As information-processing psychology won adherents, explorations of cognition became more ambitious. The preferred method for identifying cognitive processes was to compare response times under distinct conditions. Investigators identified hundreds of component processes in a wide range of verbal, figural, and quantitative tasks.

Some even broke down complex performance in this way (see Exh. Strn, p. 150).

As one example, we cite the Posner–Mitchell (1967) investigation into how efficiently people access information in memory. They asked respondents to determine whether two letters were the same. In the name-identity (NI) condition, "the same" meant having the same name (e.g., A and a). In the PI condition, "the same" meant physically identical (e.g., A and A). Typically, subjects respond more rapidly in PI. The NI judgment requires letter naming as well as perception, so subtracting PI times from NI times indicates the time needed to pull the letter's name from long-term storage.

The expectation that broad abilities might be explained in a core set of component processes has not been realized. For example, when E. Hunt, Frost, and Lunneborg (1973) administered the Posner–Mitchell task (along with many other experimental tasks) to a sample of undergraduates, they found that NI – PI times correlated about –.3 with verbal ability. No other process component gave a larger correlation.

Although scores from any single component correlate only weakly with G, their combined effect can be appreciably greater. Effects cumulate across different component processes, each of which has only a small correlation with the criterion (Detterman, 1986). They also cumulate when the same process is repeatedly applied.

Nevertheless, the search for elementary information processes has not led to the insights initially hoped for. Recall that Simon and Kotovsky had shown that a handful of simple relations could generate complex letter patterns. Those hoping to tease out a small set of information-processing mechanisms from the decomposition of ability factors failed. But writers who question whether the information-processing metaphor can be applied to abilities go too far. Analyses of abilities in this mode have taught us much.

Other critics noted that although subtraction of times may usefully highlight important components, difference scores are ill-suited to correlational research. This complaint is subtle. It says that component processes may be identified, but that individual differences in them may not be what they seem. Why? Consider the NI-PI difference. If people who make name comparisons rapidly are also fast in making physical comparisons, then subtraction will remove most of the reliable individual differences in latency.

Finally, some hold that simple experimental tasks are not the place to look for explanations of ability. Rather, ability tests themselves should be the objects of inquiry. Before we turn to the investigation of cognitive tests as tasks, we review one line of work that applied rather successfully the information-processing metaphor to ability constructs. Notably, the investigators did not derive component scores for individuals. Instead, cognitive theory was used to design tasks to emphasize the action of selected processes.

Working Memory

The most important shift in research on individual differences in cognition between 1960 and 1990 came as the result of better understanding of working memory. All information-processing models of memory and cognition posit a short-term or working memory—a central processor whose limited capacity creates a bottleneck. People differ widely on tasks designed to estimate the capacity of working memory. One suggestion is that abler individuals can attend to more information. An alternative view refers to capacity, suggesting that abler persons have larger working memories than the less able. We briefly examine both hypotheses.

Hypotheses About Attention. If attention is a general cognitive resource (rather like Spearman's "mental energy"), and if people differ in attentional resources, then tasks making strong attentional demands would be expected to be especially related to G (Ackerman, 1988; E. Hunt & Lansman, 1982). Demand can be heightened by requiring participants to do two things simultaneously (e.g., searching for a figure in a visual display while simultaneously listening for a tone).

Most studies do find that differences between abler and less able subjects are greater on dual tasks than on a single task. Stankov (1988) found this result with Gc as ability index, and even more strongly with Gf. Stankov attributed the finding not to attentional resources per se but to the abler person's better management of attention. Specifically, good performance in the dual task was achieved by momentarily ignoring one task while attending to the other. What seemed on the surface to implicate greater attentional resources seemed on closer inspection to be due to better attention management.

Further complications arise. The attention a task needs varies according to its familiarity *and* the ease with which it can be automatized. People who recognize that a task is consistent in Ackerman's sense (p. 101) make component operations routine more rapidly than those who are not so attuned. Thus, an explanation of ability differences in terms of attentional resources must make a place for attention shifting in dual tasks and for the extent of routinization. Experience in context intertwines with capacity to produce observed ability. There is no "experience-free" measure of attentional processes.

The Capacity Hypothesis.   The capacity hypothesis explains working memory in terms of the amount of information that can be held in mind at the same time. Capacity is thought of as a structural limitation, comparable to a fixed number of available slots. Some argue, however, that abler people simply refresh memory traces more rapidly and so can hold more information in readiness. This ability would be especially valuable when the information must be transformed by reorganizing or elaborating on it. Reasoning tasks fit this description. Indeed, in an early paper, Pellegrino and Glaser (1980) argued that working-memory capacity was an important factor in reasoning ability. Their study offered no quantitative estimate of the relationship. However, more recently, a measure describing reasoning ability correlated approximately .8 with a measure of working memory (after correction for unreliability; see p. 243).

Where Matters Stand.   Kyllonen and Christal (1990), finding this conclusion in four large studies, entitled the report "Reasoning is (Little More Than) Working Memory?!" (p. 389). All the punctuation is important. The parenthetical "little more than" hedges the claim; the question mark adds a caution; and the exclamation point announces appropriate astonishment.

These findings surprised many, because working memory had been noticeably absent from models that posited components executed one after another. (See the later section on components, and Fig. 5.3.) But as Kyllonen and Christal noted, most of the component processes that the models suggest, such as encoding and inference, are presumed to occur in working memory. Thus the inference component, even if effective, is limited by the working-memory resources available to it. Tasks require multiple processes. Individual differences in each may reflect in large or small measure individual differences in working memory.

The "working memory" of newer theories differs importantly from the older concept of short-term memory. The older concept assumed passive storage; the newer models, a continually active, controlled processing of information. Some speak of a trade-off between processing capacity and storage capacity (Daneman & Carpenter, 1980), whereas others speak of multiple memory systems. As an example of the latter, Baddeley (1996) posited a working memory with a storage component and also an executive system that attends to one stimulus while inhibiting the perception of another, coordinates performance, and switches strategies. Once the concept of working memory has been expanded to include executive functions, high correlations of working memory with reasoning seem less astonishing.

TESTS AS TASKS

Most works reviewed in the preceding sections sought to understand abilities in terms of processing mechanisms and their limitations. Now we turn to work directly on ability tests. Estes (1974) made the case for such analyses:

> Rather than looking to learning or physiological theory or some correlate of intelligence, I should like to focus attention on intellectual activity itself. ... We need next to consider just what behaviors to analyze in order to be sure that the activity we are dealing with is closely related to that involved in the measurement of intelligence. The simplest and most direct approach, it seems, is to begin with the specific behaviors involved in responding to items on intelligence tests. (pp. 742–743)

Understanding a complex test performance typically begins with an attempt to identify component processes that test takers use when attempting each type of item. Next, one must describe how component processes are sequenced and applied.

Components in a Complex Performance

What Are Components? *Component* has several meanings. At one extreme, the term refers to a mental operation with a well-specified input and output. For example, H. A. Simon and Kotovsky (1963) posited a component that evaluates pairs of letters to determine whether they are "same," "next," or "backward next" in a series. As we have seen, such highly specified processes play an important role in some experiments. At the other extreme, *component* means little more than a step or stage in the events that a problem-solving episode comprises.

Much attention has gone to analogy problems such as *mouse* is to *elephant* as *small* is to *???*. For a typical component model and discussion of it, see pp. 149. Component operations are shown as diamond-shaped boxes. The processing sequence is indicated by arrows.

In some types of problem, steps separate cleanly and are typically performed in the same order. For example, well-practiced adolescents doing long division will follow fairly predictable steps. In other problems, boundaries between steps are not sharp, and the sequence is less predictable. People attack a task in various ways, and a given person may use different approaches on essentially similar problems. The more consistent the behavior (efficient or not) is over items, the easier it is to infer the solution procedures.

How are components organized?   Consider this problem:

What is one third of 15 + 15 + 15?

Approaches can differ in four respects:

• Component actions. One method is to add 15 + 15 + 15 and divide the sum by 3. Another is to multiply 15 by 3 and divide the product by 3. Another is to divide each 15 by 3 and add the 5s. Yet another is to recognize that one third of any number, added three times, yields that number. Among possible components, then, are reading and understanding (i.e., encoding) each term, adding and multiplying, and recoding the problem algebraically.

• The ordering of actions. As just illustrated, multiplying and adding can be performed in either order. More broadly, one may do complete encoding before altering what is given, or may start by restructuring only the first cues examined.

• Variation over tasks in the preceding choices. Suppose that the problem solver added the three scores and divided the sum by 3. If later confronted with a similar problem, will the person solve it in the same way or shift to a more efficient strategy?

• Rate of component execution, and the range of problem difficulty over which the operation succeeds.

The Performance Pathway.   Test scores are affected by all four sources of variation. Each person *assembles* a sequence of steps that together may be called a performance program. The program is based on an initial understanding of the test instructions and a few specimen items. For a familiar task, long-term memory may also hold one or more usable performance programs. If the test is novel, a new assembly may be needed.

As the test begins, a performance program (perhaps incomplete) is applied to early items. Program components are run off in sequence. A component process may be easy for some persons and hard for others; another process, everyone carries out readily.

Especially if the test is novel, the person is likely to evaluate any retrieved program at an early stage and adapt it. Thus, the person actively monitors, adapts, and perhaps shifts among alternative programs as the items and the ongoing self-appraisal suggest. Tests whose difficulty comes from complexity and not time pressure may require more active, more flexible *control*, and conscious endurance (implicating conation).

The result of performance on one item will influence performance on the next, even without external feedback. Individual differences in assembly and control processes reverberate throughout the test. Confusion or inflexibility or an unwise change of strategy can generate an obviously faulty response; the experience will influence subsequent performance. The total test score will be a complex summation of all sources of variation, even if the test was designed to measure a single ability.

Assembly and Control Processes

What are assembly processes and control processes? Striking evidence comes from studies of patients with damage in the prefrontal cortex. Symptoms range from general impairment of attention and working memory to special difficulty with ill-structured problems, particularly social and personal ones. Behavior is disorganized; emotions are absent or flat. Such patients often retain the component skills that problems demand, but cannot coordinate them. A classic patient in the neuropsychological literature happened to be the sister of the famous neurosurgeon Wilder Penfield. She had been a competent cook before her brain injury. The injury left intact her knowledge of recipes, measurements, and cooking techniques, but she could not prepare even a simple meal because she could not assemble a plan.

Prefrontal damage can also impair regulation of responses. The cards of the Wisconsin Card Sort task show forms that vary in shape and color. The person is asked to sort according to, say, color. After the person sorts correctly, the examiner changes the dimension to shape. Patients with prefrontal damage often continue to sort by the original criterion, even after some responses are called wrong—and have even continued to sort on color while saying aloud, "That's the wrong form."

In a gambling experiment, the rule may be that (let us say) a card from Pile 1 gives a better payoff on most draws than a card from Pile 2 or 3—but on occasion brings a severe penalty. Normal subjects learn to avoid the high-risk pile; if the person draws from it, there are signs of emotion. Patients with prefrontal damage, in contrast, tend to choose the risky piles and show no emotion as they draw. These patients are influenced by a high penalty for a short time, but a few trials later revert to high-payoff, high-risk piles (Damasio, 1994).

Explanations for these cognitive, affective, and conative deficits are diverse. Although some theorists posit the existence of some sort of executive in the prefrontal cortex that is disrupted by damage, many psychologists prefer other explanations. These diverse deficits may stem from a common defect in working memory (a lowered ability to maintain images over time, in the view of Goldman-Rakic, 1987), or perhaps inability to think beyond the moment to include the past and the future (Fuster, 1997). Bringing past events (or future events) to mind while also attending to the present requires coordinating ideas. In the vein of Fuster, Damasio (1994) described his patients as having "myopia for the future."

For Kimberg and Farah (1993), the parsimonious explanation is simply a drastic reduction in the strength of associations among ideas. In other words, even if ideas A and B have been repeatedly joined, the patient with prefrontal damage may not be reminded of B when thinking of A. As Kimberg and Farah expressed it, such patients have difficulty "selecting an appropriate response when there is more than one possible response at hand, or when the correct response is not the one that is readiest at hand" (p. 191). Damasio (1994) attributed the loss to the failure to activate emotional responses typically associated with ideas. He also argued that this emotional deficit explains the peculiar difficulty some patients have with ill-structured social and personal problems.

In summary, assembly processes order a series of behaviors or cognitive processes into a plan. They are essential for nonroutine thought. Assembly is helped much by the ability to envision end-states (i.e., goals) that differ from what is currently in mind or in view. They count especially with novel or ill-structured tasks. Control processes are more diverse, but all of them require monitoring effects of actions and correcting them. Both types of processing depend heavily on the ability to keep ideas or images active in working memory, especially when several ideas must be considered simultaneously.

Reasoning Processes

Sternberg's Procedures.   If thinking might proceed in so many ways, how might one even begin to determine the way subjects solve items on any one test? Close attention to timing of partial responses has been instructive. An investigator might reasonably start with a fairly well structured item form, such as analogies. Simple items are often most accessible; data from difficult items are the result of many entangled processes. Further, because error-response latencies are ambiguous, one would probably also seek to reduce the number of errors in order to maximize the amount of usable data. Comparing response latencies across problems that vary in specific ways allows inferences about processes in play, and sheds light on how each component is executed and how actions are sequenced. In the end, one must test a model by the success of its predictions and compare its success with that of rival models.

An early and influential approach of this kind was Sternberg's (1977) "componential analysis." It was first applied to choice analogies such as

doctor : patient :: lawyer: client/judge

At least five component processes, Sternberg said, enter a successful response: encoding the terms (here referred to by the letters *A:B::C:D/D´*), inferring the relationship between *A* and *B*, mapping the *A-C* relationship, applying the *A-B* relation to *C* to generate an answer, comparing *D* and *D´* against the constructed answer, and responding. See Fig. 5.3.

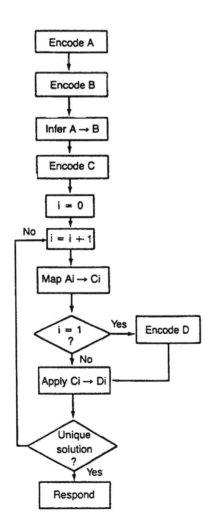

FIG. 5.3. Schematic flow chart for a successful model of analogical reasoning. From Sternberg (1977). Copyright 1977 by Lawrence Erlbaum Associates. Adapted by permission.

Exhibit 5rn. Performing a Componential Analysis

Sternberg (1977) reported several investigations into how people solve analogy problems. Figure 5.3 diagrams the model that worked best in several studies. Each box locates a hypothesized component of the response process. A component can be self-terminating, or exhaustive. For example, inference is self-terminating if the individual stops when just one relation between A and B is discovered. It is exhaustive if the person searches for all possible A-B relationships. In children's protocols (for many but not all types of analogy), the proportion of processes that were self-terminating was higher than among adults.

We can illustrate in a rough way how models are tested. (For details on such procedures, see Sternberg, 1977, and Pellegrino & Lyon, 1979.) Consider the true–false geometric analogies at the left of Fig. 5.4. The subject must encode each figure or figure-pair in the row, infer the rule(s) for changing A to B, apply the rule(s) to C to generate an ideal answer D, then decide whether the D´ shown in the item matches the generated answer. There are thus four processes: encoding, inference, application, and comparison/response.

At the right of Fig. 5.4, the numbers indicate how much intellectual work an item requires. For Encoding, the entry is simply the number of figures that must be observed. For Inference, the entry is the number of changes made in going from A to B. For Item 1, there is one transformation (in size); for Item 2, there are two changes (in size and shading). Counts for Application are necessarily the same as for Inference. Finally, the entry for Comparison/Response is the number of transformations that separate D´ from the ideal answer. With careful design of items, one can make these predictor variables largely independent of one another (except, of course, for the inference-application pair).

The model is typically tested by determining how well, for each person in turn, the four process variables predict the latencies of responses. The four regression weights from the calculation are interpreted as the person's scores on the respective components. Component scores can be reflected, so that larger numbers go with better performance.

Sternberg used "precuing" as an **experimental** procedure to trace processes with analogies in true–false form (with a D term and no D´). The person is allowed to examine just a part of the problem for as long

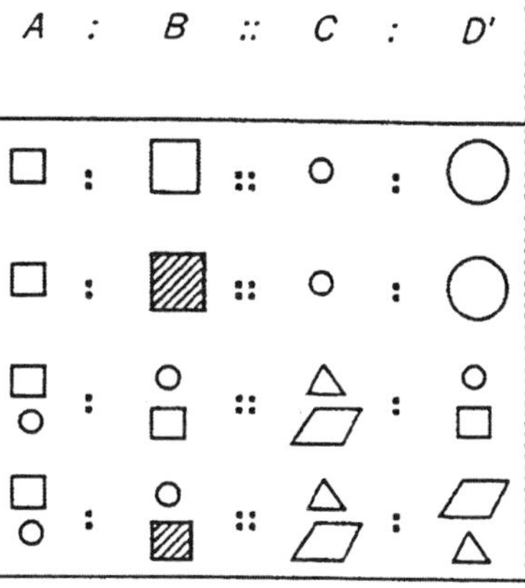

A : B :: C : D'	Encoding	Inference	Application	Comparison and Response
□ : ☐ :: ○ : ◯	4	1	1	0
□ : ▨ :: ○ : ◯	4	2	2	1
□○ : ○□ :: △▱ : ○□	8	1	1	2
□○ : ○▨ :: △▱ : ▱△	8	2	2	1

FIG. 5.4. Four true–false analogies, with counts of the number of times each component must be applied.

as necessary, then signals readiness to see the remainder. The time taken at the first step ("cue latency") and the time required at the second step to answer "True" or "False" ("solution latency") are recorded. When A:B is shown, the latency includes the time for encoding A and B, and for inferring the A-B relationship. The time on the following step includes time for encoding C and D, and for mapping, application, and judgment. Errors as well as times are recorded.

Using this or other procedures, response latencies are estimated for each step or subtask. Models are then fitted. Exhibit Strn, together with Fig. 5.4, demonstrates componential analysis of a geometric analogy.

Strategies and Strategy Shifting. Componential analyses produced process models for several reasoning tasks, but fitting the same model to everyone performing a given task is only a first approximation. Various process models might be needed to describe individuals. Younger and less able people, for example, often seem to analyze only briefly the first terms of a multiple-choice analogy before examining the D/D´ choice.

The approach depends on the person's ability profile; this was true even with simple laboratory tasks. For example, subjects have been asked to compare "The star is above the plus" with the picture at left. Persons higher in spatial ability than in verbal tend to create an image as they read the sentence, then to check it against the picture. Those higher in verbal ability than spatial tend to recode the picture into words, then to compare these with the sentence (E. Hunt & McLeod, 1978).

In the course of a single task performance, people shift strategies. Many investigators had argued that people shift strategies as items become more difficult (Bethell-Fox, Lohman, & Snow, 1984; Mulholland, Pellegrino, & Glaser, 1980).

Componential analysis makes possible a test of this hypothesis. Kyllonen, Lohman, and Woltz (1984) identified three kinds of relationships of strategy to ability:

Ability limits strategy selection.

Strategy choice is unrelated to ability, but ability determines how effectively the strategy is implemented.

Ability limits strategy and also predicts performance within strategy groups.

Instances of all three types were found in the componential analyses of a complex form-board task (Figs. 5.5. and 5.6). People tend to shift strategy as items increase in difficulty (Exh. KLW). Figure 5.5 shows how ability profiles moderated strategy choice.

Other studies have confirmed the usefulness of strategy-shift models, and have shown that seemingly minor variations in task demands can change the way people attack reasoning items (Embretson, 1986; Lohman, 1988). Although figural tasks seem particularly susceptible to alternative solution strategies, verbal tasks show similar effects when problems become difficult.

Modeling Difficult Items.   An ability test is designed to be hard for the people who normally take it. Correct answers show ability; fast response is of only secondary importance, if it affects scores at all. For example, time limits on subtests of the Cognitive Abilities Test (Thorndike & Hagen, 1993) allow most students to respond to all items on each subtest. Indeed, complex tests that load highly on G tend to be less speeded than tests that define more specific factors (and fall near the periphery of the radex).

One of the earliest criticisms of information-processing studies of abilities was that models capable of reproducing solution times in simple tasks omitted important aspects of intelligence. Investigations of verbal analogies confirmed this. Perhaps, said Pellegrino and Glaser (1982), test takers solve a verbal analogy by first abstracting semantic relationships from the stem of the item, and then evaluating the alternatives in a generate-and-test mode. But for more difficult problems, they argued, test takers must use information from the answer choices to guide the search for the appropriate *A-B* relation.

Exhibit KLW. Strategy Shifting
on a Spatial-Synthesis Task

Kyllonen, Lohman, and Woltz (1984) employed the spatial task illustrated in Fig. 5.6 (p. 157). On the simplest items, the person was asked to hold in mind an irregular polygon and judge whether a second drawing matched it. More difficult items required adding one or two polygons to the first figure, or rotating the initial figure, or both.

The 1984 report concerned only items that required combining of figures. Encoding, synthesis, and comparison steps in the performance were identified, and a model for each was constructed. Two types of model were tested: single-strategy and strategy-shift. Single-strategy models presume that any person solves all items in the same way, whereas strategy-shift models allow strategy to change with the type of item.

At each task step, strategy-shift models accounted better for the performance of most participants. For example, a person asked to combine several stimulus pieces can actually imagine their synthesis as a new shape. Most participants did this when complex pieces combined to make a simple shape, such as a square or a triangle. Instead of synthesizing, one can remember the separate pieces and test them one by one against the target figure when it is presented. Many participants did resort to this strategy when the pieces were simple shapes and the target shape was complex. It is easier to remember, say, a triangle and a rectangle than an irregular figure having six or seven sides.

Solution strategies could be predicted from the scores on reference ability tests (see Fig. 5.5). For example, those who seemed to shift strategies at the synthesis step often had high overall ability. In other words, high-G subjects were the most flexible in adaptation of strategy. Subjects who restricted their strategies had more extreme profiles; specifically, those who always synthesized figures were high in spatial ability (Gv) but low in verbal (Gc). Those who synthesized only figures presently in view (forgetting the figure on the first slide when it was supplanted) had very low spatial ability, but fell in the normal range of verbal ability.

An ambiguous *A-B* relation can be a major source of difficulty. Consider, for example, the analogy:

can:sack :: cop: [*sergeant/barrel/swipe/car*]

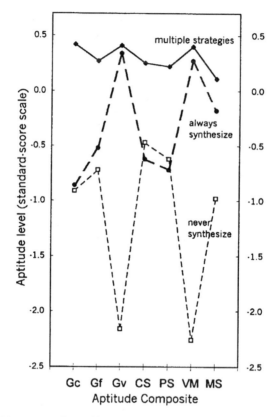

FIG. 5.5. Mean aptitude profiles for subjects who handled the synthesis step in different ways. Adapted from Kyllonen, Lohman, and Woltz (1984).

The terms *can* and *sack* are synonyms; though both often denote concrete objects, both also can replace the verb *discharge*. As a synonym for *cop*, *policeman* could complete the analogy, but it is not an option. When the person looks at the options, *swipe* brings to mind the second meaning of *cop*—to steal. The other options are designed to appeal to those whose processing was incomplete. Thus less able subjects often pick an option that is merely an associate of the *C* term—*cop*. Here, *sergeant* could appeal in that way. Others understand at least one *A-B* relation, but not the one that completes the analogy. Here, such responders may choose *barrel* because it is a member of the same category as the objects *can* and *sack*. The item writer's selection of options thus contributes importantly to problem difficulty. (Note also that when responders pick particular options they can thereby reveal something about the processes they used or failed to use.)

Other studies confirm that difficult items require more complex models. Gitomer, Curtis, Glaser, and Lensky (1987) studied eye fixations on verbal-analogy items. On easy problems they replicated Sternberg's (1977) results: Able people spent proportionately more time processing the stem (encoding, inference, mapping) than people of low ability. The pattern was reversed, however, on difficult problems. High-ability people spent more time processing stem words *after* looking at answer options than they did initially. Moreover, on difficult problems, abler people were much more likely than those of low ability to attend to all answer choices.

Why Do Gf Loadings Rise With Complexity?

Cognitive psychology—particularly the information-processing branch of it—has been characterized as task-bound (Newell, 1980). Many of the studies we have already reviewed amply demonstrate this. Most reflect intensive analysis of one or another task. Although such analyses are a useful first step in developing a theory of reasoning or intelligence, ultimately one must identify commonalities across tasks. The processes of greatest interest, Snow argued, are those common across families of tasks. (A "family" might be tasks presumed to measure inductive reasoning, or tasks that fall along the same spoke of a radex such as Fig. 3.1). The goal should be to develop a theory of constructs, not of tasks (Snow, 1978b).

Of the many processes employed in performing a given task, some but not all will be shared with other tasks. Of these common processes, only a subset will produce correlations across task scores. Processes and structures common to all tests in the inductive-reasoning family may contribute little or not at all to individual differences in reasoning performance. Therefore, although a theory of individual differences must begin with the processes in particular tasks, it must in time focus on processes that generate individual differences that will reappear in task after task.

With these caveats in mind, componential analyses, computer simulations, and demonstrations of strategy shifts can be considered together with factor analytic research. Snow used this evidence to shape an enriched theory of general reasoning ability or fluid intelligence. Tests of inductive reasoning discussed previously (e.g., series completion, analogies, and matrices), classification problems, and some performance tasks (e.g., block design) are good measures of Gf. Definitions of Gf typically mention perceiving relationships, educing correlates, maintaining awareness, and abstracting rules and concepts from sets of figures or symbols.

Chapter 3 called attention to complexity continua in the radex. Snow wanted a theory of cognitive abilities to explain not only the clustering of tests by content, but also their hierarchical organization. Tests that load heavily on Gf typically fall near the center of the radex, whereas seemingly simpler tasks are distributed around the periphery. Moving from periphery to center, one steps from task to task along spokes where tasks sometimes seem to build systematically on one another (and sometimes increase in complexity in less obvious ways). We are now in a position to examine the nature of this complexity.

Snow and his students noted several ways in which processing complexity can increase in going from edge to center:

1. The number of component processes increases.
2. Mental-speed differences within components accumulate.
3. Analytic performance components such as inferencing take on more importance.
4. Demands on working memory or attention increase.
5. Demands on assembly, control, monitoring, and other adaptive functions increase.

These explanations are not independent. For example, for greater accumulation of speed differences across components (2), the number of component processes must increase (1). Despite their overlap, these hypotheses provide a useful way to organize the discussion.

Number of Components. Tasks near the center of the radex require more intellectual work than peripheral tests. Many years ago, W. Zimmerman (1954) demonstrated that, by gradually increasing item complexity, one could make a form-board test load more heavily on perceptual speed, spatial relations, visualization, and reasoning factors—the increases coming in that order. Similar continua can be traced in Fig. 3.1. Increases in the number or difficulty of task steps beyond a certain point, however, can decrease the correlation with Gf.

An example is the faceted spatial test, shown in part in Fig. 5.6. Item difficulty was systematically manipulated by increasing the number of figures to be combined, the difficulty of the synthesis, and the amount of rotation required. Subscores were correlated with factors in reference tests (Lohman, 1988). Accuracy in synthesis correlated increasingly with Gv as the number of synthesis operations increased; $r = .21$,

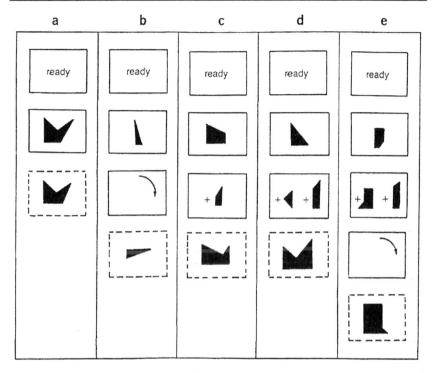

FIG. 5.6. Items from selected levels of complexity in a faceted spatial test. From Lohman (1979b). Copyright 1988 by Lawrence Erlbaum Associates. Adapted by permission. Note: Frames were shown one at a time. When the probe slide (shown here in dotted outline) appeared, the examinee was to respond "Yes" or "No."

.43, and .55 for zero-, one-, and two-piece additions, respectively. When rotation was also required, correlations with Gv were highest for trials requiring a single addition plus a rotation ($r = .67$). With still greater complexity—rotation following addition of two stimuli to the base—correlations with Gv declined, whereas correlations with memory span increased. Thus, one does not automatically increase the relationship with Gv simply by making problems harder.

Similarly, many hard problems (e.g., memorizing lists of randomly chosen numbers or words) are not particularly good measures of Gf. Furthermore, even when a task entails the type of processing that makes it a measure of Gf, good measurement requires difficulty appropriate for the test takers.

Speed of Processing. Speed can have a pervasive impact on cognition. For example, those who can access memory traces more rapidly can refresh them faster, and thus maintain information in an active state with relative ease. Faster processing also means less need to maintain memory traces for long periods—a further contribution to efficiency. The mental-speed hypothesis, as we said earlier, has sometimes gone so far as to attribute differences in mental ability to differences in the general speed of information processing (Jensen, 1982, 1998). A more cautious view is that, even when speed correlates only weakly with complex reasoning, small differences cumulate over time and tasks.

Although individual differences in speed of processing are surely an important aspect of Gf, rapid processing is not the whole of Gf in action. Furthermore, the correlation of processing speed with G varies considerably across domains, reaching approximately –.4 in the verbal domain and falling to approximately –.2 in the spatial domain (Snow & Lohman, 1989). The speed with which people carry out complex spatial tasks usually predicts overall performance much less well than does the richness or quality of the mental representations they create (Lohman, 1988; Salthouse, Babcock, Mitchell, Palmon, & Skovronek, 1990).

Demands Upon Central Components.   If Gf is not simply another name for faster processing, could it be that Gf reflects the action of particular mental processes? Spearman (1927) was one of the first to argue this (before G was reinterpreted or subdivided to consider a Gf). For him, the essential processes were "eduction of relations" and "eduction of correlates"—which resemble, respectively, Sternberg's "inference" and "mapping and application." The factor-analytic evidence favoring this hypothesis is substantial. Good measures of Gf require reasoning, especially inductive reasoning. Many school-learning tasks that resemble Gf tests can be seen as requiring induction of structure (Greeno, 1978). The frequency with which science and mathematics instruction hands the student the burden of inducing structure probably explains why reasoning tests correlate with achievement in these domains (Snow, 1980a). But such statements are not explanations.

Clues as to which central processes are important come from experiments that show how particular task requirements increase or decrease the correlation of success with Gf (Pellegrino, 1985). Using such evidence, Sternberg (1986) identified three types of processing demanded by reasoning tests:

> Selective encoding—attending selectively to information and encoding only information likely to be needed.

Selective comparison—recalling and comparing what is immediately relevant, ignoring further information in memory.

Selective combination—organizing only relevant portions of the information held in working memory.

Deductive reasoning calls primarily for selective combination, whereas inductive tasks call mostly for selective encoding and comparison.

Selective encoding depends heavily on the individual's knowledge and its attunement to the affordances present. The performer must resist distraction from salient but irrelevant information, and the temptation in choice-response items to examine the alternatives before considering the stem (Bethell-Fox et al., 1984).

Selective comparison likewise depends heavily on knowledge. Here, however, the key factor is how well the person's knowledge is organized. Comparison requires searching rapidly through memory for overlaps between two concepts. Better organization of the mental store leads to more efficient and productive search. Indeed, this is the essential requirement of most inference tasks. The task is not simply to find associations between two concepts, but to specifically characterize their relation. For example, consider the analogy:

breakfast : sunrise :: supper : dawn / evening / afternoon / sunset

The second and third choices are not unreasonable. But *sunset* is best because it refers not only to the time of day, but also to the position of the sun.

Selective combination means assembling and comparing information efficiently. Syllogistic reasoning is difficult not because statements such as "All A are B" are obscure. The main difficulty is in keeping track of all the ways in which the premises could be combined. This taxes both working memory and the ability to manipulate symbols. Thus, although certain processes may be central to intelligent thinking, individual differences in those processes may be due in part to other system limitations—such as that on working memory.

Attention and Working-Memory Capacity.   All information-processing models of cognition posit a limited-capacity working memory. As the place where cognitive operations are carried out, it tends to be a bottleneck in the system. Managing in working memory many simultaneous processes is indeed at the heart of reasoning. People differ substantially in the amount of information each can work on at any moment, and these differences correlate substantially with Gf. But working memory is much more than a limited-capacity central processor. Working memory also includes functions that selectively attend to one stimulus while inhibiting another, coordinate performance in tasks, and switch strategies (Baddeley, 1996). These functions suggest that a process model of Gf must include more than working-memory capacity.

Adaptive Processing.   Several theorists have argued that still more mental activities must be considered. Sternberg (1985) proposed that intelligent action requires metacomponents—that is, control processes that figure out what the problem is, select lower order components and organize them into a strategy, select a mode for representing information, allocate attentional resources, monitor the solution process, and attend to external feedback.

Snow and his associates emphasized the importance of assembly processes and control processes (see p. 147). More complex tasks, they thought, require more management activity. Such processes suggest a structure for the problem, assemble a strategy of attack, monitor the performance, and adapt (within an item) the strategy as performance proceeds. The analysis of the Raven test in Exhibit CJS supports and extends this hypothesis. In BETTERAVEN, the crucial executive functions were the ability to decompose a complex problem into simpler problems, and the ability to manage the hierarchy of goals and subgoals generated by this decomposition.

Working under Snow's direction, Swiney (1985) and Chastain (1992) manipulated items to change the amount of adaptive processing required. Swiney looked at change in the relevance of Gf on geometric analogies demanding various degrees of flexibility. In his blocked condition, items placed together had similar processing requirements (estimated by the number of elements and by the number and type of transformations). In his mixed condition, neighboring items were dissimilar. Mixing items hampered persons of low ability more than it did the able ones. Relations of Gf to task accuracy varied systematically with item difficulty and with task requirements. Relations were strongest when participants had to infer difficult but familiar rules, or to apply them. Gf mattered least when participants were applying easy rules or trying to discover unfamiliar, difficult rules—especially in the scrambled condition.

Participants' retrospective reports supported the conclusion that those with high G were better able to adapt their strategies to changing task demands. They reported switching to strategies that were more analytic as item difficulty increased. In contrast, low-G subjects preferred holistic strategies such as trying to "see" the answer; and on the difficult problems they were likely to report just "trying harder."

Swiney found also that those low in G overestimated their performance on highly difficult items, and consistently underestimated the difficulty of problems. This suggests high–low differences in monitoring and evaluation.

Chastain (1992) likewise contrasted blocked with mixed item ordering. Chastain's first two experiments used five types of items—arithmetic, antonyms, syllogisms, spatial relations, and number series. His third experiment used a figural encoding task and a dynamic spatial task. In all three studies, flexible adaptation was estimated by a simple difference score (mixed minus blocked) and by a residual score (deviation of mixed from the regression of mixed on blocked). Correlations of each of these scores with a battery of reference tests were small, but generally in the expected direction. Mixing item formats appears to be a less effective way to manipulate the G loading of a test than systematically altering a block of items. It thus appears that Gf has more to do with assembling and modifying a strategy for exercises of the same type than it does with shifting strategies as item type changes.

Gustafsson (1999) reported a study by B. Carlstedt that supports this interpretation of Gf. Carlstedt administered three kinds of inductive-reasoning problems to Swedish military recruits. Items were combined to form two tests: heterogeneous (HET), in which item types were mixed, and homogeneous (HOM), in which all items of one type were presented before another came along. Like Chastain, Carlstedt expected performance on HET to correlate higher with G. Instead, G loadings were higher in the HOM condition. Carlstedt suggested that HOM affords better possibilities for learning and for transfer across items. Simple logical ideas were called forth in early items, then had to be combined to resolve the later ones. The efficiency of a test as a measure of Gf, said Gustafsson, is thus partly a function of the dependence of later items on earlier ones.

This discussion of assembly and control has suggested that, although both the adaptation and within-task-learning interpretations have merit, the latter has stronger empirical and theoretical support. Assembling and tuning a workable strategy requires within-task learning, aided by careful monitoring. If items change too drastically or become too difficult, then more extreme adaptations are required. In either case, the problem solver must continually monitor her progress and work systematically to assemble, tune, and sometimes reassemble her strategy.

To summarize the discussion in this section: As one moves from periphery to center in a radex, tasks increase in apparent complexity. Tasks near the center typically require more steps or component processes, and emphasize accuracy rather than speed of response. But this does not mean that speed of processing is unimportant, or that the adding in just any type of process will increase the correlation with G. Increasing the demand on selective encoding, comparison, and combination does increase that correlation. Important to note, though, is that such processes require controlled, effortful processing, placing heavy demands on working memory. They also require more strategic or flexible problem solving, or the learning from easy items of rules that will combine to help with hard items.

LIMITATIONS AND FUTURE DIRECTIONS

The information-processing paradigm has enormously enriched our understanding of cognitive tests and of ability constructs. Investigators have moved from trait labels and vague notions of "process" to rich and detailed models of thinking. However, the information-processing approach is no exception to the rule that all paradigms have shortcomings. Two are particularly salient here: the neglect of affect and conation, and the failure to understand the role of context.

Neglect of Affect and Conation. Theorizing about the influence of affect (or feeling) and conation (or will) on cognition dates back to the Greek philosophers, yet only recently have investigators attempted to study their complex influences on each other. Some promising leads are reviewed in the next chapter.

Clearly, test takers who do well expend effort differently from those who score poorly. In general, those who score well are better at retrieving information from memory, and better able at maintaining the information in working memory while carrying out other processes. The difference is most striking when experts in a skill domain such as reading are compared with novices. The expert's time is spent on high-level processes (including comprehension); the novice must struggle just to identify words and grasp sentences.

Affect enters not only as anxiety and frustration (which constrict cognition), but also as interest and surprise (which enhance and direct cognition). In particular, those constructively motivated on a task will regulate their work more effectively than others. Situations elicit different combinations and strengths of conation and affect. Understanding the role of affect in cognition seems to demand a mode of theorizing and experimentation that attends not only to persons or to situations, but also to the aspects of situations to which a person typically attunes himself.

Need to Include Situations and Their Affordances. A theory of Gf must explain individual differences in problem solving not only on tests, but also in school and other everyday contexts. Although cognitive theories occasionally acknowledge the role of culture, they have not fully grasped that cognition is situated.

This thought must be a basis for a theory of aptitudes, in Snow's view. Abilities are reflected in the person's tuning to the demands and opportunities of each situation in turn, and thus reside in the union of person in situation, not in the mind alone:

> [T]he situation contains some pieces of what the person needs or can use to accomplish a given task. But persons must be tuned to perceive and use these pieces, and also to supply needed pieces from their own learning histories. Some persons are prepared to perceive these affordances, to use the pieces provided by the situation, and to complement these with pieces they provide, but some are not. Among those who are so tuned, each may use and supply slightly different pieces; there is functional equivalence despite idiosyncrasy. The result is that some persons succeed in learning in a given situation; they are in *harmony* with it. Others do not, because they are not tuned to use the opportunities the situation provides or to produce what it demands. (Snow, 1994, pp. 31–32; italics in original)

The idea of affordances refers not only to the physical and social environment, but also to the couplings or attunements to aspects of that environment that arise through the long evolutionary history of the species or the short developmental history of the individual. Put differently, the notions of affordances in the situation and propensities in the individual provide a way to reason about the selective encoding abler performers exhibit.

A Summary Hypothesis. A person's acts in a familiar situation can largely be attributed to that familiarity, that is, to remembering what works. In another situation, it may be implausible to attribute any part of a success to past experience with such a situation. The latter case, Elshout said in 1985, is what we should call a "problem." Tasks that can be accomplished using stored routines do not, in Elshout's view, count as problems. Sternberg (1986) made a similar but less radical distinction when he proposed that, to be called reasoning, processes used to solve problems must not be automatized. Likewise, Belmont and Mitchell (1987) contended that learners will generally be most strategic on tasks they perceive to be moderately difficult. To be "strategic" is knowingly to use a tactic that helps one achieve a goal, such as memorizing a passage, understanding unfamiliar words embedded in it, or the like. Strategy use requires effort, and people are unlikely to invest effort they consider unnecessary or unlikely to be rewarded. Snow (1989b) proposed to speak of tasks scaled along a continuum of difficulty or complexity. Elshout had argued that along such a continuum each person has a threshold. Below the threshold, fluid reasoning abilities are not required. The performance employs routines for the task that the person already has in store; activity is relatively automatic and algorithmic. Errors come mostly from cognitive slips and inattention rather than from inadequacies in the routines. In the language of Cattell (1987), these are crystallized abilities and skills.

Above the Gf threshold, however, the activity must be increasingly heuristic, improvisational, controlled, and motivated by interest in achievement for its own sake. Cognition follows a different path. Now, errors occur because the stored-up routines and knowledge are inadequate, or poorly applied, or are not tuned to the task at hand, or because motivation flags prematurely. Furthermore, the further above one's threshold one is forced to work, the more likely that heuristic processing and improvisation will degrade into helpless, even anxious, muddling.

Snow thus saw novices as having to work at or above their Gf thresholds in tasks of the type under consideration, whereas the experts on that task can work well below their Gf thresholds. The contrast is also seen in the pattern of declining correlations with Gf and increasing correlations with more specific abilities as participants acquire a new skill (Ackerman, 1986, 1988).

The goal of instruction is to raise the Gf threshold in each type of task that society (or the person) values. Raising the threshold means making nonproblematic (hence automatic) increasingly complex instances of the task type. To measure reasoning, however, problems must be perceived by the individual as located above the threshold. Fluid reasoning abilities are thus uniquely situated at the interface of person and situation.

6 The Cognitive-Affective-Conative Triad

Snow's dissertation (p. 110) was ahead of its time in considering how learning from instruction relates to affect and conation. In most of his writing about aptitude, Snow discussed qualities other than ability, and continually carried noncognitive measures into his research.[20]

OVERVIEW OF THE TRIAD

Snow and Farr (1987), prefacing their coedited volume on affcon processes, noted that, although basic research had begun to incorporate affcon processes into theories for instruction, investigators had tended to study either affective or conative processes as they influence cognition instead of considering connections between all three. Keeping these domains separate often simplifies research, but these three facets of performance are not provinces; they work together during learning and problem solving.

Both conative and affective factors can alter the perception of situations and the outcome of cognitive efforts. *How* such influences operate during learning remains to be established. Even less is known about the principles governing the cognitive-affective-conative triad when learning takes place over an extended period, as in most education. Coordinated theory on process will be developed by considering

---

[20]Writings by Snow related to substantial parts of this chapter are Snow (1989b, 1996b) and Snow et al. (1996).

the motives, goals, and circumstances surrounding extended educational performance, together with models of information processing.

Parallel Pathways for Performance and Commitment

The process analyses of abilities described in chapter 5 open a window: Persons who score high on ability tests retrieve from memory efficiently, leaving time for assembly and control. Concentrating resources on assembly and control is all the more important when complex tasks are novel, or incomplete, or call on special knowledge and skills.

Figure 6.1 offers a scheme of parallel pathways leading to achievement. The upper path summarizes some main ideas of the preceding chapter. The second contrasts performance with commitment, reflecting the affcon processes that are the topic here.

Striving toward attainment in any domain implies more than choosing a goal and working toward it. An energizing push starts the cognitive system in a certain direction; expectations and other conative processes regulate and sustain the moves. Recall Plato's metaphor (p. 7): The chariot horses provide the power the charioteer must regulate.

Even at the level of detailed cognitive processing, actions are motivated. People adapt plans and drop them. With or without reason, they rearrange priorities and goals—sometimes in midcourse. Sometimes the goal is to discover new goals. Sometimes plans are playful. Alternative plans may well carry different affective tones, especially when learning takes place in a group. Affective reactions and negative self-evaluations can alter details of plans, or disrupt plans altogether. Conation implies follow-through beyond motivated commitment.

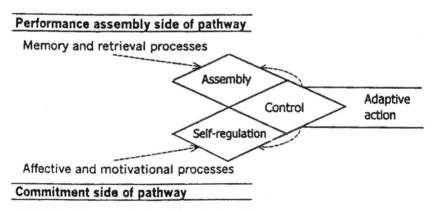

FIG. 6.1.   Processes that precede adaptive action.

When goals and circumstances are ambiguous, or just plain ambitious, efforts to stay on the plan are required.

Until recently, ideas about how to bridge between the parallel pathways of Fig. 6.1 were incomplete and often loose. Somehow mood, emotion, impulse, desire, and purpose—aspects of mental life—ought to connect directly into information-processing models of cognition. For some theoretical purposes, details of the connections can be ignored. Thus a good mood can facilitate careful attention during study; if the mood shifts, so does the quality of work.

In short-term or independent learning, a few mechanisms may account for most cognitive-affcon relations. H. Simon (1982) suggested, for example, that only two functions—interruption of information processing and arousal of attention—account for most of the relations that might be identified. For extended or group learning, we suggest adding other functions, such as directing, maintaining, blocking, and terminating an activity.

Broad psychological constructs may guide explorations of cognitive, affective, and conative processes in education, but only if such constructs are understood as processes. Shyness and persistence, we know, play roles in education. Investigations that treat these as surface characteristics cannot explain educational success; tracing processes is required. For example, an underlying tendency to reflect before taking action helps clarify how a trait such as shyness connects with ability in a given educational situation.

Affective or conative response to a learning task generates a psychological state. When that state is observably consistent across times and situations, then it becomes reasonable to apply the word *style* or *trait*. Evaluation anxiety is a state; but the state is so frequent in some people that the label *trait-anxious* applies. Traits represent the most general and stable individual differences. As few as five traits may cover most of the big picture, but each of these comprises many stylistic and strategic tendencies, and a vast number of states.

Affcon states and processes can influence sequences of information processing during learning and performance. A student engaging in strategic task management can make productive use of the concern that arises when the due date for a project approaches. That anxious concern might be troublesome in group work, however, where people must be managed as well as tasks. Process relations may be reciprocal; anxiety could trigger a strategic response, but the sense of control gained from good task management should eventually reduce anxiety. Although many affcon responses are below conscious awareness, such responses nevertheless condition a student's performance.

Process research has begun to examine details of some possible cognitive-affective-conative relations implied in Fig. 6.1. Some investigators limit their attention to one type of task. But a general label is appropriate when a similar strategy is observed in a variety of learning situations. *Self-efficacy*, for example, denotes a broad self-concept of ability, but when it is actualized a more specialized evaluation of task competence is evoked also (Eccles & Wigfield, 1995). Researchers who focus on only one level of a construct can miss important information. Ultimately, most data collection will benefit from both the magnifying glass and the panoramic camera.

AFFECT AND COGNITION

We first discuss the role of affect in cognitive processing. When possible we identify models that integrate the affcon processes.

How Anxiety Influences Reaction to Difficulty

We begin with anxiety, an aspect of the Big Five Neuroticism factor, before turning to moods.

Affect can influence the kind of effort expended, as well as the amount. A person, having alternative strategies to attack a problem, implements one. Slow progress often leads to a change of strategy. A strategy shift may be a sign of competence, or a sign that the person is in trouble.

Exhibit KLW (p. 153) shows that one key is the profile of abilities. There, very high spatial, low-verbal students attempted a demanding spatial synthesis to handle every item. Others synthesized only on easy items. Those excellent at reasoning showed the most flexibility in strategy change.

Schmitt and Crocker (1981) found a similar effect for test anxiety. They gave a test under two conditions. In the more demanding condition, students had to formulate a response before seeing multiple-choice options. In the other, they saw the choices along with the item stem and could eliminate some poor alternatives quickly. Less anxious students did markedly better under the first condition, where they had to construct an answer before matching. The anxious did better in the second condition.

Schmitt and Crocker (1981) studied only test anxiety, and Kyllonen et al. (1984) predicted only on ability. We can anticipate the finding if both were measured together. Able nonanxious students can use a demanding task, and the less able, highly anxious must retreat to an easier approach. Data are lacking on the able anxious and the nonanxious of low ability.

The explanation for the Schmitt–Crocker results is affcon: Anxiousness produces self-defeating thoughts and self-doubts; these intrude, shifting attention from task to self. The great demands of constructive matching are likely to induce such intrusions. A student comparing features in a display, on the other hand, has eyes on the task all the time, not on her feelings. If the form of the task encourages a manageable cognitive activity, it can support the anxious and self-doubting student.

This research suggests what mechanisms may operate during instruction. Many instructional treatments are novel, unstructured, and incomplete, which makes them difficult for some students. Insofar as those treatments demand more elaborate information processing, the quality of responses can be influenced by anxiety, mood, and so on.

Mood as an Influence in Learning

An elated person finds material easier to recall than does a depressed one (Bower, 1981). Moods and related emotional states are thought to act as "filters," which direct attention, with good or bad consequences for learning (Schwarz & Bohner, 1996).

A learner in a good mood organizes what is presented more systemically and meaningfully. Isen, Daubman, and Gorgolione (1987) reached that conclusion from a number of experiments on problem solving. They recruited participants in shopping malls, libraries, and other places, concealing the fact that an experiment was going on. To induce positive feelings, the investigators might hand out refreshments to a random half of the individuals. Another experimenter then called in these same people to work on tasks ranging from simple word and color sorting to creative problem solving. Those with the induced positive feelings consistently outperformed an untreated control group, according to every indicator of cognitive organization. In sorting, for example, learners who were feeling good used broader categories that allowed more grouping (e.g., "vehicles" could bracket both "truck" and "camel"). They engaged in playful exploration of novel solutions, which in turn fostered creative problem solving. In a heuristic task, said Isen et al., positive affect leads to richer interpretation, which in turn, results in more meaningful organization. (On rote tasks, no such effect appeared.)

Affect may not be the only explanation for the results, however. Perhaps stronger motives—increased confidence, desire to please researchers, or simply "trying harder"—lead to meaningful organization. People in good moods worked almost twice as fast as controls in the Isen study. However, they ignored the less important dimensions of the task, and reviewed their work less than others did. The authors suggested that if motivational factors contributed to the findings, these must somehow enable more efficient work. One possibility is a greater sense of efficacy; another is a change in goals, suggesting some affcon integration.

Integrative Process Models

According to Schwarz and Bohner (1996), people with positive affect tend to think that their goals are reachable; negative affect increases the sense of risk. A sense of risk suggests that the person needs to change the given situation somehow, or to give up. Before making a change, however, people are likely to inspect their options closely, proceed with caution, and consider details with care. Experiments on attitude change, and studies of school learning, support the hypothesis that elation leads to playfulness whereas depression or slight anxiety leads to care and vigilance.

Another integrative model offers a definition of positive affect that goes beyond mood. According to Klinger (1996), people have "current concerns" that combine thoughts and emotions about goals, interests, and values. Like moods, their concerns sensitize individuals to information that could guide potential cognitive, emotional, or behavioral response. Klinger measured current concerns via introspective interviews and questionnaires.

In a series of studies, participants responded to audiotaped narratives associated with either their own current concerns, or the concerns of someone else. Both narratives were played at the same time, one to each ear. The participant used a toggle switch to indicate the side she was attending to. Participants reported and rated their thoughts as they listened; also, during a break, they described in their own words the last segment of narrative that they could recall.

Participants spent considerably more time listening to passages related to their own concerns. They recalled those passages best, and their expressed thoughts involved those passages more than passages referring to someone else's concerns. Concern-relatedness of words and emotional-arousal ratings that respondents assigned to them were strongly correlated. According to Klinger (1996), current concerns dispose individuals to respond emotionally to associated cues: "What people notice, recall, and think about is ultimately governed by their concerns, and ... this relationship is mediated by the emotional responses evoked by concern-related cues" (p. 184).

Exhibit Kln. Temperament-Related Differences in Desire for Directions and in Efficiency

In Strelau's self-report reactivity scale (p. 172), many questions refer to emotional stability and self-regulation. Reactives are thought to differ from low reactives on a characteristic of the nervous system. According to the theory derived from Pavlov, reactives have the temperament to respond to even low levels of stimulation.

In Klonowicz's 1986 study, students from the top and bottom quarters of the reactivity distribution were to construct two physical models—each under a different condition:

H. Heuristic instruction indicated the desired product, but left individuals to organize their own activities and work methods.

A. Algorithmic instruction described the goal of the task and, step by step, the procedure for the construction.

Almost two thirds of the reactives, polled after completing the tasks, said that they would prefer to use A in the future. Among low reactives about 40% preferred A. These preferences support an image of reactives as impulsive, and appreciating the regulation imposed by the algorithm.

A second phase asked these participants to form a square of tape and clamp an eyelet to it. Half of the sample worked under instruction of type A; a matched half, under H. Judges rated the quality of the products. Reactives and nonreactives scored about equally well in condition A, but the reactives' quality fell off markedly in condition H. Quality was unrelated to preference.

Klonowicz recorded each person's ratio of corrections made to number of errors. The averages of this "effort index," taken at face value, showed a marked interaction. Low reactives made much the same effort in both conditions. The reactives put forth noticeably more effort than low reactives in condition H, and somewhat less than nonreactives when told what steps to take. To put the finding simply, reactives wasted effort in condition H. They made far more moves than low reactives to reach the same average quality. Klonowicz judged that, on the heuristic tasks, reactives made a greater overall investment of skills, forces, and knowledge than their low-reactive counterparts.

Relation of Reactivity to Instructional Response

Early research on temperament in the Pavlovian tradition emphasized reactivity, which is associated with activity level and responsiveness to weak stimuli. Such temperament differences purportedly contribute to an individual's behavioral style (Thomas, Chess, & Birch, 1968).

Strelau (1983), moving away from traditional laboratory measures of reaction time and excitability, collected teacher ratings of students' excitability and sensitivity to stimulation in such areas as:

Shows initiative in organizing play or work with others.

Does not abandon current activity when encountering an obstacle.

Seeks the company of others. (p. 347)

The opposite poles of each scale were anchored as in the following delineation of "Seeks the company of others":

During breaks prefers to remain in class. Does not join others in play or talk. Prefers to be alone or with a close friend (low reactive).

Spends breaks in the hallways. Participates in games, usually of movement, with others, or talks in a large group (high reactive). (p. 348)

A "reactivity" score summarized the ratings. Reactive students are characterized by "intensity or vigour of movement" (Strelau, 1983, p. 349). Students at the high and low ends of the reactivity scale adopt different styles on an extended task, and prefer different kinds of instruction. Moreover, different kinds of tasks bring out the best performance in the contrasting groups.

Exhibit Kln describes differences between high and low reactives in their preferred mode of instruction. Sixty-five percent of reactives preferred algorithmic, step-by-step instruction over heuristic instruction—which required them to devise a response. Only 40% of low reactives had that preference.

Strelau (1983) added that, when reading texts, reactives are more likely than low reactives to engage in auxiliary actions—underlining, writing summaries, and reviewing. Summarizing many studies on instruction, Strelau concluded that reactives deal with their straying attention by reducing stress and tension, taking breaks to avoid overstimulation, and alternating activities. Low reactives do not need rest breaks—they seek out the stimulating novelty and complexity that reactives try to block out.

Low-reactive learners, it has been suggested, perceive the outer, instructional environment as low in either structure or challenge, so much so that they create challenge (e.g., raising standards, or complicating a task). Reactive learners have no such urge; they rest their mental functions between subtasks. By taking notes and reviewing, reactives control their activity level. Organizing and control processes thus serve a compensatory function.

Conative controls also can compensate for affect that interferes with coping; Exhibit Bkrt illustrates. Conceivably, reactives would profit more from a problem-focus than from a "rest break" strategy. Focusing on the problem is one way to bring stress under control and restore a sense of well-being (Boekaerts, 1996). Mood and cognitive ability should play into this situation as well. A good mood can make it easier to handle perceived stressors, irrespective of reactivity level.

Exhibit Bkrt. Problem-Focused and Emotion-Focused Styles in Coping With Stress

Boekaerts (1987) investigated how adolescents worked at computer mathematics related to their coursework. She distinguished problem-focused response to stress from emotion- focused response. Problem-focused students try to alter perceived stresses, often through planful problem-solving or strategy-shifting. *Emotion focus* refers to attempts to regulate negative emotions generated by stress, or to regain self-control.

Boekaerts classified students according to the pole each was closest to, having interviewed them about common academic stresses (e.g., tests, homework, failures, and conflicts with teachers and peers). Each student presumably prefers one mode of coping, but most coping models accept that anyone may use both forms of coping, even in dealing with the same stress.

Students, as they worked the computer problems, answered questions about their confidence, state of anxiety, and effort expenditure, and about the perceived relevance of the task. Students who reported anxiety when under stress adopted the problem-focus style more than emotion focus. Problem-focused coping was especially frequent among highly anxious girls.

Action control is thought to help restore well-being under stress. Boekaerts (1993) used Kuhl's (1984) Action-Control Scale (see p. 177) to register students' methods of regulating action in the presence of intrusive thoughts and/or feelings of anxiety. Students who controlled their actions by focusing directly on the task and away from themselves appeared to have more positive feelings about their performance, lower state anxiety, and higher average performance on the computer problems. Boekaerts saw action control as regulating state anxiety and reducing ruminative thought; that is, a conative process moderated affect.

Strelau has now begun to study, in adolescents and adults, the connection between activity level and ability. Researchers collected measures of fluid, crystallized, and social intelligence as well as Strelau's own self-report measure of reactivity (see Strelau, Zawadski, & Piotrowska, 2001). Only the matrix test and measures of divergent thinking (the production of varied responses to a problem that has multiple solutions) correlated with reactivity. Strelau hypothesized that able low reactives are more resistant to stresses. Their resistance to intrusion actually draws them into tasks and helps them persist. They seek opportunities for development and achievement, or take better advantage of their educational chances.

Facing complexity, abler people turn to analysis. Low reactives also find ways to make less complex tasks more interesting or challenging for themselves; their wish for stimulation pulls them into the task and they gain more. Of the four possible combinations, high ability combined with low reactivity would respond best to complexity.

People with lower ability would not be so able to handle the deep analysis and would tend toward surface processing. But a reactive person with low ability may compensate by pausing to review before moving ahead, or by using notes and summaries. With too many rest breaks, however, these students lose intellectual ground. The less able reactive may spend half his study time reviewing completed work, rather than forging ahead. In instructional situations, such students benefit from added structure. Strelau et al. (2001) suggested that researchers study the dynamic relations between fluid ability and reactive aspects of temperament. Presumably, these studies would include detailed experiments investigating high-high and low-low aptitude combinations as well.

The conclusions reviewed so far point to influences of affect on such intermediate processes as strategy choice, concentration of attention, risk assessment, cognitive efficiency, and coping. Some studies trace the influence further, to effects on quality of learning during instruction and problem solving. In the next section, the review of the substantial educational research on conation moves on to examine strategic actions in academic situations, then relates data on strategy to criteria such as grades or achievement tests. Strategies observed across various learning and performance situations are stylistic regularities of a comparatively general nature.

THE RUBICON MODEL

In most tasks, a person has goals, chooses a plan of action, and sets out to execute the plan. The predecision period during which an intention is formed is distinguished sharply from the postdecision period, so sharply that Heckhausen (1991) called the theory elaborating this distinction "the Rubicon model" (p. 175). He and Kuhl (1985) identified as "motivational" the conative processes engaged prior to fixing on an intention; after action begins, the processes are considered "volitional."

The Commitment Pathway

As Heckhausen and Kuhl (1985) described the conative aspect of the commitment pathway (Fig. 6.1), one proceeds from wishes to wants to intentions to actions. *Motivation* refers to the processes involved in the decision to pursue one or another goal. Wishes and wants lead to intentions. A "wish" is a value attached to a goal. Individual emotional histories and interests dictate wishes at least in part. A person has an expectation about the chances of attaining this or that goal; expectancy-value theories predict what goal will be chosen. A wish becomes a "want" when expectation exceeds a critical level.

A want can become an "intention" when it is seen as relevant to a future action. Wanting to do well in high school is intensified, becoming a serious intention, when a person expects to go to college. The motive to succeed, intrinsic motivation to learn, expected rewards, and self-confidence all refer to such underlying motivational, predecisional tendencies (Pintrich & Schunk, 1996; Snow et al., 1996).

Volition, coming into play after an intention is formed, includes implementing and protecting goals, and managing resources to protect intentions. Intentions lead to action when they are protected against competing intentions, and when the person hopes for success. Problem-focused coping, described in Exhibit Bkrt, is most relevant in the intention-action segment of the pathway. So are the action controls involved in self-regulation during learning:

> Predecisional motivational ideas [bring to mind] possible incentive-laden consequences of one's actions and ... the likelihood of possible consequences .... Once a goal intention has been formed, the volitional mind-set is implementation-oriented. (Heckhausen, 1991, p. 176)

Participants do not generally go back and reconsider their goals, once thoughts about implementation have begun. Some of the evidence for this conclusion comes from ingenious and varied studies by Gollwitzer and his colleagues (many summarized by Heckhausen, 1991, pp. 177–183; see also Gollwitzer, 1996). In one design, students were assigned a short exercise that required selection among possible tasks, or planning for a task already chosen. The selection mode triggered motivational reactions; the planning mode led to volitional reactions. A second move asked participants to complete three fairy tales. Then—third move—the investigator interrupted the writing before it was completed, and introduced a seemingly unrelated activity. The activity, a kind of projective technique, yielded a score thought to indicate what was "on the mind" of the participant at this time.

Participants in an (induced) predecisional state reported thoughts about the value of various decision alternatives. In the writing task, they also displayed superior memory, a sign of enhanced receptivity to incoming information. In contrast, participants in the postdecisional state (again induced) reported procedural concerns, and thoughts about translating the decision into action. They showed comparatively poor memory.

Although crossing the Rubicon sets a person firmly on task, unbending pursuit of a goal is not always for the better. If winning a chess contest is an unrealistic goal for a boy, then losing several times ought to lower his sights. If a girl's personal goal to exceed her best time in a sport is not reached after extensive coaching and practice, perhaps she should reconsider the goal. In academics, it may be best for teachers to hold fast to a few primary goals for which their students can be well prepared.

Whether motivation should be distinguished from volition remains in dispute. Some theorists propose constructs that bridge the pathway, for example, "impulse, desire, volition, purposive striving, all emphasize the conative aspect" (English & English, 1958, p. 104; see also Exh Csk, p. 47). Others (see Mischel & Shoda, 1998) are beginning to construe motivational and volitional processes, such as expectancies and self-regulatory plans, to explain situation-bound expressions of propensities (e.g., conscientiousness). The distinction does allow new emphasis on the volitional side of the path, which had been lost in other theories on motivation (Weiner, 1990).

We do not discuss predecisional (motivation) processes further, preferring to orient readers toward the full range of conative processes instead. The model of Fig. 2.1, however, fits squarely in the predecisional portion of the commitment pathway; and Table 3.3 presents those predecisional constructs given prominent consideration by Snow et al. (1996). Volitional processes can be categorized as contributing to performance or interfering with it. Motivation is more diffuse, both because it is less linked to steps in information processing and because it often lacks the good/bad polarity. Many motivational qualities (e.g., anxiety, self-efficacy, and level of aspiration) are likely to have an optimal level for a given task or situation. Either an excess or a deficiency is potentially detrimental.

Volitional Processes

The most noteworthy constructs on the postdecisional end of the pathway are aspects of self-regulation: action orientation, action controls, mindful effort investment, and self-regulation in learning. Generally, the four have been studied separately rather than considered together. We examine their similarities and differences.

Action Orientation. State-orientation implies fixation "on past, present, or future states—for example, on a past failure to attain a goal, on the present emotional consequences of that failure, or on the desired goal state itself" (Kuhl & Kraska, 1989, p. 366). State-oriented persons also hold stubbornly to unrealistic goals or intentions that they ought to reconsider. Although he conceptualized action orientation as a stable propensity, Kuhl (1981) induced action or state orientation by experimental manipulation. For example, he induced state orientation by confronting subjects with unexpected and uncontrollable failures on a task. Kuhl demonstrated also that people can be oriented toward action by asking them to think aloud while solving problems.

Kuhl (1984, 1993) has measured action orientation by self-reports organized into subscales. Correlations of the subscales range from –.20 to .54 with measures of test anxiety, vulnerability to stress (negative), self-control, and achievement motivation (positive). Obviously, action orientation is largely independent of these other variables (see Kanfer, Dugdale, & McDonald, 1994).

State orientation lowers performance on difficult tasks through its relation to affect (Heckhausen et al., 1985; Kuhl, 1985). In one trial, for example, subjects who had succeeded on several tasks were faced with uncontrollable failure. The state-oriented ones reported considerably more thoughts about failure and more worry than those who were action oriented (Kuhl, 1984).

State-oriented students, in contrast to action-oriented ones, show an increased tendency to choose activities that require little self-regulation. Kuhl (1982) asked sixth graders to rate their intentions to engage in each of 22 after-school activities and report the next day how much time they actually spent on the activities. Correlations between strength of intentions to engage and actual time spent ranged from .40 to .80 in action-oriented samples, and from .30 to .40 among the state oriented. In routine but required activities (e.g., brushing teeth), this difference in correlations was reversed.

Action Controls. Action controls are devices for maintaining intentions (Kuhl & Kazén-Saad, 1989, p. 387). Action-oriented individuals deliberately use them to complete tasks. Such questions as "Should I consider a different way to solve this problem?" and "Am I reacting too slowly?" are action controls. Action controls can be evident also in school learning, as in prioritizing the intention to study for a test as a way of getting going. An activity assigned a lower priority, such as exercise or a conversation with a friend, might then be set aside.

Using action controls requires the capacity to envision one's own intentions. According to Kuhl and Kraska (1989), very young children exhibit rudimentary action controls, but adolescents and adults become better and better at them. Exhibit Msch (p. 88) referred to research on delay of gratification in children, where action control was rewarded. Even in Mischel's artificial situation action control predicted adjustment in schooling. Conditions common to both situations may explain the continuity—including interesting distractions, competing intentions, and the value of focusing.

Learners regulate their action by four types of control: environment, attention, motivation, and emotion. (For more complete taxonomies see Kuhl, 1984, and Corno, 1986, 1989.) Kuhl reported on action-control strategies that protect intentions from competing tendencies. Suppose, for example, that a student intends to do homework and needs to inhibit the preference to do something else. The first step is controlling the environment, for example, choosing a quiet and well-lighted work space and having necessary materials ready. The next step is prioritizing tasks and judging roughly the time each should receive. Attention is thereby channeled toward the academic work and away from distractions. The student also should monitor the time spent on each subtask. If the work becomes difficult, motivation controls can be used—looking ahead to the sense of satisfaction from completed work, for example. Negative emotions can be controlled by taking a breather, and trying consciously not to get upset. Recalling previous successes is a way to boost self-confidence; with that momentum in place, learners can reconsider the source of difficulty and try again. Beyond these four types of control, deliberate development of a preferred way of working (i.e., a work style) establishes habits conducive to perseverance.

To investigate origins of action control, Kuhl and Kraska (1989) questioned children using what we refer to as MKT (for Metamotivational Knowledge Test). This measure consists of pictures depicting situations in which it is difficult to stick to one's purpose. Questions are asked about alternative ways to carry out intentions and resist distraction. For example, one picture shows a student working on homework while friends play outside the window. Researchers ask children to explain why it is difficult to stay focused on homework in such a situation. Such action controls were observed in Mischel's research on delay of gratification.

Motivation control and attention control increase regularly from first to fourth grade. (Emotion control, however, seems not to develop until late in childhood.) Scores tend to correspond to teacher ratings of compliance with classroom rules and of overall adjustment to school. Taken together, results from this research program and that of Mischel suggest that knowledge and strategic use of action control may be a significant aptitude for school adjustment.

In further work, Kuhl and Kraska (1989) developed a computerized performance assessment of action-control efficiency that approximates a process analysis—in the version for children,of choice-reaction time by a task shown on the monitor. Successful performance earns money for toys. As children work, an interesting distraction occasionally appears on part of the screen. Children understand readily that they will earn less if they interrupt performance on the speeded task to watch the distraction, so they intend to resist the distraction.

Children low on MKT tend to vary in response time over episodes, though their average time is not longer. In one study, children with low MKT scores varied four times as much in interresponse times across episodes with distractions as they did across episodes without distraction. Those with high MKT scores had essentially constant response times even with distraction. According to Kuhl, children who become distracted, then notice that their performance has slackened, try to compensate by working faster on later trials.

Because performance-based measures of self-regulation are rare, the convergence between this indicator and MKT is noteworthy. Both measures correlate moderately, in the expected directions, with self-reported test anxiety and Kuhl's action-orientation scale. In second to fourth grade, the children whose response times varied most tended to be rated low on attentiveness in class and concentration (range of correlations, –.22 to –.72).

Mindfulness. Intentional use of nonautomatic, effort-demanding mental processes (Langer, 1989; Salomon, 1984) is another aspect of self-regulation. The difference between what a person can do and what he does is often an effect of mindful effort. Most novel situations require not only knowledge and skill but an intention to mobilize and apply them.

The distinction between mindful and effortless learning parallels that between controlled and automatic cognitive processing. However, mindfulness becomes conative by its emphasis on the taxing quality of intellectual effort. Some instructional conditions promote mindful effort directly and indirectly. Perceived complexity in a task, lack of structure, multiple goals, and demands for participation all stimulate mindfulness. Mindfulness is slight when skill can proceed without conscious guidance, or when completing the task looks easy (and also when a task appears too demanding). In such cases the person allows events to unfold without vigilance, so time and energy can go elsewhere (Bargh & Chartrand, 1999; Salomon, 1983).

Streamlining effort to reach desired goals is an aspect of mindfulness that H. A. Simon (1982) called "satisficing." Satisficing can be an efficient reaction to exhausting or extremely difficult tasks, helping to restore well-being under stress (Exh. Bkrt). Flexible adaptation of mental effort serves important functions in complex learning and performance, as we saw in chapter 5. Occasional rest breaks and shifts in goals need more study as adaptive devices in complex learning.

Salomon (1981) assessed mindfulness with a self-report scale on the number and kind of nonautomatic mental elaborations a person uses in various situations. He found that mindful learners perform better when given loose guidance and freedom to work independently; they react negatively to intensive guidance. The opposite occurs in learners low in mindfulness (including those Strelau would class as reactive). Mindful learners tend to work better alone than in teams. In teams that encourage independent activity, however, mindful learners act as if alone, whereas those who are less mindful tend to loaf (see also Salomon & Leigh, 1984).

People vary in their "need for cognition"—that is, in their wish to engage in effortful cognitive activity (Cacioppo, Petty, Feinstein, & Jarvis, 1996). Optimal levels of anxiety and self-efficacy for academic achievement also are associated with mindful effort investment (Ames, 1992; Kanfer & Ackerman, 1989a). Mindful learners seek opportunities to invest mental effort. They are selectively mindful about some aspects of the situation while ignoring other aspects.

Even when goals are not currently "held fast before the mind" (James, 1890/1983, p. 1166), they continue to exist in some deep recess. Just knowing that a goal is there, without taking action to reach it, is a mindful event that aids persistence. Gollwitzer (1999) called these "implementation intentions." His experiments indicate that intending to implement fosters follow-through. For example, Gollwitzer and Brandstatter (1997) asked a group of their students to write a report on how they spent their Christmas Eve. The report was to be finished by December 26. To encourage intent to implement, half of the group completed a questionnaire before leaving school stating exactly where and when each would write the report. The other half saw no questionnaire. Three fourths of the first group produced their reports on time, compared with one third of the controls. Gollwitzer (1999) said that "implementation intentions ... cause the mental representation of the anticipated situation to become highly activated and thus easily accessible. ... [These] perceptual, attentional, and mnemonic consequences ... help to overcome problems of action initiation" (p. 497).

Intent to implement relates to other conative propensities. Middleton and Midgley (1997) measured sixth graders' approach and avoidance goals for academic work. Those who specified how they planned to reach goals were higher than others in efficacy, seeking help, and self-regulation. Students who set out to avoid effort were lower in efficacy, avoided help, and had more test anxiety. Additionally, students with lower GPAs were more likely than students with higher GPAs to focus on performance rather than mastery, and to hold both approach and avoidance goals at once.

Self-Regulation in Learning.   Many predecisional thoughts occur without conscious intent (Winne, 1997). The expectation of a valued reward (parental approval, say) is one example; another is the expectation of efficacy. Kuhl (1984) would have it that learners who reserve deliberate application of mental effort for selected situations thereby can better sustain goal-directed action.

Still, self-regulators do apply learning strategies deliberately, with the aim of promoting deeper learning or more efficient problem solving (Corno & Mandinach, 1983). Thus some make tables and charts, think of examples, self-test on the material, and evaluate ideas. The choice of style is again influenced by situational and motivational factors, such as knowledge of one's effectiveness as a learner, and by self-efficacy (Pintrich & Garcia, 1991; Zimmerman, 1990).

Students who self-regulate see themselves as able to pursue chosen courses of action. Winne (1995, 1997; see also Winne & Hadwin, 1998) offered a process analysis of self-regulation during study. The model includes awareness of personal limitations or task difficulties that may impede progress, deliberate use of cognitive strategies to achieve study goals, and thoughtful control of affect and cognition. Self-regulated studying thus reflects cognitive, as well as affcon processes. Winne fit his definition within J. R. Anderson's (1991) model of rational cognition, relating it to costs and gains that a learner's cognitive system seeks to balance during study.

Learners perceive cues selectively. To organize this information for input into memory, self-regulators use cognitive strategies. Thus, one would expect confident learners who anticipate success to opt for more demanding, more constructive learning strategies. Those with lower expectations, reactive learners, and those with strong evaluation anxiety might use weaker algorithmic strategies. To protect their sense of their own worth, they may reduce their effort.

Postdecisional processes often retain the colloquial sense of volition as deliberate action to monitor and control one's processing. Other specialized forms of control permit self-observation of automatic motivational and affective processes. (Example: "I notice that whenever the teacher calls on me my face turns red and I want to hide.") In principle, unproductive habits may be broken deliberately, and that is the aim of many clinical applications of cognitive self-monitoring (see Meichenbaum, 1977).

Students can fit a strategy to a type of motivational difficulty. Wolters (1998) asked students how they would maintain effort when attending a lecture, reading a textbook, writing a paper, and studying for a test. He described three situations where motivation lagged—when the material seemed irrelevant, or was difficult, or was boring. When the material was considered irrelevant or boring students would use more postdecisional, protective, and control strategies than when the material was considered difficult, they said. They would use cognitive elaboration and organizing efforts.

Kanfer and Ackerman (1989a, 1989b) provided evidence that laying out detailed goals to encourage self-regulation can benefit early learning, but the advantage tapers off. Notably, less able trainees reported anxiety and ruminating thoughts when given goals at an early stage, and this made them less likely to work according to a plan.

Belief in one's probable success is not in itself the key; thinking through how to do the work is a necessary support for many who aspire to do well. Kanfer and Ackerman concluded that motivation without regulation and control is not enough for successful learning, and that direct instruction can promote self-regulation (see also Kanfer, 1996, and Winne, 1995).

Research on self-regulation in response to instruction has had many goals (see, e.g., Schunk & B. Zimmerman, 1994; B. Zimmerman, 1988; B. Zimmerman & Schunk, 1989):

Developing self-report measures on use of self-regulation, and relating them to measures of other variables.

Understanding more fully how self-regulation develops.

Predicting important educational outcomes.

Evaluating interventions to teach self-regulation.

B. Zimmerman and Martinez-Pons (1986) used a structured interview to prompt students to describe their use of self-regulation in various academic situations. Among nine strategies reported, five correlated above .40 with standardized tests of academic achievement. Zimmerman and Bandura (1994) also found that college students who believed strongly in their own ability to self-regulate aimed toward better grades and did receive better grades. Another questionnaire on self-regulation correlated .22 to .36 with college grades on exams, quizzes, essays, reports, and seatwork (Pintrich & DeGroot, 1990). The strongest predictor of grade average, using a combination of cognitive and conative factors, was self-regulation; self-efficacy was the only other significant predictor. It is worth adding the observation that high achievers do not uniformly report heavy use of self-regulation (Risemberg & B. Zimmerman, 1992). (Self-regulation does not correlate with SAT scores; Ablard & Lipschultz, 1998; Pintrich & Garcia, 1991; B. Zimmerman & Bandura, 1994.)

One would expect self-regulation scores to correlate with some cognitive or learning styles. One theory holds that students build up a "schoolwork module," a program for schooling, which provides a work style for academic contexts (Bereiter, 1990). The possible connection merits more thorough study.

Conative Styles

Messick (1994) and some others saw styles as representing processes more directly than abilities or personality constructs do; styles express preferred or habitual use of abilities:

> Because ... styles refer to consistencies in the *way* psychological substance is processed rather than to consistencies in the substance itself, they may entail mechanisms for the organization and control of processes that cut across substantive areas. (Messick, 1994, p. 121, emphasis in original)

Some styles can reasonably be called conative. Messick (1987) described cognitive controls as styles of regulating attention and avoiding distraction. Habitual ways of explaining success and failure ("attributional styles") are conative (Dweck & Leggett, 1988), as are learned industriousness and helplessness (Eisenberger, 1992; Seligman, 1975). Defensive styles organize and channel negative affect.

Preferring teaching loaded with visual presentations is not necessarily better than alternative preferences. And which style works best will depend on the outcomes measured as well as the nature of the task (Sternberg & Grigorenko, 1997). A measure of recalled lecture material should be a nice match for students who prefer to learn by hearing, but not for those who prefer a visual input. Many preferences are malleable, modifiable with the situation.

A Deep Approach to Learning.   Entwistle (1987) contrasted a deep approach to the processing of information in learning situations, with surface processing. This distinction summarizes a large number of other style and strategy differences.

In deep processing, students regard the text to be learned or problem to be solved as the means to gain understanding of underlying or "big" ideas. Those adopting a surface approach regard the material to be learned as it stands, not linking it to larger themes. Students who learn for the sake of learning, with no great concern about their performance and how others will evaluate them, are likely to take a deep approach. A neutral or positive mood will typically produce deeper learning than a defensive mood. There is some analogy between Entwistle's idea and the preferences of low and high reactives for heuristic and algorithmic learning tasks reported by Strelau. Low reactives are more likely to adopt a deep approach.

With a deep learning style, construction is more active. The student may engage in construction even when a task does not demand it. The surface approach seeks primarily to satisfy demands others place on students; the style goes hand in hand with reactivity, anxiety, or depressed mood, and extrinsic motivation. Learning in that mode often consists of passive acquisition from learning materials, with emphasis on systematic checking, memorization, and short-term recall.

As is true for most of the affective and conative propensities we have discussed, the deep/surface dichotomy has elements that are both statelike and traitlike. An extensive series of studies in English universities started with the idea that each student had a consistent inclination to use or not use the deep approach. Naturalistic data on how students did their course work indicated substantial variation from situation to situation. Some courses elicited one style more than others, but the student's interest in the task, expectation as to what was wanted, and relationship to his or her tutor made a difference (Marton, Hounsell, & Entwistle, 1984; see especially the summary at pp. 213–221).

Entwistle and Ramsden (1983) added a third distinct approach—"strategic." In this learning style, thinking and behavior aim mainly at impressing instructors and obtaining the highest possible grade, by whatever means necessary. The approach apparently reflects efficient resource management (an aspect of action control) coupled with ego orientation; it may appear when learners adopt task-mastery and performance goals at the same time (Blumenfeld, 1992; Corno, 1992).

A questionnaire measure of approach would be likely to ask about intention to understand, active interest, relating ideas, and use of evidence. Intention and interest seem to be predecisional, although interest sometimes shifts as work proceeds. Relating ideas and using evidence seem to be postdecisional, but refer to cognitive processes rather than conative controls. The same questions permit describing the surface approach in terms of passive learning, unrelated memorizing, and fear of failure. Fear of failure could again be predecisional, or could be evoked by the task. The strategic approach includes the display of an intention to excel, alertness to assessment demands, organization of study, and time management. The questionnaire should also include some scales for lack of direction, subject-matter interest, and academic self-confidence.

Entwistle (1988) summarized many findings associating intentions, performance, and outcomes with deep, surface, and strategic styles, relating his own inventory to one developed by Schmeck, Ribich, and Ramanaiah (1977). A factor analysis of all the subscales yielded four distinct dimensions:

Deep approach, elaborative processing, and intrinsic motivation.

Surface approach, fear of failure, and orientation to task details.

Disorganized study methods and social motivation.

Achieving orientation and strategic approach (found in only some samples).

A deep approach might reflect independent, intentional learning, and perhaps also a task-mastery orientation that contrasts, for example, with a social orientation. A more complete correlational network of this sort remains to be developed.

Alternative Ways of Capturing Conative Styles.   As with personality, self-reports predominate in research on styles and other assessments are underused. Grigorenko and Sternberg (1993) developed three ways to measure "thinking styles" in adolescents and adults: a conventional self-report, questions on preferences among tasks, and teacher reports on a student (e.g., "prefers to solve problems in her or his own way"). In addition, they recorded each teacher's preference among student styles.

Teachers gave more positive evaluations and higher grades to those students who displayed the teachers' preferred thinking style (Sternberg & Grigorenko, 1995). Moreover, students tended to alter their styles to match whatever their teacher preferred. Relations between styles and achievement changed from school to school. For example, correlations of achievement with a "conservative" thinking style (agreement with items calling for "return to the good old days") ranged from –.39 to .49 across schools. "What is valued in one environment may actually be devalued in another" (Sternberg & Grigorenko, 1997, p. 709; see also Grigorenko & Sternberg, 1997).

Ainley (1993) investigated how student work styles related to their beliefs and goals. Clusters of high school students labeled "detached and disengaged," "committed, hopeful, and engaged," and "keen-to-do-well" were identified. Detached students, for example, scored high on ability, but well below average on "academic achieving"—a style reminiscent of Entwistle's "strategic" approach. They tended to use a surface approach. All this suggested a low level of engagement in school.

The students in different clusters prepared for tests differently. Committed and engaged students reported using an active, deep-study approach, whereas the keen-to-do-well and hopeful used passive, surface approaches. At each level of ability, committed students achieved best. Ainley's cluster analysis discloses the multidimensional character of engagement (see also Pintrich, 1989).

Styles, viewed as expressions of personality and preferred or habitual use of abilities, are constructs taking on new shadings. The deep approach to learning reflects a style of cognition that handles complexity, even seeks it. But it also reflects a more general work ethic: action orientation, mindful effort, and action control.

A PROGRAM FOR THE LONG TERM

An individual's mental store contains not only knowledge and skill but also wishes, wants, and intentions. These influence appraisal of challenging situations. Challenging situations arouse interest, and press for control. People adopting a deep orientation will tend to use regulation and control differently from others. They manage their time better, handle disruptions that come their way, and are more likely to monitor and control effort and emotion. They are also likely to approach a task more actively. Part of working smarter, apparently, is rising to the occasion and accepting challenges. The perceived level of press for regulation or control in a task signals how much effort to invest.

Anxiety, mood, and reactivity exemplify the role of affect in cognitive activity. In the face of complexity, and distraction, affcon resources serve cognition. The affective energy students bring to carrying out intentions deepens the level as well as the organization of cognitive processing.

Similarly, beliefs about personal capabilities and current concerns, goal coordination, and control of attention and emotion—all conative— influence academic work. When affect interferes, then conative processes can serve disciplining, directive, and control functions. Recall that depressed moods lead to more caution, and that reactives perform auxiliary actions to regain a sense of control under stress. The implicit self-instruction in such events is "buckle down." Similarly, high anxiety can increase distractibility and interfere with recall, but self-regulatory processes or routinized work styles can keep the work going.

For the person engrossed in the work, spending mental energy to "run the self-regulatory program" is a waste. Such a person's cognitive system is free to process deeply and playfully, without careful monitoring and control. Thus low reactives seek stimulating tasks. And happy, able learners inject challenge and play into tasks.

Unfortunately, the present state of the research on affect and conation in education provides little direct evidence on hypotheses relating them to cognition. Too few studies examine processes along both pathways of Fig. 6.1 together. Affcon research has moved toward multivariate correlational studies in which details of treatments are all but ignored, and writers pay little attention to parsimony.

Research on cognition "gets inside" a performance by tracing eye movements, by microtiming, and by asking students to teach what they learn. In a nutshell, the research described in chapter 5 is rooted in experimental psychology; not much of the literature available for this chapter has such roots.

Affcon states can be manipulated experimentally, the studies by Isen et al. (1987) being examples. And even without experimental control more intensive study of affcon processes in context is productive, as in the beeper studies of Csikszentmihalyi (1997). In cumulative academic work such as portfolio construction, periodic nondirective interviews could trace the moves of individual students.

Despite these limitations, the studies sampled here do show how thoroughly intertwined are affect, conation, and cognition. Belief that cognition and learning can be understood apart from conation and volition will fall only with broader, empirically supported theories. We have now passed the end of the beginning of such efforts. To quote Snow et al. (1996):

> We ... need an integrated model of affective and conative with cognitive functioning and development. ... However, [we also need] another kind of integration ... one that views individual human functioning in educational settings as a whole, open, adaptive system, and assesses it as such. ... Fragmentation of human personality into particular variables and pursuit of multivariate empirical relationships is a fruitful research strategy up to a point. But individuals are more than lists of variables. Somehow we need to find ways to put the fragments and relationships back into a pattern that describes integrated activity. ... The trick may be to find multiple models that criss-cross in ways that help fill in the information that any one model leaves out. (p. 295)

7 The Education of Aptitude

MAKING READINESS AN AIM OF INSTRUCTION

Snow believed that aptitude was the most important raw material of education, and its most important product.[21] Aptitude theory must account for both relations. Chapters 4 to 6 were concerned with the ways that propensities influence, at any moment, adaptation to tasks and instruction. This chapter examines how educational experiences can enrich the repertoire of propensities for future use.

Educational experiences, planned and unplanned, create the circumstances for unceasing but gradual changes in propensities. A person has insights during educational activities—finds a good example of a principle, or connects two previously unrelated ideas. Such insights lead to change in propensities. Planned educational experiences provide more such opportunities than arise by chance. On the largest scale, by teaching the facts, concepts, procedures, and cultural underpinnings of a society, educational institutions foster readiness for further stages of individual and collective life. Successful completion of any stage of formal education is literally a "commencement."

Education should develop attainments that will be used in the future. Learning to learn, to represent information, to find problems and solve them, to be committed, to cope in the face of difficulty, are examples. Certain propensities lead to full participation in a community of learners; readiness depends on skills of discourse and negotiation, and attitudes of open-mindedness and of accepting responsibility for a

---

[21]For writings that foreshadow this chapter, see Snow (1994, 1995, 1996a, 1997).

group product. Teachers and educational planners confront an array of choices in working toward these goals: How to teach which students? With what materials and procedures? How to tell whether teaching has succeeded?

The conventional style of classroom teaching—where one teacher manages 25–30 students—affords many opportunities for verbal, abstract, and logical thinking and listening. Students learn to comprehend the spoken word, and to read and write words and mathematical symbols.

A conventional teaching style requires the learner to listen for extended time periods and to understand symbolic expressions. Students ill-suited or unprepared for that style will struggle more than others, though they may eventually develop a readiness to learn from conventional teaching. As soon as goals move away from comprehension of verbal and mathematical abstractions toward, for example, representational drawing or group leadership, a conventional teaching style falters. Sociocultural diversity in a classroom and a broad range of learning abilities also prompt a search for alternatives to conventional teaching.

A teacher rarely commits all his or her instruction to one style. Targeting a range of outcomes demands flexibility. Best practice will keep pace with social and technological change. Teachers today can select from a smorgasbord of options in curriculum, teaching, and assessment. Instead of simply teaching lessons from a textbook, teachers learn to vary the approach to a given topic, to use new technologies, and to create their own materials. In a curriculum, topics should be chosen that resonate with student interests. Content organizations, explanations, and examples should be sufficiently varied to reach all learners. Research now supports many options for differentiating instruction: ways of grouping students, types of modeling, and forms of computer-based learning, for example. Various materials and electronic media also accommodate student diversity.

Many commonplace teaching activities can have considerable cognitive value. When students rearrange subject matter, or group objects and observations sensibly, they improve perception and memory. When teachers call attention to key features in complex visuals and to important points in verbal presentations, they demonstrate the usefulness of pulling images and ideas out of their original surround. Reminding students of end-goals in a project maintains their forward momentum (Schank & Joseph, 1998). When students systematically present and evaluate evidence, the teacher can refine skills of collaboration and argument (Chinn & R. D. Anderson, 1998).

Developmental histories influence who will profit from each form of instruction. Teaching without an understanding of students' past experiences and attitudes (and also of community attitudes) can be a little like excavating with neither ecological information nor a topographic map. Thus teachers wishing to prepare students for future learning in diverse environments assess them in ways suited to their level.

An ability profile derived from test scores is a snapshot of only a fraction of the significant propensities. At a finer grain, individual performance monitored daily adds information about aspects of student work. Students' remarks can signal misconceptions that should be corrected. Such informal cues are often lost unless teachers document them accurately. Assessment of readiness will note students' expressed attitudes and aspirations. It will look for potential talents. An assessment procedure that suggests for one student instruction to build confidence and alleviate anxiety could lead to a different suggestion for another. Individuals are given experience in areas where they show promise as well as those where they show problems. Increasingly, educational environments grow out of accurate, periodic descriptions of particular students or small groups of students in situ.

ABILITIES AS PRODUCTS OF EDUCATION

What is the evidence that education actually develops adaptive cognitive abilities? What sorts of educational experiences support such gains?

Gains in General Ability From Schooling

J. Hunt (1961) successfully promoted the idea that general abilities are not fixed; measured ability levels can increase, and rankings can change. More recently, Ceci (1990, 1991) documented the effects of regular educational programs on ability development. Compiling the evidence comparing children with differing educational histories, he developed several points:

G measures in adulthood correlate strongly and positively with years of school completed.

G scores typically decline during summer vacation, especially among low-SES children whose summer activities are unlikely to have instructional components.

Intermittent schooling lowers ranks in G. The shortfalls cumulate; children initially performing at average levels fall further behind as they miss more of school.

Delay in beginning school beyond age 5 tends to reduce G standings substantially.

G scores of those who have left school early lag behind the scores of others, lagging further with each year the others stay in school.

Assessments designed explicitly to reflect school achievement show increases and lags similar to those described previously for mental-test scores.

These correlational findings must be interpreted with caution. For example, years-of-schooling-completed correlates with G in part because more able students typically stay in school longer than others. Still, the evidence Ceci reviewed shows unequivocally that education improves Gf as well as Gc.

Huttenlocher, Levine, and Vevea (1998) related amount of schooling to cognitive abilities for a large sample of kindergarteners and first graders. Language and spatial scores improved as expected. A less familiar finding emerged when the authors compared changes from April to October (*a*) with October-to-April changes (*b*). (The divisions were made at midmonth.) In each grade and at all pretest levels, average gains in concepts and skills were much greater during the *a* period when children were generally in school than in the *b* period (end-of-year wind down, and vacation). Clearly, schooling exercises abilities and summer vacation breaks the momentum.

Exhibit MSMGL. Earlier Intervention Produces Greater Intellectual Growth

Among many evaluations of large-scale interventions to help children of poverty, a study carried out in Colombia is especially instructive (H. McKay, Sinisterra, A. McKay, Gomez, & Lloreda, 1978). The treatment combined education with health care and better nutrition. An average treatment day consisted of 6 hours of health, nutritional, and educational activities. The educational activities included curriculum elements drawn from some of the more successful U.S. compensatory-education programs, beginning with instruction in language, social, and psychomotor skills, and eventually reaching reading, writing, arithmetic, and decision making.

Poor, undernourished children were assigned at random to groups receiving longer or shorter treatment. All these children were tested on five occasions—the first around age 3½, the last near age 7—on verbal, figural, numerical, memory, and reasoning tests whose composite provided a broad index of ability. Each treatment period occupied about 10 months out of a year, with Group T4 receiving four periods, starting at age 3½ and ending at age 7. Figure 7.1 shows the timing of treatments for other groups.

The start of treatment did not always coincide with a testing date.

In the figure, the lowest broken line can be thought of as a baseline reflecting growth without special intervention. Compared with the baseline, the T4 children grew impressively during the first year of treatment, and maintained their advantage. Groups T3 and T2 also profited.

Individual mental tests at age 8 showed a similar progression of means across groups, but the range of abilities was noticeably wider in the groups receiving longer treatment. Among untreated children similar to the intervention groups, roughly 20% had IQs below 75 at age 8, and this dropped only to around 15% in Groups T2–T4.

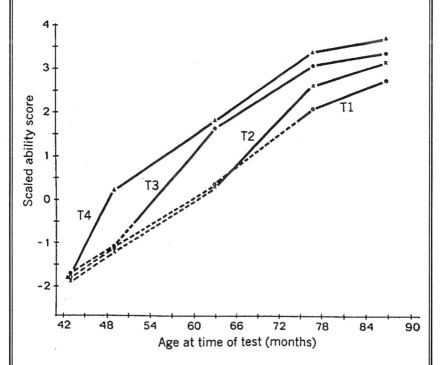

FIG. 7.1. Ability changes among children receiving intervention of long and short duration. From H. McKay, Sinisterra, A. McKay, Gomez, & Lloreda (1978). Copyright 1978 by the American Association for the Advancement of Science. Reprinted, with modifications, with permission. Groups T1, T2, T3, and T4 received treatment for 1, 2, 3, and 4 periods respectively, each starting at about the age where the corresponding solid line begins. The scale to which test scores were converted is not a standard-score scale, but the zero point corresponds to the performance of a nondisadvantaged group of Colombian children at 48 months.

In the United States and other industrialized countries, the number and variety of educational materials and media in homes has expanded throughout this past century. Books, computers, television, and facsimile machines have increased opportunities for intellectual discussion in the family and in peer groups. The Internet provides for access by children everywhere to rich information (though access is unequal). The influence operates more on Gc than on Gf or Gv, probably because most educational activities emphasize words.

Decade-to-decade gains in Gf have been larger than in Gc, according to Flynn (1984, 1987). This effect surely reflects the spreading influence of schooling and improved nutrition and health care. It suggests that improvements in Gf may be one of the more important outcomes of an educational system that challenges students to reason rather than to memorize. Perhaps parallel extensions of intellectual affordances in homes and in schools have been accelerating ability development.

Climates for intellectual development may also be benefiting from declining birth rates (Zajonc & Mullally, 1997). Zajonc's confluence theory (1976) holds that the first children born to a family reap the advantages of parents' undivided attention, and then solidify their knowledge by teaching younger siblings. An age-place cohort having more of these "early borns" is expected to have higher average ability, hence abler peer groups and school classes; the consequence is a favorable intellectual climate for all members of the cohort, not just for early-borns.

Effects of Planned Instructional Supplements

Exhibit MSMGL demonstrates how much planned intervention can accelerate development of ability. This large study checked on one of many attempts to extend education via preschool, summer school, or after-school programs.

Among Head Start programs, the Carolina Abecedarian Project had a particularly strong evaluation. For a controlled experiment the staff monitored, from birth through age 15, the cognitive and social development of high-risk children (F. A. Campbell & Ramey, 1994, 1995). Risk (taking into account 13 variables including parents' education, income, welfare status, and counseling history) determined which infants from poor families went into the sample. In half the sample, the child received full-day care at the project center from age 6 months to 5 years. The program included a range of developmentally appropriate activities, and had a low child-to-caregiver ratio. The other half of the sample were left untreated during this time.

At about age 4, IQs were used to match children from the preschool and control groups. One of each pair was then assigned for treatment during kindergarten and the three early grades. The treatment at this stage consisted of customized at-home lessons suggested by a resource teacher, who worked with each family as advocate and academic coach. The second member of any pair received regular schooling only. There were thus four groups: early supplement plus late, early supplement only, late supplement only, or neither. At ages 8, 12, and 15, groups were compared on IQ, academic achievement, and classroom behavior.

Effects were substantial and consistent. Early-treated children out-performed controls on all measures of intellectual development from age 18 months to the end of preschool (Ramey & F. A. Campbell, 1984). They displayed significantly higher IQ and academic achievement at age 8, and were much less likely to have been retained in grade. The preschool treatment, not the late supplement, accounted for most of the difference. Effects on adjustment paralleled those on achievement. Follow-up at ages 12 and 15 also showed group differences. When the children who had been treated the most and those with no supplementation were compared, the effect on IQ was quite large at age 36 months, and no more than moderate at age 15 years.

Direct Training in Processes

Direct instruction in cognitive skills and strategies outside regular subject-matter courses has produced mixed results. Many early experiments assessed effects of training or coaching; students were trained in using Venn diagrams on syllogisms, for example, or were taught means–end problem solving. The skills rarely transferred from trained tasks to novel ones, and initial improvements were likely to fade with time (see Baron & Sternberg, 1987; Chipman, Segal, & Glaser, 1985; Resnick, 1987). Moreover, the nature of the instruction often determined who improved.

Computers now offer sophisticated tutorial options. Investigators attempting to train general cognitive skills often neglect, however, to design their studies to accommodate learners with atypical propensities. The value of an ATI perspective was illustrated by a dissertation from the Snow project that used a computer game to train reasoning and general problem-solving skills (Mandinach, 1984, 1987). The game required goal setting, planning, and risk taking, in addition to deducing which moves were hazardous. Learners had to monitor their moves to avoid strategic mistakes. Instruction in effective moves, and coaching, augmented the game.

Able students improved in strategic planning just by being given examples of effective moves. Less able ones required instructional support; suggestions, hints, and feedback on moves helped them. A number of low-ability students, and a few able ones, never displayed meaningful improvement in strategic planning, regardless of the type of practice. The more games a student played, the more reasoning and planning of moves improved. But those whose reasoning improved most were good at the outset, or were markedly engaged by the game.

General problem-solving skills are difficult to train in a short time, when the problems are not meaningful in themselves. But, in the longer term, subtle changes in organization and problem-solving processes occur, changes that cannot be seen in short-term data.

Although tradition has directed effort toward skills and strategies of thinking, components of verbal and reading abilities might be trained more easily (Calfee, 1982; J. Frederiksen & Warren, 1987). Brown's work with small groups exemplifies a successful way of teaching skills and strategies of reading comprehension. The teacher invites students to collaborate in understanding a passage, and guides them in extracting meaning. Records of conversations in the group can suggest ways to improve responses. It is hoped that students will become adept at framing questions such as a teacher might ask. This skill is to be evaluated as much as the reading itself. More basic skills, such as letter-sound correspondences and phonological awareness, are exercised in children's reading and listening at home as well as in school (Calfee & Norman, 1998). Reading aloud with a child is one way to provide assistance with decoding; it serves in another way the reader who will miss some meanings unless comprehension is monitored.

Some types of spatial ability can be developed through training. For example, orthographic projection (OP) transforms three-dimensional objects or figures to two-dimensional drawings. If one sets out to make sense of front and side views (for example), an efficient strategy is to reconstruct mentally a representation of the object. For her Snow-project dissertation, Lajoie (1986) designed a computer program to tutor college students on OP. A treatment group who had low spatial ability mastered the OP rules and then applied them, working at their own pace for up to five sessions. The tutor also modeled strategies for translating objects into two dimensions, and provided online coaching to correct student errors. A comparable control group practiced OP exercises without tutoring, but had a chance to reflect on the answer key. Thus, treated students received more, and more detailed, instruction than the controls. (We ignore one additional control group that only took the pretests and posttests on OP.) The training worked. People in most of the range of the data showed some improvement.

Most of the large gains were made by the initially incompetent. People who started with a raw score of 10 finished at 21.5 on average, whereas those who started at 40 finished at 38. In the group that merely practiced OP, those who started at 10 finished at 16; those starting at 40 (a perfect score) finished at 36. The failure to improve of people who started near 40 does not tell the whole story, because the test was too easy to appraise them fully. Individual rankings were not much altered. In the treated group the pre–post r was an astonishing .99; in the control group, .91. The sample was small, so another study might well find values of .70–.80; but .50 is unlikely. Other investigators have demonstrated successful training of spatial skills and even transfer to untrained tasks. (See the summary by Ackerman & Lohman, 1990.)

Moving Toward Mastery of a Domain

Education builds new concepts and associations within domains, and deepens and extends existing concepts and associations. Also, it can cause a person to rehearse stored knowledge to the point where responses can be routinized. Having basic domain knowledge and skills ready for automatic recall and flexible use facilitates higher level analysis on difficult tasks.

Most subject-matter learning demands both Gf and Gc. Especially as teaching methods build on prior instruction, Gc and domain knowledge foster success. Any subject matter will be more familiar to some students than to others. Novel content seems to demand general knowledge and reasoning skills. But these demands change as students progress in a subject. As children rise in grade level and tasks become more abstract and difficult, they need specialized knowledge and self-regulation (Demetriou, Gustafsson, Efklides, & Platsidou, 1992). In mathematics, for example, early learning requires discrimination of shapes and visual layouts as well as knowledge of numbers and elementary reasoning. When the lessons reach word problems, students must actively coordinate linguistic, mathematical, and perceptual information—a different level of reasoning. In time, word problems call higher reasoning into play also.

Good instruction in later grades enables students to participate in the conversations among domain practitioners. It does this by introducing students to pertinent concepts, and by socializing students into the way practitioners speak and reason. (Cf. Exh. DeC.) Teaching of such processes—drafting and revising in writing, estimation in mathe-

Exhibit DeC. Building Expertise in Mathematics

Contemporary reforms in mathematics education are converging on the situational features that provoke students to think and solve problems as mathematicians do. A program developed in the Netherlands illustrates principles common to many such reforms (DeCorte, 1995):

> Students in groups that reinvent mathematics knowledge learn well.
>
> Familiar contexts, models, and tools facilitate the move from concrete materials to abstract representations.
>
> Children's own constructions are starting points for reflection.
>
> Students who interact and cooperate attain higher levels of problem solving.
>
> Instruction should explicitly link basic mathematical operations; this helps students understand the various ways of solving mathematics problems. (p. 42)

DeCorte related how a lesson in long division leads students to devise a procedure that approximates a standard division algorithm.

The teacher first poses a real-world problem: "The PTA meeting at our school will be attended by 81 parents. Six parents can be seated at one table. How many tables will we need?" The teacher asks students how to proceed; the simpler proposals rely on addition whereas others move to multiplication. By comparing these methods, many students begin to see the value of more sophisticated solutions, which eventually lead the group to invent a workable procedure that all students are then taught how to use.

Such realistic problems are chosen to push at the edges of students' developmental reach (cf. p. 36 ff). The teacher's request that students construct ideas freely provides a forum for reflection about which ideas work best and why. As discussion proceeds, the teacher can present visual models, manipulatives, or symbols that gradually move individuals from concrete to abstract conceptions. Hearing teachers and peers ask reflective questions, students begin to ask similar questions themselves. More efficient solutions then appear in later attempts to solve problems. "Interaction and cooperation mobilize reflection" (DeCorte, 1995, p. 43).

Notably, the program puts emphasis on explicit connections between the basic operations of mathematics. Although multiplication and subtraction both enter into long division, teaching of-

> ten fails to make students aware of such connections. In the new program, teachers prompt students to discuss connections of decimals with fractions, measurement with geometry, and so on.
>
> In one field experiment (Treffers, 1987), students in the program learned long division in about half the time controls required, and performed better.

matics, and the scientific method—has been attempted through "cognitive apprenticeships" (see, e.g., Bereiter & Scardamalia, 1987; White & J. Frederiksen, 1998).

Apprentices are drawn into the kinds of thinking and analysis that expert writers, mathematicians, or scientists use. A "cognitive coach" thinks aloud, modeling the skills and strategies of interest. The coach then guides students to try similar moves. Gradually the tutor reduces the amount of feedback she gives on thoughts they put out for inspection. Eventually students use their apprentice skills independently on new tasks (A. Collins, J. S. Brown, & Newman, 1989). Greater domain knowledge and skill can also lead to better methods of organization and higher levels of discussion, and to interest or even commitment to the field.

In each major domain, educators aspire gradually to develop full expertise: intellectual discipline and ways of imposing order, command of established knowledge and accepted standards of reasoning, testwiseness in the domain, and capability of knowledge-based invention. These several aspects of domain knowledge and skill should more often be made explicit goals of teaching. Expertise is attained only after many years of deliberate practice and good coaching (Ericsson & Smith, 1991). Motivation matters in this process, because students who develop commitments are the ones who persist to reach the point of expertise. The richer the educational environment, the greater motivation is likely to be.

One way to enhance the required curriculum is through intelligent tutoring systems and other microinstructional environments, made possible by present-day personal computers. These systems are sophisticated integrations of knowledge about individual differences, instruction, and assessment (see Lajoie & Lesgold, 1992). Goals for instruction can be based on cognitive analyses of tasks. This is common in technical training—for avionics troubleshooting, for example, or for mammogram interpretation. The task analysis produces a performance model, which specifies expected performance (and anticipates what learners are likely to do). A competence model specifies the learning state of the student for each instructional goal; this estimate is updated continually during tutoring. Seeing one's own performance record on screen encourages self-monitoring and self-assessment.

Monitoring identifies strengths and weaknesses in declarative knowledge and in procedures. The computer program records changes in knowledge, then compares the learner's moves with those programmed as "expert." Feedback, more or less continual, provides hints on moves that are just beyond those already under the student's control. In such a tutoring system, principles of instruction include recognizing multiple goals and alternative paths to success, allowing choice among activities and self-pacing, accommodation to individual differences, and real-world tasks. Such fine-tuned stimulation is next to impossible for a human tutor to provide for student after student.

Another approach to motivational enhancement takes affect and conative processes as curricular goals.

DEVELOPING MOTIVATIONAL READINESS

Readiness to learn entails more than cognitive ability. Unlike a species that becomes adapted for the long term in a particular environment, learners must adapt to many environments in the classroom and beyond. Ultimately, learners should become students in the sense of the Latin *studere*—able to strive zealously after learning in whatever context invites their participation. Striving brings us back to affcon processes.

We unite the affective and conative here because educating one affects the other. Many interests and preferences develop because the situation offers something that suits a particular temperament or characteristic mood. Habits of mind and workstyles have attitudes and aspirations as by-products. And styles and habits often come about through the pursuit of interests and short-term goals.

Development of Affcon Propensities

Snow intended to use the report of Haritos-Fatouros on the selection and training of torturers (Exh. HFG) to remind readers that there can be aptitude for evil actions as well as good ones. It can serve here, ironically, as very nearly the epitome of time-tested practices for shaping and strengthening motivations, and putting them to work. The formula can be boiled down to:

> Select people who already show a good start toward the desired propensities.

Exhibit HFG. *Detecting and Developing Aptitudes of the Torturer*

During the Greek junta (1967–1974), military policemen were selected and trained for service in special torture units. Court testimony, interviews, and case studies indicate what aptitudes were sought and how the training was tailored to those aptitudes (J. T. Gibson & Haritos-Fatouros, 1985; Haritos-Fatouros, 1983a, 1983b).

Selection sought "proper" political beliefs (strong support for the military regime and opposition to communism), identification with parental authority and supportive behavior toward authority figures, and a strong need to be approved by and to be the "right hand" of authority—combined with low self-esteem. Other characteristics of those selected were heavy body build, endurance in heavy exercises, and low socioeconomic level. These characteristics were thought likely to foster negative attitudes toward potential victims.

These attitudes were promoted by daily lectures during basic training and later in military prison camp. A second 3-month training camp required obedience to illogical and degrading commands, and exercise was carried to the point of exhaustion. Unpromising trainees were deselected. In a third camp, for the special units where torture was actually carried out, a final selection was made. An initiation ceremony—a beating—was administered to successful recruits.

Then, on their knees, they swore allegiance to the junta. The idea conveyed was that they belonged to the father-authority of the commander, who was to be obeyed without question.

Training had crushed any will to resist. It sought to bind individuals to the military police corps and, later, to the subgroup of torturers. The corps was portrayed as the strongest, most important, most elite service in the regime. The torturers were encouraged to develop a jargon all their own; they used nicknames for one another, for the prisoners, and for the different methods of torture. Daily routines of flogging and exhaustive exercise adapted trainees to the idea of torture. A systematic desensitization routine prepared them for contacts with prisoners. Authorities asked the trainees to "give blows" to prisoners, posted them as guards where they watched torture, then had them participate in group floggings, next as individual beaters, and then graduated them as torturers. Part of a prestigious military unit, they were heavily rewarded materially and socially, even after they retired from service.

Provide opportunities to exercise these on progressively more challenging roles.

Provide ample reward to those who perform well, and opportunity for self-satisfaction.

The practices of the Greek trainers were not driven by theory nor does the exhibit offer a theoretical explanation. But the reader will be able to see illustration in the practices of a great many of the general motifs in this chapter. Thus, in connection with Exhibit DeC, we spoke of "introducing students into the way practitioners speak and reason." And, a few pages hence, educators are advised to "establish the classroom as a learning community." We leave the reader to carry this ironic game further, not at all intending to suggest that principles that worked for barbarians are thereby falsified.

Learning From Lessons and Living.   Affcon processes, like abilities, can be cultivated directly and indirectly. Because most explicit educational objectives point toward the cognitive domain, affcon objectives tend to remain implicit—especially those (e.g., overcoming stage fright) not tied to a school subject. Nevertheless, U.S. education has seen waves of interest in affective education (see, e.g., Rubin, 1973) and, even earlier, in character education (Hartshorne & May, 1928).

Character education is now recast as social and emotional learning. Some schools no longer rank students in classes, and post honors for effort and help giving instead. Some class groups address self-esteem directly, asking students to draw upon their deepest resources to set personal and relationship goals. Others give lessons on teamwork and mutual respect, on differences and on conflict resolution, and on ways of avoiding risky behavior (one's own and that of others). Embedded within such lessons, often, are traditional goals of character education: dependability, honesty, ethical decision making, and the like. Goleman (1995, Appendix F) emphasized the preventive intentions of the new programs, and their potential for changing how students relate to each other. Improvement in participants' emotional awareness and skill, he said, could be expected to follow.

Some parents and educators see these school character-building programs as providing an important counterpoint to the pervasive ways that today's society exposes children to violence. They note that many popular video games, for example, reward players for point-and-shoot tactics and strategic moves that foil imagined enemies. The U.S. Marine Corps has actually used one such game ("DOOM") as a simulation tool for training tactical thinking and quick reactions to the unexpected—"the "mental side" of warfare"

(Grossman, 1996). Although millions of children play violent video games without untoward consequences, the dark side of these games should concern society ("Gaming of Violence," 1999). For more on motivation toward violence, see Exhibit HFG.

In real life, reactions of parents, peers, and teachers encourage some affcon propensities and discourage others. The same can be said for the simulated reactions of characters in interactive video games. The reactions may contribute to readiness, or reduce it. "Don't get out of line," for example, is advice that inhibits experimentation. Similarly, engagement in simulated violence cultivates a casual attitude toward it. Various attitudes, interests, self-evaluations, and attempts at self-control surface during the play and everyday conflicts of very young children, just as they do later in formal tasks.

Behavioral interaction, whether with adults, peers, or characters in a virtual environment, calls attention to affcon processes; feedback during modeling shapes and extends them. The adult's aim in deliberate shaping is to bring the response toward an optimum. For example, in a student facing challenging tasks, one wants not too much investment nor too little willingness to engage. As we saw in Exhibit Csk (p. 47), balance between challenges and skills produces "flow," which leads to cumulative investment and learning. Even without deliberate shaping, some aspects of affcon response such as self-regulation of emotion and motivation become more sophisticated and perhaps more automatic, over the course of experience.

The Role of the Educational Community. Earlier in this chapter, we reviewed the unambiguous reports showing that more schooling makes for stronger cognitive functioning. No one has examined how more schooling affects affcon attributes, however. Many influences other than school, of course, make people individual. And the nature of schooling may matter here more than the amount.

Some schools have a pervasive sense of community. Whether having this sense makes schools more effective was a principal question in a comparison across 24 elementary schools (Battistich, Solomon, Kim, Watson, & Schaps, 1995). Their student bodies responded to a questionnaire appraising sense of community; analyses related scores on this measure to concurrent self-reports on several affcon (and cognitive) variables. In most social research, correlations calculated from group means are typically much larger (i.e., further from zero) than correlations of scores for individuals. Even recognizing this, some of the group-level r's in this study were remarkably high. For example, the r of "sense of community" with "intrinsic academic motivation" was

.84; with "liking for school," .66; and with self-reported "conflict resolution skill," .94. Within schools, pupils' scores showed moderate positive correlations of their personal sense of community with desirable
affcon scores.

An exceptional feature was an analysis of interactions at the be-
tween-school level. The statistics are too intricate to recapitulate here,
but we give one specimen finding. "Enjoyment of helping others learn"
was reported to be distinctly lower in schools with high poverty and a
weak sense of community than in other subsets of schools. Several
findings led the authors to conclude that "a caring, supportive, and responsive community would be particularly important in schools with
poor student populations" (Battistich et al., 1995, p. 649).

Compatibility between a student's environment, in home and neigh-
borhood, and the style of the school impacts motivation in school. Cole
(1985) described how teachers can use students' absorbing individual
interests and out-of-school expertise (e.g., fishing, the Civil War) to promote motivation for schoolwork in biology or social studies. On a larger
scale, teachers can build a sense of community by altering incompatibil-
ities between students' home cultures and their own styles of teaching.
Observations in the homes of native Hawaiians identified a widely used
form of oral storytelling (Au, 1980). In reading instruction, the school's
usual emphasis on systematic decoding was alien, making no use of the
rhythms of talk-story. By replacing the traditional reading program with
one that provided for more congenial classroom cross talk, Au was able
to raise reading achievement of the Hawaiians substantially above national norms within a year. A change in instruction such as this can also
enhance students' perceptions of the worth of their cultural traditions.

Teaching Self-Regulation.   Educators can influence affcon development by encouraging conscious self-regulation as an integral part of
lessons in subject areas, without special affcon programs. Schooling
often demands self-regulation. This is the case when tasks require sus-
tained attention and the assimilation of information, or when students
are pulled by competing goals. Teachers can help students find ways to
juggle their priorities, and lead them to revise goals on occasion. They
can help students observe their own emotional states and responses.
They can lead students to use a range of mechanisms for assimilating
information and mastering skills. They can heighten students' awareness of the need to persist on difficult tasks, and of the need to recognize when perseverance is unlikely to pay off.

Teachers now sometimes collaborate with researchers to design instruction that seeds such elements of self-regulation into subject-mat-

ter instruction. They identify self-regulation strategies (including planning, monitoring, and evaluating progress toward goals) as objectives in mathematics, reading comprehension, or science. Various procedures for teaching these objectives have been successful (e.g., Schunk & B. Zimmerman, 1994, 1998). However, some students who have had explicit instruction in strategies fail to use them in similar situations later on, unless prompted (Pressley, Goodchild, Fleet, Zajchowski, & Evans, 1989).

We describe as an illustration one approach (Randi & Corno, 2000) that uses the quest genre in secondary-school literature or humanities courses. The Golden Fleece, the journeys of Odysseus, and other stories introduce students to literary characters who are self-regulatory (resourceful, mindful, resilient). The plots display how such characters meet challenges—accepting a call or summons, resourcefully passing tests of strength and wit, returning to the community wiser for the experience. The teacher ties the quest stories to principles of self-regulated learning, and this of course enriches students' understanding of the literature as well.

In small multitask groups, each student embarks on an assignment, a quest. For example, the task might be to find evidence of self-regulation in a certain narrative. As the research advances, the student becomes a "topic expert." Topic experts have to integrate their knowledge (A. Brown, 1994). To do this, students write about the research they have done, incorporating instances of self- and task-management in the narratives. They then present their narratives to the whole class. Because the narratives spring from students' own preoccupations (sports, selecting a college, etc.) and also from the teacher's challenges, personal knowledge is linked with a growing explicit knowledge of self-regulation. According to the theory, self-regulation strategies, once solidified and articulated, are ready for future use.

The quest genre provides a suitable curricular match for learning about self-regulation as psychologists define it. Educators should search for such correspondences. Thus Solomon, Watson, Battistich, Schapp, and Delucchi (1992) suggested various children's stories for use as springboards for class discussions of empathy, caring for friends, and the like. In principle, this style might highlight in turn each affcon process in the full range, at a suitable point.

Socializing Motivational Orientations

Brophy (1998) reviewed the vast literature on techniques teachers use to motivate students, seeking approaches that work under ordinary classroom conditions. Brophy listed these principles, among others:

Think in terms of shaping students' motivational development.

Teach things that are worth learning, in ways that help students to appreciate their value.

Establish the classroom as a learning community whose members collaborate.

Emphasize informative feedback rather than grades or comparisons among students.

Provide extra support to struggling low achievers.

Praise and reward students for meeting performance improvement standards.

Embellish traditional learning activities with simulation or fantasy elements.

Model motivation to learn, communicating desirable expectations and attributions. (pp. 258–259)

These guidelines mostly reflect experiments in classrooms. We discuss a few examples and cautionary notes, moving from change in classroom management and structure to more subtle changes directed at groups of students within a class.

Collaborative Learning.   A classroom that functions as a learning community can promote many affcon goals (A. Brown, 1994). Even students who come to class with little motivation to achieve may become task oriented once they identify with the group. How teachers manage student work can boost motivation; one key is to reward students for getting the most out of tasks and for working cooperatively. When teachers compare student abilities publicly, and emphasize grades, students are more likely to adopt surface goals, that is, to seek good grades or to "beat" others. They become less concerned with mastering tasks. Evidence for this pattern of results comes from experiments by goal theorists (e.g., Dweck, 1986), as well as research on classroom cooperative learning (see Slavin, 1995). Ames (1990) also worked with teachers to develop a learning community.

Ames adopted for her program Epstein's (1989) acronym of *TARGET*, which Brophy (1998) later decoded concisely in this way:

*T*asks are meaningful.

*A*uthority is shared among teachers and students.

*R*eward structure emphasizes improvement and progress rather than comparing students.

*G*roups work together toward goals, and students teach one another within groups.

*E*valuation occurs in multiple ways, including self-evaluation.

Time schedules of individuals and small groups for completing activities are flexible. (pp. 258–259)

Preliminary evaluations of *TARGET* indicate that with it teachers can not only change the climates of their classrooms, but also promote motivation to master tasks, especially in high-risk students (Maehr & Midgley, 1991).

Exhibit Frn. Affordances Can Be Tailored to Match Motivations

French (1958) illustrated neatly that aptitude is elicited by features of the situation. Two propensities of military trainees were assessed: achievement motivation (see Exh. Atk, p. 44) and affiliation motivation (related to sociability but not identical). Two pools of students were selected:

Achievers: high on achievement motivation and low on affiliation motivation

Affiliatives: high on affiliation motivation and low on achievement motivation.

Each pool was divided randomly into four-person groups. A check ensured that ability was distributed similarly in all conditions.

A brief narrative was cut into 20 pieces and sorted into four packs. Each member of a four-person team received one pack. Each team was to fit the cards together by exchanging information orally; letting another member see one's cards was forbidden. Ordering the cards, a group could create a coherent story. Half the teams (condition G) were told to produce a final single story that satisfied the team as a whole. Teams in condition I (individual) were told that the group could prepare a team solution but that any member could turn in an independent version instead. Many individuals in this condition did draft independent stories for a time, but no one turned in an independent final story.

Twice during the work, the experimenter intervened and applied to each team either treatment E or C:

Condition E: Experimenter praised the team for the group's efficiency.

Condition C: Experimenter praised the team for members' cooperation.

Illustrative acts of the pertinent type were mentioned. Then the team resumed work.

For the final stories, the scores on a 0–45 scale ranged as shown here:

Score Ranges in Two Motive Groups Under Four Treatment Conditions

		Achievers	Affiliatives
GE	(agreement required, efficiency praised)	36–45	24–36
IE	(agreement not requested, efficiency praised)	33–45	20–32
GC	(agreement required, teamwork praised)	25–37	30–45
IC	(agreement not requested, teamwork praised)	27–36	19–45

Note. Data are from French (1958, p. 404).

The means and *SD*s convey the same impressions as the ranges. The effects are remarkably strong; a doubly motivating treatment made for a large difference among affiliatives.

Affiliatives got their best results under GC conditions, where they notably outscored achievers. Achievers were at their best in GE and IE; they valued efficiency. It was expected that G would elicit better responses than I from affiliatives (confirmed), and poorer responses from achievers (not confirmed). Achievers praised for affiliative behavior (conditions C), and affiliatives praised for achieving (conditions E), were comparatively unproductive. The match between the situational cues and the propensities brought to the situation is what maximized scores.

For related discussion at another place, see p. 101.

Informative Feedback. A dissertation supervised by Snow illustrates how feedback on student work functions. Cardelle-Elawar (1982; reported in Elawar & Corno, 1985) trained 18 sixth-grade teachers to tailor feedback on homework to individuals. Teachers addressed four questions in grading homework:

What is the key error?

What is the probable reason for the error?

How can I guide the student to avoid the error in the future?

What did the student do well that could be praised?

During 10 weeks, half of the students received feedback of this kind on homework; the students in the other half were told only the number of problems answered correctly. Several motivational outcomes were assessed before and after the experimental period, along with math achievement. The students receiving personal and informative comments on homework outperformed others by a wide margin, on all measures of achievement. Their enjoyment of mathematics and the value of mathematics in their eyes (judged by questionnaires) went up markedly from the beginning of the study to the end. The effects on attitude were even stronger than those on achievement. Perhaps most important, mathematics anxiety was reduced, and self-concepts and attitude toward school improved. A small study by Cardelle and Corno (1981) found similar results in college students who were learning a second language. There also, personalized, informative feedback was an effective means to promote academic motivation.

As Exhibit Frn illustrates, students may respond best of all when the type of feedback matches their motivational orientation and the nature of the task. The *R* in *TARGET* suggests the motivational value of a reward system that emphasizes individual progress rather than comparison. Such a system might eventually reshape students who come to class with a grade-getting, rather than a mastery orientation. Brophy's suggestion that teachers reward improvement was also intended to encourage mastery motivation. Exhibit Frn suggests another way to use praise for supporting immediate achievement when time is limited. The task and the reinforcement can be adapted to fit the motivations of a given group of students. Both types of adaptive support will be useful when ability and motivation are both low.

Support for Struggling Students.   Students who seem reluctant to learn perhaps do not know how to cope with difficulty, or perhaps lack basic skills. Schunk and Rice (1985) taught fourth- and fifth-grade remedial readers how to search for key words (and other subskills). In half the sample, teachers modeled procedures and asked the students to describe them in words and then use them. The other half observed the teacher's procedures but were not asked to describe them. On later days, the ones pressed to verbalize the strategies showed that they were getting more from their reading.

In learning-disabled fourth graders, Vauras, Lehtinen, Kinnunen, and Salonen (1992) were interested in boosting mastery motivation, task-oriented coping behavior, and metacognitive skills. One group was trained in social and emotional coping (e.g., in self-monitoring and in crediting themselves for successes, rather than crediting luck). A similar group was trained in skills, comprehension of text, and reflection on their own techniques of study. Training in a third group considered both coping and skills. Each type of training spread over 16 weekly 2-hour sessions. Effects favored the third ("combined") group, as measured even 8 months after the intervention.

Students who had some motivation for task mastery at the outset improved in coping skills more than others. For students who initially were more social and compliant, with no motivation toward mastery at the start, progress was short-lived. Only extended classroom intervention produced lasting improvement for them. The authors concluded that struggling students need task-mastery motivation to perform effectively over the long haul. "Extra support" has to counter directly strong and often stable tendencies toward defensiveness or social compliance.

Over the history of psychology, interest in using education to promote aptitude has waxed and waned. Snow (1996a) clearly viewed education as a long-term aptitude-development program. We speak of children in their early years as being "cared for," then "schooled," "brought up," and "educated." All these terms imply a person–environment interplay that changes both.

Improving readiness to learn continues to challenge educators. The evidence available for this chapter suggests the value of getting the reasoning processes counted in Gf to work as a team with conceptual knowledge. Conceptual knowledge in use is an enhanced Gc; self-regulation and coping are critical. The trick, for educators, is to plan school activities that exercise components such as deep subject-matter reasoning, meaningful organization, and visual-spatial representation. Reluctant participants should be pressed to get fully into the swim. This requires explicit attention to affcon processes that moderate cognition and learning outcomes. These processes are as central to readiness as the verbal abilities and conceptual store that are the staples of schooling. If educators can design experiences that exercise cross-connecting processes, then more students should become ready for lifelong learning.

8 Toward a Theory of Aptitude

In numerous ways, Snow reshaped the concept of aptitude. He identified readiness as its defining feature. As affective and conative characteristics of the person clearly contribute to or impede readiness, "aptitude" extended far beyond "ability" or "intelligence." Aptitude emerged as a complex concept seen in active person–situation engagement. In summary, Snow argued forcefully that conceptions and inquiry methods should depart from those of yesterday.[22]

The aims that led to this book emerged in a 1991 article, where Snow spoke of *aptitude* as a term for "an old concept still widely used, but also widely misused and misunderstood" (p. 249). He went on to list key questions:

> But what is aptitude, really? How is the concept used and misused? How might behavioral and social scientists better understand, describe, and use aptitude, and individual differences in aptitude, as a basic property of human functioning? What form might theories of aptitude take? What research methods apply? How can we gear theory and method for research on aptitude to meet the prescriptive, decision-making requirements of educational, clinical, personnel, or other professional practice? (p. 249)

Previous chapters dealt with some of these questions. The focus of attention here is "What form might theories of aptitude take?"

---

[22]Articles where Snow dealt most directly with the topics of this chapter are his; 1991, 1992, and 1997.

In 1991 Snow committed himself to locating aptitude in the joint action of person and situation—that is, to the "a-in-p-in-s" conception. Even his earliest work had thought about properties of situations—recall his analysis of consequences of darkening a physics classroom to show films. Still, in his pre-1991 writings, *aptitude* referred chiefly to what the person brings to the situation. Our Seminar decided that in speaking of Snow's intentions for theory we should call such knowledge or response tendencies *propensities*, and that in this chapter we would consistently restrict *aptitudes* to the p-in-s interpretation. In previous chapters reviewing and quoting from older work, we did not generally alter uses of *aptitude* in the a-in-p sense. In this chapter, however, we go so far as to replace, in quotations from Snow, some appearances of *aptitude* with [*propensity*] or [*predictor*]. In the preceding quotation and in this chapter generally, *aptitude* is to be understood in the p-in-s sense. Propensities, of course, remain a major interest.

PLACING APTITUDE THEORIES AMONG OTHER THEORIES

To put aptitude theories into perspective, Snow (1991) set out a version of Fig. 8.1. Boxes in this figure identify prominent kinds of knowledge that anchor the wished-for theories. Placing aptitude theory among neighboring theories characterizes its mission. In addition to the boxes, the diagram contains many arrows. Arrows connecting boxes are a reminder that theories shape each other, and that contributions between theories can run in either direction. For example, the behavioral theory of operant conditioning (bottom box) gave rise to such instructional designs as the token economy and programmed instruction (right box); experience with them in turn raised further questions for basic motivation theory. Similarly, identifying features of expertise (top box) can feed back into ideas about situations (right box).

The Anchor Boxes.   Four boxes at the outside point to fields that are or should be the environment of aptitude theory.

At the base of the structure are general scientific theories of human individual and cultural functioning; any theory or practice represented in other boxes must be in harmony with the basic science. A theory of aptitude would rely strongly on general cognitive and motivational psychology. Physiology, especially neurophysiology, is becoming increasingly able to map the physical sites where mental processes do their work. A very short list of further relevant disciplines would have to include cultural anthropology, genetics, and linguistics.

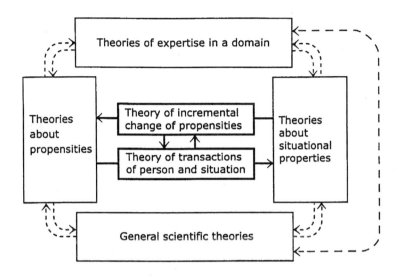

FIG. 8.1.   Where theories of person-in-situation fit.

The theories at the top explain expertise in a domain. To date, such theories have referred to specific and narrow domains such as chess, computer programming, or batting a baseball. In education, theories of expertise include statements about the structure of an academic domain as well as value judgments about learning objectives. The degree to which a person is an expert or shows promise of becoming one is of interest in evaluating students and the program in any instruction on the route to excellence.

The rightmost box represents theories of situations, concerned primarily with the structure and operation of environments large and small. The situation explicated may be as broad as the ecology, or as narrow as the plan for the dosages and other standards of a clinical trial of a medicine. The explications may focus on material elements, or on a plan of organization, or on actual operations under the plan. All the social sciences offer theories in this category, with cultural anthropology and organization theory being prominent suppliers. Ergonomics, grounded in experimental psychology, fits here also.

Instructional situations are of greatest concern to us, of course. Theories about them may derive, for example, from field studies addressing effects of instructional styles or media, or of discrepancies between a curriculum plan and the instruction delivered. Of special interest are attempts to produce theories of design for instruction, analogous to theories of design in architecture and engineering. These transcend the particulars of specific projects or instructional programs (Reigeluth, 1999). Snow encouraged development and application of principles of instructional design, based on theories of situations and permitting some degree of generalization from experience in one situation to others that meet appropriate specifications.

Theories about propensities, represented at the left, have been a main objective of differential psychology for a century. These aim to account for what people can do and are inclined to do, and why. Topics within this category include the unity or diversity of mental abilities, the origins and manifestations of anxiety, and the family's influence on motives and values. The theories have both psychological and biological components; questions about the role of the culture and the family bring in social-science disciplines.

Left-box theories also consider how propensities develop and can be further developed. Piaget's work on how children gain command of various aspects of the world is a prime example. Such a theory makes only vague reference to the class of situations in which propensities may later be applied. A theory of aptitude would go beyond Piagetian stages to account for their activation in some contexts and not others.

The distinction between the left box and the top box lies in the user's current interest. An employer concerned with hiring high school graduates for training will see as a left-box topic the attributes and predispositions the job applicant brings. Dealing with persons hired, the same manager will see training and supervision in the light of expertise: What is the firm's target of development for this new hire? What degree of expertise can be hoped for and how it can be promoted will depend on the propensities that developed over a long time. Such relations drive all the traditional interest in selection for employment and for higher education.

Aptitude Theories: The Central Bands.   Aptitude theories draw on the outside boxes. The central configuration in Fig. 8.1 symbolizes what is needed.

Two bands in the central area of Fig. 8.1 distinguish two kinds of process. It appears that these are theories of microevents such as were highlighted in Fig. 2.4 (p. 52). The lower band refers to theories about how and why the person copes in specific situations. Upper band theories treat the way experiences in a situation cause change in one or more propensities. Both these subtheories describe parts of a coherent system.

Lower band questions examine how propensities and features of situations combine to generate a performance. Conventional constructs such as reasoning ability, domain knowledge, achievement motivation, and anxiety all remain in the new aptitude theory. But documenting a correlation between such propensities and various criterion performances is only a starting point.

Chapter 7 considered some upper band theories of how situations affect propensities. Under what circumstances do young people develop interest in machines and their workings? Or develop anxiety about mathematics? Or change from being impulsive to comparatively reflective? As we said earlier, developments such as these can be seen as the cumulative residue of momentary experiences in situations (p. 50 ff). But cumulation is more than an unorganized piling up or accretion. It is a highly structured process by which a complex configuration of interrelated propensities evolves and matures.

Snow's Call for Integration. Each box, Snow thought, ought to commingle general theories and theories of individual differences. For maximum utility, theories have to share their language or express any unique concept in terms those developing new theory can adopt. We see powerful hybrid sciences developing; this is notable in genetics, which began as a study of individual differences but now relies heavily on biochemistry.

New language is needed to describe person–situation interchanges. In Snow's (1992) words:

> The process description of the person–situation interface ... is the step on which today's aptitude research has been stumbling. ... [T]he conceptual limitation derives from our tendency to think of persons and situations as independent variables, rather than [to see] persons-in-situations as integrated systems. To build the aptitude theories of tomorrow, we need a language for describing the processes that connect persons and situations—the processes that operate in their interface. Put another way, we need a language for aptitude constructs that is [compatible with] concepts of individual differences in learning, achievements from learning, and instructional treatment designs. ... (p. 19)

The candidate theoretical language Snow offered was a patchwork of several languages, each having advantages for different parts of the problem. But it is to some degree bewildering. Another goal for tomorrow's theory, then, is to replace today's quilt with seamless fabric.

Prominent sources for the language Snow proposed (and for theses on which we later expand) include James Gibson's concept of affordances, Herbert Simon's *Sciences of the Artificial* (1969), and various information-processing models—for example, of comprehension, and of reasoning (chap. 5). Snow reached back to E. L.

Thorndike and Thomson's connectionism, referring especially to the modern version of this elaborated by Humphreys. He made use of systems of ability factors (chap. 3), and work on situated learning and distributed intelligence. Even phenomenological perspectives entered Snow's purview, along with dynamic personality theory.

Snow never got to the point of meshing these conceptions. He would, however, urge that language move away from aptitude-in-person toward aptitude-in-person-in-situation. For example, replacing the idea of individual "strengths" and "weaknesses" with "attunements" or "matches," and "mismatches" would be consistent with Snow's reasoning. Note that even a situation-conscious reference to "aptitude *for* a situation" does not fit Snow's thinking. Aptitude emerges in the course of person–situation transactions.

PERSON–SITUATION TRANSACTIONS

Examination of transactions calls for new styles of research. Interaction studies of the traditional ATI variety assess from a distance; to describe the influence of propensities on performance, they estimate the percentage of variance in a summary measure of instructional outcome that person and situation variables jointly account for. Process analyses from a similar distance (e.g., retrospective interviews) enrich ATI accounts. Statistical interactions and even process analyses, however, cannot build a sufficient foundation for aptitude theory.

What "Union of Person and Situation" Means

The essential concept is the union of person and situation. At the least, *union* suggests that to understand the effects of person characteristics on performance, one must specify the performance situation. Similarly, understanding situational effects on performance requires knowing the personal qualities capable of influencing response. Beyond this, Snow insisted on interpreting aptitude in terms of a stream of transactions between person and situation, with special attention to events at the interface.

How should theorists conceive of that interface? In what sense can we say that person and situation engage each other? *Webster's New Collegiate Dictionary* defines *transaction* as "a communicative action or activity involving two parties or things that reciprocally affect or influence each other." *Interface* is "the place at which independent and often unrelated systems meet and act on or communicate with each other" or "the means by which interaction or communication is achieved."

Perception as the Bridging Element.   Features of situations affect thinking and behavior. An experimental psychologist will usually think of those features as defined objectively, prior to the transaction, but in the present context a subjective element counts heavily.

Objective ordinarily means something like what an all-seeing, impartial, nonselective video camera would record of, say, a student doing homework problems. The situation runs deeper, however. If previous class periods had been recorded, the history would show, objectively, events that are a significant ingredient in the present events.

Participants affect even what the objective record shows. Nominally objective aspects of tasks (e.g., materials, content, mode of delivery) are often elastic, susceptible to manipulation. A learner can omit steps in a task, for instance. Social situations are even more defined by the participants. A student in a classroom can press a teacher for a better explanation of some process, or ask a peer for a useful example. A student chooses to become more involved in group activities, or less.

In the course of a transaction, person and situation change. Snow (1994) wrote:

> [A] person working on a task learns to change strategy, which affords use of different abilities in the task performance; the task changes as the abilities and strategies brought to bear on it change. Thus, a person who shifts from verbal analysis to spatial visualization midway through a task has changed the task psychologically. A task that affords such learning has changed the person psychologically. Such changes in person and task at one point in time may change the person–task interaction not only later in the present task sequence, but also later in other task sequences. A person who learns to shift strategy in one task may start a new task with the new strategy, but also with the transferable idea that strategy shifting sometimes helps. ... Thus, learning in the task can change both the types and the levels of abilities that apply to this task performance, and to other task performances, and can do so differently for different individuals. (pp. 6–7)

Objective description of a task that will change as a person completes it is of some use—but it leaves out a large part of the story.

J. J. Gibson (1979) made this instructive comment:

> An important fact about the affordances of the environment is that they are in a sense objective, real, and physical, unlike values and meanings, which are often supposed to be subjective, phenomenal, and mental. But, actually, an affordance is neither an objective property nor a subjective property; for it is both if you like. An affordance cuts across the dichotomy of subjective-objective and helps us to understand its inadequacy. It is equally a fact of the environment and a fact of behavior. It is both physical and psychical, yet neither. An affordance points both ways, to the environment and to the observer. (p. 129)

A major feature of the inquiry Snow advocated is that he saw virtue in regarding perceptions of events studied as key elements. The view that an "objective" position stands in opposition to the "subjective" positions of participants or observers is misguided. (See also Gould, 2000.)

Principal Processes

An early version of Snow's thinking about events during a transaction was referred to as a "response sampling" model (Snow & Lohman, 1984). Snow strove for an integrative explanation of how a person's cognitive, affcon, and behavioral responses relate to the intricate system behind a transaction. Snow's model described how transactions in situations shape and maintain the organization and functions of a person's response system. The model recognizes within-person adaptations, and accounts for many between-person differences, within and across situations.

Snow borrowed the terms *inner environment* and *outer environment* from H. Simon (1969) to distinguish psychological constructs and processes within a person (the human environment) from external influences. *Environment* denotes surroundings; one can imagine surroundings of units within a person as well as conditions on the outside

Sampling.   The propensities and situational features sampled in a transaction reflect the match between the individual's inner environment or system and the demands and opportunities in the situation. *Attunement* (person–situation matches), then, refers to the process of a person "sampling" what he or she needs that a situation offers. Likewise, as a situation taps what the person offers, it samples only certain of the available propensities and responses. Assembly and control processes along the performance and commitment pathways govern this bidirectional sampling process and the resulting response.

Some response sets and propensities—those most stable and familiar abilities and other predispositions—will be more readily available than other potential resources and thereby preferred. Use of these resources will likely affect performance consistently across situations, accounting for some cross-situational stability in performance. The more tentative or fragile aptitude resources will gain prominence when appropriate to the situation.

The outcome of a transaction will be predictable to the extent that the person retrieves and applies well-established response sequences. Snow (1992) noted that:

Each person's learning history will influence this perception-selection process to some degree. Thus, the sampling is designed in part by the demands and opportunities afforded by the performance situation presented and in part by the possibilities and constraints afforded by the assembly and control history of the performing person. (pp. 23–24)

Snow's view that sampling is prominent in a transaction leads naturally to the question "What is being sampled?". Snow made general references to the inner environment; suitable elaboration can be found, for example, in the CAPS (cognitive-affective personality system) formulation of Mischel and Shoda (1998).

They spoke of "various types of mental events—thoughts and affects—that become activated characteristically and stably within a given individual in relation to certain features of situations or of the self" (Mischel & Shoda, 1998, p. 237). They identified five main categories of units in the CAPS formulation. The five categories are encodings (categories of declarative knowledge), expectancies and beliefs, affects, goals and values, and competencies and self-regulatory plans (Mischel & Shoda, 1998, Table 1). Like Snow, these authors conceived of the human response system as a fluid organization of patterns. Sensitivity to situational features (attunement) activates the organization of patterns on a more or less continuous basis. The more stable propensities are products "of the individual's cognitive social learning history in interaction with the biological history, such as temperamental, and genetic-biochemical determinants" (Mischel & Shoda, 1998, p. 238).

Assembly and Control.   Snow saw transactions as regulated by a within-person system:

Each individual's inner environment contains a vast assortment of response components. They are probabilistically interconnected in multiple associative networks; that is, the connections vary in strength to reflect the person's learning history. (Snow, 1992, p. 23)

The hypothesis that motivated the search for key assembly and control processes was that some differences in learning seem to reflect adaptations to the continually changing demands and opportunities in tasks. Learners construct their performances by drawing on resources and assembling, reassembling, and controlling them to adapt to perceived needs and opportunities in the situation (see p. 146 ff; see also Snow, 1989a). As Snow saw it, aptitude then shows through as the extent to which the mutual sampling by person and situation results in success, as defined by some recognized criterion.

Chapter 5 described how a task's novelty and complexity create cognitive demands. For any person in any task, novelty and complexity can be optimized. Like Vygotsky's ZPD, optimal functioning occurs in a limited range where assembly and control functions are at their most flexible and efficient. The optimum is not a property of the situation or the person alone but of their synergy.

The performance assembly pathway (see Fig. 6.1) starts with deliberate retrieval of knowledge or the automatic application of skills from the person's repertoire of propensities. A person organizes a performance to effect some match between the menu of affordances and the repertoire of propensities. An analysis of the situational profile with respect to a person's readiness for novelty and complexity highlights the situation's cognitive aptitude requirements and opportunities. As Snow (1992) explained it:

> Many sorts of assemblies of these components can be constructed in different ways for different situations. These assemblies are also decomposable so parts can be used in other assemblies as needed. The products of past learning are components already assembled into units to be triggered anew by situations similar to those previously faced. The products of continuing learning are additional components, new assemblies of both new and old components, and strengthened connections between them. But learning also exercises and thus strengthens the assembly and control functions themselves. ... Since [the human mental system] reflects personal learning history in this regard, it is also highly idiosyncratic. (p. 23)

When a person cannot address a situation adequately by employing propensities already within the repertoire, new responses must be constructed or imported. A rearrangement of existing patterns of responses may also be required. As we have said, fluid ability reflects competence and efficiency in assembling appropriate responses under conditions of novelty and complexity. Crystallized ability, in contrast, reflects competence and efficiency in using existing response patterns and knowledge. Kuhl's (2000) theory adds the hypothesis that novel situations challenge the person to form an explicit intention to act, a conative response.

In tandem with the performance assembly pathway, which accounts for the appearance of cognitive aptitudes such as Gc and Gf, there is a performance commitment pathway. This accounts for the appearance of affcon aptitudes such as anxiety or flow. Again there is a link to complexity in the situation, but the need for affcon aptitudes arises especially when there are distractions and other stressors.

Some Reflections.   A review of what present knowledge might contribute to educational assessment led Snow and Mandinach (1999) to this comment:

> We are left with a structure of abstract thinking and reasoning skills that may be hypothesized as general and transferable to much of school learning. Yet we are also left with the intriguing but difficult hypothesis that what is left out of such a structure is the crucial ability to assemble and reassemble such skills into flexible strategies during learning—to construct and adapt one's performance to each particular situation as it occurs. (p. 32)

Thus there is a store of resources within which aptitude can be found. This store or repertoire is, as it were, aptitude in waiting. The situational response is aptitude in action, here and now. These are different.

Much is known about how control operates given what a person brings to the situation, and what sorts of transactions matter. Assembly, however, remains much less explained. Thus, another lower band question is what mental sets, skills, and the like lie behind successful assembly. Similarly, we have adequately documented in previous chapters that strategy shifting has correlates, but what propensities predispose or trigger a strategy shift remain ill-understood.

A few words of caution on another matter are in order also. It is natural to judge readiness by asking whether the performance "results in success, as defined by some recognized criterion." (The quotation comes from our p. 219.) A criterion, however, most often is intended to represent the values of an institution. Those managing training are charged with producing the results the institution wants, to the degree possible. Once an observer steps back, other values can be brought to bear. Exhibit HFG (p. 201) illustrates the general truth that from a larger or alternative standpoint the "successes" of an institution may be socially damaging.

Even where no overt conflict of philosophies is at issue, a recognized criterion may give faulty information. Recall the finding in a study from the College Board, that the usual grade average was a poor representation of what colleges wanted to produce in students. Changing the criterion changed the relevant propensities.

Emphasis on short-term success in school lessons may be similarly shortsighted. A value judgment that the person coped well or poorly may be based on the record from a given situation; but the heart of the matter is the response process. Successes achieved in different ways may leave different residues in the repertoire of propensities. And some short-run "failures" prove to be highly instructive in the long run.

Compounds of Propensities

Earlier we discussed Snow's interest in "aptitude complexes," sets of propensities that have joint effects (p. 116 ff). Snow's research moved in other directions after 1978 and he did no studies of joint effects after the ones summarized in chapter 4. His writings of the 1990s repeatedly urged more investigations of that nature.

In this connection, Snow consistently referred to propensities, to properties of the person. Here, then, we speak of CP, where P refers to properties and C stands for complex, compound, constellation, and the like. (Snow used the first two of these terms; the third was used in a recent review by Lubinski.) Lubinski (2000) reported that the CP hypothesis is now under active investigation by various successors of Snow, notably Ackerman (1996; Ackerman & Heggestad, 1997).

It is inadequate to treat propensities as independent variables, to study them one at a time or in additive combinations. Investigating CP can only be accomplished by specifying combinations that seem likely to act jointly. The number of possible combinations is very nearly unlimited, and in a shotgun study chance results will obscure any genuine, replicable interactions. Focused hypotheses can be suggested by a collection of qualitative case histories. Prior to any kind of quantitative validation of a compound, there should be substantive argument to support the plausibility of the joint effect.

Some hypotheses will pair abilities, or an ability such as Gf with specialized prior knowledge. Some will combine aspects of personality. And both Snow and Ackerman have found promise in hypotheses that pair an affcon variable with an ability. A joint effect may apply to many situations or may be found only in one type of situation. "For any performance situation in which success can in principle be predicted, there will be [a CP], a mix of personal predispositions ... needed as preparation to achieve success ..." (Snow & Mandinach, 1999, p. 41).

These conditions correspond to the complexity and novelty dimensions already discussed. Kuhl also described how needs, values, and other internal states are compounded into self-representations. People call forth self-representations when they have to operate with incomplete information or handle stress.

The work on CP has not been recast in a-in-p-in-s terms. The possibility is intriguing, but even to pursue hypotheses at the a-in-p level tests the limits of research technique. Results may, however, be as situation-conscious as Kuhl's recent thinking. Kuhl thought of propensities acting in combination, while avoiding mathematical formulation like that in Exhibit Ptr.

CHANGES IN THE REPERTOIRE

Our discussion shifts now to the upper band of Fig. 8.1, theory of incremental change in propensities. The a-in-p-in-s view accepts that the person acquires qualities—propensities—while engaging with situations. (It would add that in transactions the person refines the qualities.) The needed theory will connect theory of transactions with the "acquisition metaphor" of Sfard's formulation.

Explaining change in propensities over comparatively long periods is central to educational psychology; even so, theories of propensity development through education are far from mature. Debates over whether the study of geometry improves logical reasoning evolved to recognize the many ways of studying geometry, and the fact that some children learn about geometry outside school from parents and math games. However, the product of the work to date consists of isolated propositions rather than strong developmental theory. The nature/nurture argument is another much-discussed aspect of change in propensities over long time spans.

These matters have been discussed in the aggregate over persons, in terms of antecedents such as gender, social, and cultural background—or in measured propensities—rather than as micro-processes. The research on development in chapter 7 was dominated by studies of score change after instruction that was at least somewhat extended.

Studies of heritability likewise have relied on aggregate measures of abilities or traits. But work in genetics is beginning to say how genes modify functions by modifying a chemical reaction here, an anatomical structure there (Lander & Weinberg, 2000). More important for us, there are reports that genes not only influence propensities, but that to do so they interact with each other ("aptitude complexes"!) and with variables in the social life of the developing person. This decade, then, may see the beginning of explanations of how human behavioral differences derive from genes and experience jointly.

Whereas the research to date (notably that considered in chaps. 5 and 6) provided rich material for lower band theory, we can offer only meager sketches for the upper band. Explaining development in terms of p-i-s transactions is nearly virgin territory. The neo-Vygotskian studies of interventions seeking to modify the ZPD (see p. 36 ff) stand as a rare exception that does look for effects of brief transactions.

The many successive transactions going into completion of a task have transformed the situation and, cumulatively, may change the learner. The responses of the situation to her moves help her gain insight into the nature of the problem, to think of external resources that could help (for example, the Internet), to become more aware of her own resources, and to seek new solution paths. Her next line of attack may combine propensities in a fresh way.

A changing situation generates change in the repertoire already in place, by modifying the conditions of use of propensities and their likelihoods of use. A propensity may be added if, for example, some aspect of the transaction brings to consciousness an explicit rule of strategy. Rules are one of many internal associations that, when confirmed, save much thought. Likes and dislikes are another example of such compressed experience.

A schoolchild can learn to make mental summaries of experience, to look for rules and to be skeptical of a generalization until she has tried it repeatedly. We speak here of an aspect of learning to learn, a higher order propensity that fosters powerful propensities. The skills of building knowledge and attacking problems are now often the subject matter of lessons, but they should be prominent among the objectives of everyday instruction.

As a propensity is used in many contexts, it becomes increasingly likely to be sampled on subsequent occasions. Mere exposure to a situation is not likely to account for a meaningful and lasting increment in this or that propensity. Rather, as one deals with situations that generate much the same perception, a response pattern stabilizes.

More generally, both lessons and incidental learning equip the learner with resources: information-processing algorithms, visual images that can be used in modeling abstractions, learning sets, schemas, and representations of internal states. A person gradually incorporates these new response systems and assemblies of intentions into the more stable organizational core. An important task for tomorrow's aptitude research will be to document how elements within the cognitive-affcon system are tied together.

In a sense, the person never meets precisely the same situation again. The altered propensities will be to some degree decontextualized so that they can be applied fluidly. Some new response sequences in time will be largely decontextualized, becoming available for use in even loosely related situations. Some elements of the repertoire will be highly transferable, still contingent on affordances but essentially detached from their situations of origin. Others will be situation-specific.

It is subjective experience with situations that carries forward, not the transactions that could be objectively recorded. Readiness to grasp (or not grasp) an affordance is an attitude or a sensitivity, or a blockage—either way, a deposit laid down in the person. The person is prepared to act when the target comes into view for whatever propensities she has ready.

Diagnostic efforts should identify and analyze patterns of matches (or harmonies) and mismatches (disharmonies) for the person–situation union in view. As Snow (1992) put it, "research on aptitude requires a detailed analysis of the affordance-[propensity] ... matches of different learners and different instructional treatments" (p. 25). Bronfenbrenner (1993) echoed Snow in calling for research designs that address what he called "force-resource" matches or mismatches. Such diagnostic conclusions, in turn, can lead to design recommendations that target specific aspects of the mismatch. For example, some current reforms in mathematics instruction follow from diagnostic research on young children's misunderstandings of mathematical symbols (Schoenfeld, 1999). In addition, designing instruction that prompts learners to use their more fragile resources when they might not do so otherwise extends the repertoire.

THEORY BUILDING: STRATEGIC CHOICES

Snow began this book largely to persuade members of the next generation to develop the aptitude theory he envisioned. He knew that advice on how to go about the task would be useless; only the investigator's own experience and creativity can provide direction. There are, however, some basic issues our seminar examined, and comments here may clarify them for investigators of the next wave. Snow's own thoughts about paths research might well follow we leave mostly to the end of the chapter, as a capstone for the book.

The questions before us are: What language might serve for theory of a-in-p-in-s? What forms of research question and data collection could provide a promising base for the theory?

Generalizing Over Unique Events

Our seminar was puzzled by a paradox that surfaces even in the first few pages of chapter 1. Snow laid great stress on aptitude as readiness "for a *particular* situation" (italics his). And he called for a scientific theory of aptitude in that vein. But because the particular is identified with the humanities, this will be "a different sort of theory" than science usually offers.

Propensities function instrumentally, as meaning-generating or response-generating regularities that direct the ongoing transaction. A would-be chef comes to a cooking school with some nonprofessional experience, knowledge of tools and ingredients, and probably some important gastronomic sensibilities and cheflike dispositions. These propensities help to ensure that the school experience has meaning, but do not guarantee successful response. The lessons on baking include many examples of the tacit knowledge that distinguishes a master from an average chef—using a metal cup instead of glass to measure flour, adding baking powder from a freshly opened can. Readiness for this was built up by the student's noticing that some things mark a superior baker, and by the student's inclination to ask about things that others might consider superfluous details. This activity is itself a response generated by propensities applied to the situation. Readiness is not highly particular. The qualified baker adapts to the particulars of the situation, yet brings to bear attitudes and ideas that are widely applicable.

A useful aptitude theory will generate specific predictions about the likely behavior of individuals with propensity profile P* when placed in a situation with affordance profile S*. And yet, a theory obviously must generalize. One cannot have an aptitude theory for every situation, or even for each narrow class that theorists might regard as similar in their affordances.

Perspectives.   An important step in understanding the affordance structure of a situation is to see it from the perspective of respondents.

At some level, everyone and every situation is unique, and every perspective on person-in-situation is unique. However, it is as wrong to assume that perspectives are completely unique as it is to assume that they are all the same. Saying that a situation must be understood from some perspective does not endorse a chaotic relativism, with as many perspectives as there are participants and observers. We can view perspectives as attunements to the affordances in a situation. If we model perspectives as circles in a Venn diagram, the circles should show considerable overlap, which can be described by a menu of affordances. We can describe individuals similarly by their repertoires. Some commonalities among the affordance profiles of situations will stem from shared biological preparedness of participants and observers. Others will stem from shared experiences, education, or culture.

Questions of Grain Size.   How best to accumulate evidence is much debated. Should a researcher collect many case studies of person-in-situation transactions and then try to infer an organizational structure? Or is it better to frame hypotheses about sets of propensity profiles, or sets of situations, that permit reasonably firm predictions of responses. Probably it is best to seek a simultaneous partitioning of persons and situations, limiting a cell to those propensities that the situation calls forth or that are needed for success. A case study of the details of a transaction can suggest where to start, but generalization requires comparison with other person-in-situation combinations.

The theorist faces a dilemma. Fine partitioning allows more accurate predictions; and broad categories, less accurate but widely applicable generalization.

When we think of transactions we necessarily think of short-term processes, which are expressions of propensities evoked. Kuhl's thinking, elaborated in chapter 6 and also a major source for the "taxonomy" in Table 3.4, is close to the language of a-in-p-in-s. In observation, think-aloud trials, or retrospective interviews, one can see signs of, for example, acts indicative of the present goal orientation. One can easily extend these single manifestations to statements about propensities such as, "In academic contexts Jeff is likely to aim at a performance standard higher than the task specification requires." Even though a numerical probability is hard to estimate, this has the classic if–then form. The probability can be raised in some cells, and simultaneously lowered in others, if the class of situations is further partitioned.

Most of the motivational and volitional variables in Table 3.4 are readily seen as summaries of feelings or emotional processes that enter at the microlevel, attuned to the immediate situation. This is in marked contrast to the trait names traditional in a-in-p analyses, such as anxiety and spatial ability.

The Carroll taxonomy of abilities (Table 3.2) is an instructive recapitulation of the historical approach to abilities. But chapter 5 speaks of processes on a much smaller scale. Thus, facing a figural representation, a person does not bring to bear "spatial ability" as a whole. Rather, there will be microprocesses. The display will have to be encoded. Being able to draw on a rich vocabulary of spatial concepts—diagonal, symmetric, clockwise, and so on—is no more than an element of the "spatial ability" of psychometrics. Moreover, we should not lose sight of such propensities as the probability of encoding thoroughly and where possible in alternative codes. These propensities affect transactions during both learning and criterion performance. They also contribute to a good score on a test of spatial ability; but "spatial ability" is too gross a category to suggest much about which subprocesses are readily available for transactions.

Similarly with trait anxiety, and, to some degree, with state anxiety. What one sees during transactions, for example, is some degree of arousal and focus of attention, conditional on specifics of the task and the state of the work at a given moment. A person has a certain propensity to escape stress by closing off the work hastily, to "leave the field."

Snow's thinking moved steadily toward the idea that an aptitude theory would point first to processes within transactions, studying how propensities and features of situations mesh. The propensities are evidenced in tendencies to do things and to have feelings. To report on acts and feelings requires a fine-grain description—not "I can (cannot) do it" but "I can come up to such and such standard." Once such propensities are seen as probabilities for narrowly described responses, it is reasonable to move up the spectrum toward coarser categories: not "self-confidence," for example, but "confidence in carrying out familiar mathematical operations." This is not the same as, for example, confidence in thinking through a novel problem. Whether it is profitable for theory to shift to a higher level remains to be examined. Appropriate grain sizes will no doubt differ with the subject matter and the purpose of the inquiry. The next section considers these issues further.

We break off this discussion to cover some other aspects of strategy. We return later to Snow's writings on the subject for a conclusion.

Expanding Inquiry on Constructs and Processes

Traditional construct validation proceeds piecemeal, amassing mainly correlational evidence on one psychological construct at a time. To validate constructs for the new aptitude theory, researchers must describe the complexes of cognitive and affcon variables that operate as resources in various classes of situations. Furthermore, to support the claim that an aptitude complex or profile of propensities is *needed* as preparation to achieve success in a given situation, evidence beyond correlation of predictive measure with outcome is wanted.

Validating an aptitude construct means first identifying the prominent features of criterion situations that evoke propensities and their assemblies similar to those evoked by actual learning or achievement situations. The magnitude of the predictor–criterion correlation then reflects the degree of overlap between the structure of the aptitude measures and a range of criterion situations for which inference is sought. Because this overlap is expected to vary across criterion situations, Snow (1991) argued that:

> [T]he particularity of aptitude-situation-criterion links implies *differential validity*. ... Thorough differential validation research is required to set substantive *boundary conditions* on the aptitude construct.
>
> Demonstrating differential validity across situations actually turns out to be a most important aspect of aptitude construct validation because it suggests how the predictor–criterion relations can be *experimentally* manipulated. To the extent that one can manipulate [predictor]–outcome

relations, one shows to that degree that the *particular* ... links hypothesized are being validly interpreted. (pp. 257–258, italics in original)

Researchers base decisions about placement or selection on conclusions drawn from differential validity studies. Made at medium and large scale, such decisions look toward a person's future. They rely on studies already made on a more-or-less related situation or set of situations. The studies might be sheer empirical work with a shotgun battery of predictors, or a job analysis, or the curricular equivalent of a theory of the job or situation class to which the decision points. However, these are all too specific to be "theories of situations."

One can often monitor a recurring situation so that its parameters on each appearance are known, and, perhaps, controllable. Relating such situational parameters to responses or outcomes is instructive but, again, limited. One must hope that in time such parametric studies give way to process explanations with explanatory power across a range of situations sharing common features. Some situations will overlap considerably in features such as level of structure and complexity. By describing participants' perspectives, an investigator can disclose overlaps among person–situation unions, such as classes of tasks perceived as novel.

Process explanations require a significant expansion of research strategy. Existing cognitive and affcon process studies offer some useful strategies. However, tomorrow's aptitude research will need to develop a more coherent and systematic framework to progress toward the ambitious goals of aptitude theory as envisioned by Snow. One challenge facing Snow's successors is to develop sound methodology for the study of assembly and control.

Unlike aptitude construct validation, which can be conceived as an extension of currently accepted methodology, process explanations require development of substantially new inquiry methods. These will integrate intensive longitudinal designs, a variety of instruments to record situational variations, traditional measures of propensities, and introspective or other perspective-taking techniques (such as think-aloud and teach-back). The aim is to follow the progression of transactional events along identifiable phases of the performance assembly and commitment pathways from the standpoints of both participants and observers. A carefully selected battery of measures for cognitive affcon propensities may indicate approximately the potential resources available. Similarly, detailed task analysis, coupled with instruments that gauge introspections and interpretations, will permit assessment of situational affordances as perceived by the person and by observers. These will help to make an initial evaluation of the person–situation match.

Think-aloud episodes obtained as a performance develops provide insight into assembly, control, and other processes. A researcher can use experience with a task as described by the person to structure protocols, moving from free-form to more focused specifics of the performance under investigation. Such structured protocols at successive points will seek answers to several questions: What resources are perceived as available? How are these resources used in light of perceived situational demands? How is a performance strategy determined, maintained, and revised (or abandoned) as performance progresses? How does the person maintain and revise commitments? And, what patterns of cognitive and affcon resource activation in the situation appear to promote or impede successful performance?

In learning situations that extend long enough, a terminal administration of the initial battery of propensity measures can highlight cumulative changes in the person's repertoire. These changes may then be linked to key aspects of the rich record of performance and commitment processes collected throughout engagement with the task. Keeping criterion performance in view together with process protocols and evidence of change in propensities should provide insights.

Detailed work such as this in educational, clinical, or industrial settings will be arduous, but some version of it seems necessary for worthwhile theories of aptitude. It is clear that such a program of research and development, operating through more immediate feedback loops, has two vulnerabilities. One is the high cost of intensive monitoring. The more the assessment considers students individually and tailors revisions to each of them, the higher the cost. The second is the comparative unreliability of information collected on the fly.

Theory Into Action

In translating the conclusions of construct and process studies into decisions about treatment, the most profitable questions will consider adapting the situation or removing the present inaptitude. Answers to such questions will require a theory on a microscale that treats how situational variables and propensities interact, what consequences follow treatment modifications of various kinds, and what treatments can enhance a repertoire that appears to be inadequate for the situation or class of situations.

An additional layer of monitoring and control would feed process information into proposed treatment modifications and evaluate their effects on ongoing performance. In business firms of moderate size, no one outside the personnel office sees the record of job qualifications at entry; propensities are indicated there but fresh local information guides assignments. Modern design experiments are a good resource for ideas on how to conduct research in this style, but most such studies to date have pointed toward program development rather than to aptitude development or theory building.

Figure 8.1, like the spiral figures in chapter 2, can be interpreted with reference to a variety of time scales. Microscale analyses speak mainly to questions raised in the lower band in the center of Fig. 8.1. Upper band questions of aptitude development, typically addressed at the macrolevel, may look ahead over a long time or a comparatively short one—over a career, in some instances, over a semester in another. "Aptitude or inaptitude?" generally will be less profitable to answer than the question "What aspects of the situation will prove troublesome for this person? And what adaptations can be proposed?"

Aptitude development should recognize that although the term *expertise* is usually associated with the fully trained adult, some kinds of expertise are attained earlier. The 3-year-old who has grown up with a language is expert in forming its sounds with a quality that an adult who comes new to the language is unlikely to attain. The left box in Fig. 8.1 can be read as including both inherited and formative influences on early speech. Language theory includes the finding that the very young child can make all the sounds in any language; however, this propensity is lost as months pass and the child hears the "foreign" phonemes infrequently.

One way to improve learning opportunities in a subject is to expand the situations it presents to learners. In transition bilingual education, for example, one may examine which topics and questions a child answers in the dominant language of the culture, and which are addressed in the language of the home. Change in this texture is an important developmental step.

THEORY BUILDING: SNOW'S PROPOSALS

Snow's several prospectuses for theory in the 1990s made evident the many aspects of person, task, and context that he would want a theory to consider jointly. The challenge is formidable. These writings did not suggest definite research strategies.

Some aptitudes will be uniquely situated, reflecting the demands and affordances of one situation that call forth a singular blend of aptitude complexes and processes not to be duplicated in another situation. In effect, the persons studied in any natural or laboratory context actively participate in creating that context. These persons give meaning to and construct critical elements of situations—including goals, means, and criteria for success. Individuals can, for example, set new goals for themselves over time, or change goals through communion in some social group. Group goals may shift as a result of the influence of larger organizational units. All of this occurs in ways that researchers cannot fully anticipate or control. Thus, ecological perspectives on individuals and groups will remain important sources for ideas about future aptitude research.

The place of aptitude theory within the field of neighboring theories (Fig. 8.1) suggests that generalizations can be imported from elsewhere to serve as initial questions put to specific design problems. These are not, however, prescriptions to be applied and tested blindly there. The research product is an enriched set of questions and concepts about what may count as aptitude in the new contexts, not a more refined answer to a fixed and general question.

We cannot expect to find, even ultimately, a network of laws about aptitude that hold generally, without qualification, over persons, situations, and time. Principles of aptitude will develop within research contexts, and these principles will evolve in adaptation to local conditions through continued tinkering, monitoring, and careful descriptive research.

If research on aptitude requires analysis of affordance–propensity matches at a level that identifies the unique person–situation synergy in ecological terms, then the kinds of aptitude theories such analyses serve must initially be local in nature.

Snow advocated a style akin to formative evaluation for most aptitude research:

> Whether a particular [complex of propensities] then becomes the object for further research investment depends on its perceived importance with respect to the local agenda, and the costs of ignoring it in this regard. As this local research proceeds, evidence will accumulate regarding each of the [goals] of an aptitude theory. A coherent, integrative story will be formulated about what counts as aptitude in the particular situation at hand, for the particular persons served. The story will interpret how and why person and treatment characteristics match or mismatch as they are observed to do. Local prescriptions may also be formulated, about the further design of adaptive instruction in light of this aptitude concept. Continuing evaluation reports on the prescription then add further to the descriptive story, as well as signal the need for still further revisions.
>
> But does this story count as *theory*? The answer of course depends on what meaning one gives to the term. If the story merely records what hap-

pened, as a series of events in some time and place, then most would say there is no theory apparent. But if the story offers a conceptual explanation that is a tenable, responsible interpretation compatible with the observational record, then I would argue that it is a theory just as historical interpretations are theories. It is a local theory, however, not a general theory (Snow, 1977). Its usefulness as theory rests on the degree to which it sheds new light on local events, problems, and objectives today and tomorrow, raises new questions for further work, and advances audience understanding. (Snow, 1991, p. 274, italics in original)

Snow did offer an apposite strategic plan in, astonishingly, the 1977 article cited in the preceding paragraph. The article was intended as a response to the suggestion, current in the mid-1970s, that instructional events were proving to be so complex and contingent that theory was impossible. The demonstration of ATIs does not make instructional theory impossible, Snow said, but "it will be a rather different sort of theory from what we usually think of as theory" (p. 12).

Old though the statement is, it is imbued with the same emphasis as his more recent writings—"the essential importance of detailed description of both specific instructional situations and specific groups of people" (Snow, 1977, p. 12). Snow advised investigators to study a single course as it is being taught in a single school, in sufficient detail to reach an *understanding* of good and poor outcomes. He spoke of research much like the design experiments of the 1990s, in which theoretical conjectures serve to modify some aspects of instruction. The success of the modification or an unanticipated shortcoming steers course improvement *and* shapes the theory.

In some instances, such work in a number of sites would identify a subset in which conditions, processes, and effects were sufficiently similar to warrant a generalization over a specified range of sites and subpopulations. Concepts useful in local theories would be suggestive for programs elsewhere, but the developer of instruction would have to learn much about a new site before identifying it with a cluster whose "laws" might apply. Some fresh confirmatory research undoubtedly would be needed.

The two-way traffic between closely observed instructional development and abstract conceptualization that Snow advocated in 1977 is one of the main messages of a contemporary AERA presidential address (Schoenfeld, 1999) on how research should proceed in the century that is dawning.

From our brief recapitulation the reader might wonder why, in the 20 years after he advocated this research program, Snow did not pursue it directly. Snow indeed did not put his main efforts into instructional development, as Ann Brown did. Nevertheless, he saw the studies he directed, and those done by investigators he had trained, as making progress along the lines he proposed, on a scale and at a pace suitable to gain intensive understanding. The two examples he gave in the 1977 article are the studies of Peterson and Porteus. Both were instructional experiments embodying prototheory about individual differences. The work on tutoring that Snow directed in the 1990s (Snow, 1994) again took the form of hypothesis-inspired instructional development, with an eye to individual differences.

Snow abandoned at an early date all visions of a synoptic theory, or of theory that merely links up variables from refined but separate taxonomies of person characteristics and situation characteristics. Adequate theories would give thorough treatment to behavior in situations of one or another type. Here is how his 1977 prospectus ended: "General instructional theory, I think, is a holy grail" (p. 15).

Then what *can* be hoped for in the next generation? As Snow put it in 1991:

[S]ubstantive aptitude theories linking individual difference constructs with important achievements in the fields of human living, in ways that show how treatments can be designed not only to promote these achievements but also to promote aptitude development through them. (p. 259)

Appendix

TERMS USED IN DESCRIBING RESEARCH STUDIES

This appendix introduces several terms used in analyzing and interpreting research. Much more could be said about any of the terms, but the limited entries here should enable readers unfamiliar with a term to make sense of the accounts of research in this book. The reader not wishing to read through the appendix may consult the Table of Contents to select topics for attention.

Psychological Constructs

A scientific concept used in explanations is often called a construct. Theories consist of networks of statements that interconnect constructs. Everyday terms may be elaborated into constructs. "Temperature" and "water," as chemical constructs, are abstractions having many features remote from everyday experience. The everyday experience of being anxious is likewise transformed into the psychologists' construct "anxiety," which traces features or properties that help explain observed regularities in behavior. In this instance, psychologists have found a need for two constructs, "trait anxiety" (persistent or recurrent) and "state anxiety" (variable from hour to hour or moment to moment).

In psychology, a construct applied to a person's thought, action, or feeling is a label for a hypothesized psychological function—that is, for a mental system, process, state, or the like. Explanatory constructs evolve. Some are judged unsatisfactory and discarded ("instinct," e.g.);

others ("mindfulness," e.g.) are recently minted, and will survive if needed to account for behavior of interest.

When two variables are associated with similar observed responses, over diverse occasions and situations, they are tentatively said to reflect the same construct. An underlying commonality among the indicators is inferred and, usually, the inferred construct is identified with a short label—*spatial ability*, say, or *conscientiousness*. A science often needs to separate seemingly equivalent terms as it advances. (*Weight* and *mass* provide the obvious example.)

Two tests that are highly correlated (see *correlation* discussed later) are often said to measure the same "thing." Tests that do not correlate are said to measure different "things." This compact language is unfortunate, because "thing" hints at physical reality. Some tests may be taken as signs of underlying biological structures (e.g., tests of color blindness). Some tests reflect, perhaps fairly directly, occurrences in particular parts of the brain. But one should never *assume* "thinghood" in psychological interpretation of a test performance.

Individual-difference constructs are designed to account for observed differences among persons in behavior and, sometimes, for changes in one person's behavior from occasion to occasion. State anxiety is such a dual-purpose construct.

Although some constructs—notably those for ethnicity—categorize people, the typical construct refers to a continuum along which people might be ordered. The person is said (for example) to have an estimated vocabulary of 27,000 words, or to outperform 42% of college applicants on a vocabulary test. Any propensity discussed in this book envisions a dimension along which all persons can be placed (at least all persons within some broad cultural category). Psychologists will say that certain persons are not neurotic, for example, but they are still prepared to judge these persons with respect to degree of neurotic tendency.

Treatments

At places in this book, the term *situation* is used for a broad and vague concept. In some uses it is more or less equivalent to the ecology of a place and time; in others, it applies to the momentary context of a person's action. The term *treatment* refers to the situation seen narrowly, through the eyes of a planner or director. The term has been used since the 1700s for conditions being contrasted in an experiment, but it came into psychological statistics most directly from agricultural research of the 1920s.

Experiments on instruction contrast alternative styles or arrangements. The term *treatment* is most obviously useful for aspects of a situation that were deliberately arranged. But naturalistic observations can be classified after the fact—distinguishing, for example, first graders whose parents made an effort toward early instruction in reading from those who "received a nonreading treatment." That language suggests that in some homes we can recognize events that constitute a reading treatment, and that differences in the pattern from one reading-treatment home to another are unimportant for the research in hand. If some parental efforts are beneficial and some are not, the construct will in time be specified more narrowly.

Standard Deviations and Standard-Score Scales

The everyday term *average* is generally replaced in research reports by *mean*. We need not expand on that familiar concept, but a bit needs to be said about the companion term *standard deviation* (SD), which is rarely encountered outside research reports. When a measurement is made on many persons, the scores spread along on a range. The mean locates (in a sense) the center of the distribution; the SD reports on the spread of scores.

The "normal" or "bell-shaped" curve is a convenient fiction used to interpret SDs. Its mathematical equation extends infinitely far on each side of the mean, whereas an actual score scale has endpoints; and the bell shape may fit an actual score distribution well or poorly. Even so, the following rules of thumb generated by the normal curve provide an approximation that helps in reading a table of means and SDs:

> 50% of the scores fall above the mean.
> 16% of the scores fall at least 1 SD above the mean.
> 2.5% of the scores fall at least 2 SD above the mean.

Symmetrically, 2.5% fall below the –2 SD position, and 16% below –1 SD. It follows that 95% of scores lie between –2 and +2; hence 4 SD indicates a range within which nearly all scores fall. And two-thirds of all scores fall between –1 and 1.

Many research reports, including some in this book, report statistics on a *standard-score scale*, so that readers need not bear in mind the unique scale of a particular measurement. If, for example, the mean is 27 and the SD is 6, scores of 21 and 31 are converted, respectively, to –1 and 1.83.

Variance is a basic term in statistical theory that appears a few times in this book. A variance is simply the square of an *SD*. The variance is commonly used as an index of the extent of individual differences in a variable. Thus a report might say "After this training the variance of performance was only 60% of the variance prior to training." Other uses of the term appear later in this appendix.

Correlations and Their Interpretation

When two scores are available for each of many persons, a correlation coefficient can be computed. It describes, on a scale from −1.00 to 1.00, how closely placements on one dimension agree with placements on the other. Chaotic disagreement produces a coefficient of .00; a value of −1.00 implies complete reversal of the ordering.

Some simple data help to illustrate correlations of various sizes. Each column in the table that follows represents scores of one person on four tests and, for simplicity, all tests are given the same distribution. Persons *a–i* are ordered according to their scores on A.

	a	b	c	d	e	f	g	h	i
A	1	2	3	4	5	6	7	8	9
B	3	2	1	6	5	4	9	8	7
C	3	6	2	1	5	9	8	4	7
D	3	9	4	2	5	8	6	1	7

Inspecting, you can see that the order on *B* is much like that on *A*. The usual formula (*product moment*) gives a value of .80 for r_{AB}; note the correlation symbol *r*. The value of .80 is impressive. Generally, two testings with forms of the *same* instrument will produce score sets that correlate .80 or above, still higher values coming from very long tests. (See *reliability coefficient* discussed later.) Now consider *A* and *D*. Three of the four persons who scored above 5 on *A* remain above that level on *D*; of those below 5, three of the four remain there. Even so, the radical changes in position of b and h bring the correlation down to .03; overall, agreement between Rows *A* and *D* is at a chance level. The *A,C* correlation is .50; such middling consistency is fairly common in predictive studies. A predictive correlation is likely to be much higher only if the pretest and outcome measures are similar in kind—for example, two tests in mathematics.

The range of the group studied affects the correlation. If a study is carried out on a narrow-range group (an Advanced Placement class, say), the correlation will be far lower than in a group representative of the student body. On p. 17 we described a predictive study where the correlation of prediction with outcome was .45—in data from airmen allowed to enter pilot training *after* screening by a broad test of intellectual ability. The correlation rose to .65 in a special study of an unscreened group (DuBois, 1947).

Convergent and Discriminant Validity. A construct should be identified with more than one measure; otherwise it is impossible to separate the meaning of the construct from peculiarities of the measure. Since Binet's work a century ago, differential psychologists have invented tasks that will, they hope, measure abilities that are interesting and practically important. Also, starting around World War I, they have assembled sets of self-report questions, each set thought to measure a segment of personality. Inevitably, each test was identified with an attribute, and the test developer tended to stress the uniqueness of his or her instrument rather than the construct(s) it shared with other tests. Attribute names proliferated to the point of confusion. Sometimes the same label was associated with several tasks or scales; and highly similar scales were given distinct names. (For examples, see p. 72.)

Thus a critical pair of questions for research (and theory) during much of the century has been: How many attribute names are needed to represent the variety of differences within a domain? Which tasks or scores can properly be classified as measuring the same construct? There can be no firm answer, because both coarse and fine classification systems have their uses. Current classifications nest narrow categories in broader ones. D. Campbell and D. Fiske (1959) summarized the reasoning needed to answer the foregoing questions by bringing *convergent validity* and *discriminant validity* into the language of psychological measurement.

Table A1 is a simple example displaying correlations of four tests. No description of the two verbal tests is needed, but it is worth pointing out that one is typically part of an "achievement" test and the other is usually part of a test of "verbal intelligence." (For Letter Series items see Exh. SK, p. 130; and for a matrix item see Fig. 1.1, p. 12.)

In the Campbell–Fiske language, two tests converge if they have a sizable correlation. There is sufficient convergence throughout the table that a coarse grouping would lump all the tests under one construct.

Matrix and Achievement, however, correlate less than Matrix and Letter Series. The table as a whole suggests two groupings (Matrix with Series, Achievement with Vocabulary), which can for the moment be referred to as reflecting Ability A and Ability B, respectively. The within-pair correlation supports the claim that members of either pair

TABLE A1

Four-test layout of correlations for examining convergent and discriminant validity

	(Ability A)		(Ability B)	
	Raven Matrix	Letter Series	Verbal Achievement	Wechsler Vocabulary
Raven Matrix		0.70	0.50	0.50
Letter Series			0.60	0.60
Verbal Achievement				0.70
Wechsler Vocabulary				

Note. Data are approximations based on figure in Marshalek, Lohman, & Snow (1983).

converge on the same construct—converge, in the sense that two spy-glasses converge on the same sailboat. Abilities A and B exhibit "discriminant validity." That is, the rankings on measures of A and B disagree sufficiently that it will often be profitable to discriminate them from each other. Some people rank higher in A than in B; and that is a fact in need of explanation. On the basis of the limited evidence of Table A1, it would make sense to call Ability A "inductive reasoning" and B "verbal ability."

The Campbell–Fiske article was motivated more by concern with personality measures than concern with abilities. In that context Campbell and Fiske raised a further basic question. When two procedures or methods claim to measure "the same variable," how can one check the degree to which the choice of method affects the score? They laid out a so-called "multitrait–multimethod matrix." The simplest example would again have four rows and four columns, assigned to variables patterned like this set:

    Questionnaire score:Sociability
    Questionnaire score:Extroversion
    Rating by peers:Sociability
    Rating by peers:Extroversion

(The pattern would usually be extended to more traits and perhaps to more methods.)

One wants the measures of sociability and extroversion to diverge, to justify retaining two constructs. Campbell and Fiske stressed also the importance of convergence across methods that claim to report on the same variable. Applying the construct of sociability—not further qualified—to either Sociability score would be hazardous, unless self-reports agree substantially with the perceptions of peers. In the ability field, a similar example could be developed for constructed-response and choice-response tests, or for a conventional science test and a performance assessment. For advances in the analysis and use of multitrait–multimethod data, see Shrout and S. Fiske (1995).

Recognizing method influences is potentially important to the understanding of propensity measures. It is rare for a study of outcomes in relation to an initial propensity to measure an input variable by two distinct methods. When—even rarer—outcomes have also been measured by two distinct procedures, the analysis has treated them in turn, not jointly. That leaves a large gap in the experience of the profession.

Factor Analysis and Related Methods. Once a collection of measures—often called a *battery*—is administered to many persons, a correlation can be obtained for each pair of measures. The pairwise correlations are tabulated as in Table A1. When a correlation table has many entries, it is difficult to judge by eye how many explanatory constructs are appropriate. Factor analysis sorts measures according to their correlations, usually forming clusters that can be identified with constructs. The clusters are described in terms of a few dimensions presumed to underlie the observed correlations. The analysis starts with a mathematical model, and adjusts numerical values within it to fit the matrix of correlations as well as possible. The method thus helps determine how many constructs should be interpreted and which measures are most closely related to each construct.

Factor analysis is actually a family of methods, not a single method. But all the variants have the objective of accounting for the correlation matrix with a simpler set of variables. There are exploratory and confirmatory factor analyses. In brief, exploratory methods try to discover a plausible set of construct interpretations for a correlation matrix. A confirmatory method imposes on the matrix a prespecified model and determines how well it fits the data. Hence exploratory factor analysis helps to suggest a mapping of person characteristics, whereas confirmatory analysis evaluates a structure already proposed.

Recognizing Measurement Error. Errors of measurement require serious consideration in all quantitative sciences. In much of psychology, however, they are less troublesome than the sampling errors discussed in our later section on uncertainty. When the research issue is, for example, the relation of memory scores to the ages of children, it is important to have comparable and reasonably large samples at each age. Measurement errors affect individuals' standings; but positive and negative errors tend to balance out and thus have comparatively little net effect on the age-group averages.

It is important for a test interpreter to know how much error is typically associated with scores, in order to judge how seriously to take the finding that a student scored 5 points below the passing standard, or scored 5 points higher in verbal ability than in quantitative (assuming comparable score scales).

The size of errors in a particular test, applied to examinees from a defined population, is identified conceptually with the SD of scores of a single individual retested many times; this is the so-called *standard error of measurement* (*SEM*). Repeated measurement works well in physical science but not with behavioral tests, where effects of memory, boredom, and fatigue violate the crucial assumption that what is being measured is not changing between measurements. Psychologists and educational measurers apply various techniques to estimate the *SEM*; all the techniques compare measurements of the same kind, usually from alternative sets of questions and, perhaps, of examiners and scorers. We have not reported values for the *SEM* in our chapters, so we need say only that the rule of thumb for the SD applies here. If the estimated *SEM* for the test mentioned earlier is 5 points, on any one trial how many students exactly at the passing standard (if thoroughly tested) will fall below that score by 5 or more points? From the normal curve, 16%.

The procedures that estimate the *SEM* also yield a *reliability coefficient*. This can be thought of as the expected correlation between two independent applications of a procedure to members of a group. One of many formulas for the coefficient is $1 - (SEM/SD)^2$. The test score can be thought of as having two parts, *true score* and *error*. The true score is what we would reach if we could average a great many measurements of the person. In what follows, V stands for variance. $V_{observed}$ (i.e., SD^2 for actual scores) is the sum of V_{true} and V_{error}. SEM^2 is V_{error}, so the formula reduces to $V_{true}/V_{observed}$.

Inevitably, the correlation of X with any other variable will be shifted toward zero when inaccuracies enter measures of X. And, if true scores on X and Y are equally related to Z, r_{xz} will be less than r_{yz} if the measure of X is less reliable than the measure of Y. Moreover, when true scores on two variables are strongly related, the observed correlation will nonetheless be low if the measures are inaccurate. Low observed correlations, then, are ambiguous. (This was a central concern in chap. 3 in evaluating the claims of Gardner and Sternberg.)

Much research on aptitude has been interested in how large correlations would be, or how they would compare, if errors of measurement did not reduce them. Spearman suggested in 1910 a correction formula that addresses precisely this question; it still serves today, with cautious interpretation. Basically, it combines the reliability coefficients of X and Z along with r_{xz}, to estimate what the correlations of true scores on X and Z would be in the sample observed. In this book we refer to such a result as a "correlation corrected for unreliability." In factor analysis, a correlation of a factor with a test—the "loading" of the test on the factor—is always corrected for unreliability of the factor.

Regression and Interaction

The correlation coefficient is admirably suited to statistical studies of individual differences, because the calculation deliberately loses sight of means and *SD*s.

The original problem that concerned Francis Galton (inventor of the correlation coefficient), however, was the relation of son's height to father's height. If, on this or some other variable of interest, the second generation has a higher mean or a wider range, that potentially important fact is lost from sight when only the correlation is calculated. Galton, aware of this, laid the groundwork for regression calculations.

Regression Lines and Planes. Think of a "scatter plot" with one characteristic on the X scale and another on the Y scale. A point is plotted for each person, that is, for each X, Y pair. The resulting cloud of points for height (and for most psychological and body size) variables, will form an upward-tilted ellipse—or a less regular, but usually tilted, shape.

We could average the adult height of sons in a select subgroup whose fathers are, for instance, 70–72 inches tall. If, in the total group, the average height of all fathers and all sons is 66, the son's height in the selected group will average perhaps 68 inches. A taller father is likely to produce a taller-than-average son. But sons tend to "regress" from the fathers' height toward the mean, as from 71 to 68. With 60- to 62-inch fathers, the average son's height will regress upward to perhaps 64. The *regression line* summarizes the trend of the data. For example, see Fig. 4.1. (The slope of the line is represented numerically in a regression coefficient. The coefficient is a useful partial summary of the relation of pretests to outcomes, but we have almost never reported such coefficients in this book.)

Two predictors are often employed together—for example, an ability test and a grade average from prior years. The simple graphic summary of the trend will be a tilted plane. The regression formula indicates what weighting of the two variables gives the best prediction. For an example, see Exhibit Ptr.

Although a correlation coefficient describes the accuracy of prediction, analyses often report "the percentage of outcome variance accounted for." (Such numbers appear in a few of our research summaries.) Basically, if r is the correlation, the predictor "accounts for" the fraction r^2 of the outcome variance; the rest of the variance comes from influences, known and unknown, not entering the prediction formula. With predictors X and Y, it makes sense to report r^2 for the better predictor and then the increase in "variance accounted for" when the predictors are used jointly. As regression equations become more complicated (see later discussion), one can report how much prediction improves with each step—with addition of an interaction term, or a curvature term, or whatever.

Interaction. *Interaction* can refer to communication between people, but in the aptitude literature it usually has a technical meaning from statistics, referring to the joint effect of two variables.

Suppose that with Variable K set at 100, an experimenter finds this trend:

Variable J	20	30	40	50
Outcome	20	40	60	80

There is a 2-point change in outcome with each 1-point change in J. Now suppose K is reset to 120 and the data points change to:

Outcome	30	50	70	90

This is an additive change; the rate of change across values of J is still two-to-one. The contrast with the earlier result would not be called an interaction. But suppose the values with K at 120 had been:

Outcome	15	45	75	105

The outcome now changes 3 points for each 1-point change in J. This, together with the trend at $K = 100$, is an interactive effect, because the level of K determines the effect of a change in J.

In Exhibit Psc (p. 21), a small table describes two trends. With "Low Support," outcomes were much better for students who did well on the pretest. The regression has a rather steep slope. Under the "High Support" condition, there was little relation of final achievement to pretest status. When the pretest score changed by a fixed amount, the outcome score changed far more if support was high. There was, then, an interaction between pretest score and instructional support.

Nonlinear Regressions. Some studies use complex regression procedures. (Standard computer packages are often applicable.) An adequate explanation would take more space than is appropriate here, so our description is brief.

Sometimes the data points seem to have an arch-shaped trend, outcome scores dropping off toward the right. A *nonlinear* (i.e., curved) trend line could be fitted. Figure 2.2 shows an idealized curvilinear trend.

A regression equation with multiple predictors can describe a curved surface. This technique was used in Peterson's study. One of the regression equations for predicting outcome from verbal ability (*V*) and anxiety (*Ax*) was:

$$Achvt = 24.87 + 0.35V - 2.51Ax - 0.31(V)(Ax).$$

This equation describes a "twisted plane" or "saddle surface." The scale used had a zero mean. Making some substitutions, say +10 for *V* (high) and –10 for *Ax*, makes clear that the outcome tends to be comparatively high if *V* is high and *Ax* low—or if *V* is low and *Ax* high. Outcomes tend to be low in the other two corners. (Think of the surface as sloping down toward stirrups at those corners.) Again, there is interaction; the outcome-on-ability slope changes from one level of anxiety to another.

Past studies of individual differences were strongly criticized by Atkinson et al. (1976) for almost always limiting themselves to linear regressions. Atkinson's group found that affcon variables had curved trend lines. There are two sides to the story. One cannot make a discovery if one's statistical model rules it out. Yet making the statistical model more elaborate requires substantially more data if one is not to increase the uncertainty associated with estimates of trends. One also must conclude, from Heckhausen's (1991) review of research on personality, that theoretical arguments for expecting curvilinearity are far more numerous than well-documented and replicated curvilinear patterns.

Recognizing Uncertainty

All data are subject to sampling error. Consider any randomized educational experiment intended to compare two treatments. The investigator samples—formally or more often informally—the persons to be pretested, the time at which a pretest is given, the items for the pretest, the treatment for each subject, the teachers who will administer a treatment, and so on. Many choices of teachers, for example, are possible, and each could be an appropriate representative of the class of teachers about whom a conclusion is to be drawn. Each act of sampling introduces presumably random variation into the result. (For example, if a gifted teacher is chosen to apply Treatment A, that assignment tends to put Treatment A ahead in the competition.) On average over many repetitions of the study, the net effect of sampling fluctuations would tend toward zero. But in any one study the sampling will make the key statistic larger or smaller than it would be on average over replications. The usual statistical reports recognize formally just two of these kinds of sampling variation, the selection of subjects and their assignment.

Confidence Intervals.   Suppose that the mean outcome score of the group given Treatment A is 87. We can, by considering the number of students in the sample and the *SD* of their scores, estimate how far the means in other samples of students, exposed to precisely the same treatment, would be likely to range. That is less important than a second question: How far is the population mean—the average—likely to depart from 87 as more and more such samples are pooled? The answer might be that one would obtain a mean of 87 in fewer than 5% of experiments of the same size—*if* the population mean is below 75 or above 99.

This range of not-unlikely values—75 to 99—is referred to as a *confidence interval* for the population mean in Treatment A. More specifically, it is a "95% confidence interval"; we expect to be wrong 5% of the time if we locate population means in intervals constructed by such a rule. A confidence interval guards against overinterpretation. If the treatment means in the sample are 87 for A and 99 for an initially similar group in B, the evidence seems to say that B is more effective. When told that the A data are consistent with means from 75 to 99, we recognize the possibility of a tie. When we make a further calculation and estimate an 87–111 interval for the mean in Treatment B, we see that there is a real chance of the A result being superior in the population. With the same means and with larger or less variable groups, the two intervals might be 82–92 and 94–104. Now the population mean for B is highly likely to exceed the mean for A. One can calculate confidence intervals for other statistics as well, for example, for correlation coefficients. Enlightening as confidence intervals can be, they have not been the usual form of report on sampling variation, partly to save space in reports, and partly because of tradition.

Significance Tests.   The most traditional practice is a "test of statistical significance." This formalizes the intuitive argument of the preceding paragraph and, from the original numbers, calculates how likely it is that the A and B population means differ. We spoke of a 95% confidence interval. It would have been equally easy to form a 99% interval or an 88% interval, under the usual mathematical assumptions. Many a significance test on a mean difference is summarized as "significant at the 5% level" or, more succinctly, "$p < .05$"; that indicates that a zero (or reversed) difference in the population is unlikely. (Confidence equals 1.00 minus the risk of a wrong conclusion.) In practice, one sees reports of $p < .05$, $p < .01$, and $p < .001$—that is, 5%, 1%, and 0.1% risk. The 95% confidence interval for a correlation coefficient might be –.10 to .30. This includes $r = .00$, so we cannot be confident that the population correlation is positive in the population. If the interval is .02 to .30, one can append "$p < .05$."

Psychologists have come to accept a result tagged "$p < .05$" as "statistically significant." That does not mean that the conclusion is established as valid in the population. It means only that in 20 investigations where there is no relationship in the population, just one false report of significance is likely to be made. All scientific results are to some degree uncertain. The profession has settled on the 1-in-20 risk as a generally sensible rule for separating the reportable from the suspect; in serious science there will in time be follow-up studies that identify whichever correlations or differences are not genuinely present in the population.

Experienced readers of statistical reports bring many cautious questions to a "$p < .05$" report. One that is particularly critical in research on personal characteristics looks into the number of statistical tests that the investigator made. To take a simple example, a novice investigator might administer an interest inventory that yields 12 scores. Each of the 66 correlations between score pairs can be tested for significance. Approximately three of those correlations (5% of 66) would probably be "significant" by chance. On the basis of these data alone, no one knows which they are. Even though technically accurate, "$p < .05$," has to be discounted when many p calculations were made. It is often appropriate to speak of a difference as "nominally significant" when, in the context of a large set of analyses, the conventional interpretation is untrustworthy.

Effect Sizes.   Statistical tests are much influenced by sample sizes. A result from a large sample is likely to be close to that in the next; but results from small samples are typically inconsistent. Small studies typically "lack power"; that is, even when a hypothesis about differences between means is valid in the population, the test on the observed difference is likely not to report statistical significance.

For that reason, professional opinion in psychology has reduced the emphasis placed on the significance test. (See, e.g., Harlow, Mulaik, & Steiger, 1997; Kirk, 1996.) What should concern the reader of a report, according to much current thinking, is the *effect size*.

A difference or correlation of impressive size may well be worth reporting to fellow investigators even though not "significant." Such findings are suggestive, worth tentative attention from investigators trying to build theory. Although Snow's writing said little about this question, it was evident in the research he directed or supervised that he valued highly the study that demonstrated worthwhile effect sizes of new combinations of variables, even where the result was only nominally significant or perhaps nonsignificant.

Reporting a sizable but uncertain result may encourage others to collect similar data so that evidence accumulates. This opens the way to a so-called *meta-analysis*. A meta-analysis extracts a composite statistical conclusion from many estimates of the same effect (Cooper & Hedges, 1994). Successive studies are almost never exact replications, and therefore pooling the studies requires considerable substantive judgment (see p. 91).

An effect size may be in familiar units: inches, dollars, IQ points, and so on. A correlation, with its zero-to-one scale, may also be considered a direct report on effect size. But most dependent variables in psychological research have scales reflecting the instrument design or the spread of scores in a sample from some population. So an average difference of 2 points (or 20) is unlikely to have the same meaning from study to study.

For this reason, it is usual to look at the "standardized" effect size, the ratio of the mean difference to the *SD* calculated within the contrasted groups. Such a ratio can also be defined for statistics other than mean differences (Kirk, 1996).

Cohen (1988, 1994) and others have given much thought to a simple system for describing effect sizes in plain language. They offered rules of thumb, with the caution that the qualitative judgment might change with the topic studied. A standardized A – B difference is interpreted thus: .8, "strong"; .5, "medium"; .2, "small." Most intermediate values can readily be classed accordingly. For correlations, the suggested translations are: .5, "strong"; .3, "medium"; .1, "small."

In this book we describe many numerical findings in terms of a rough effect size where the information needed for an accurate calculation has been missing from research reports. Not infrequently, for example, means are reported without standard deviations. Many of our classifications are therefore impressionistic. Still, we are almost always reporting studies for their heuristic value, not as firm conclusions. Even precisely calculated effect sizes are uncertain until evidence accumulates from multiple sources.

Recent controversies about the hazards of inference in psychological research led to the formation of a blue-ribbon committee that summarized the issues and cautions to be considered in reporting *p* values, confidence intervals, and effect sizes. The document was circulated widely and comments were taken into account. The final version (Wilkinson & the Task Force on Statistical Inference, 1999) will be important for all readers of statistical reports as well as for investigators.

Uncertainty Associated With Regressions. Sampling error affects regression statistics in a more complicated way than it does means and correlations. The complication can be presented simply by examining again a trend from an earlier illustration.

Variable J	20	30	40	50
Outcome	20	40	60	80

The mean is, let us say, 35 for *J* and 50 for the outcome. The confidence interval for the outcome mean is, let us say, 47–53 (6 points wide). Now at *J* = 40, the confidence interval widens to perhaps 55–65 (10 points), because the regression slope in the population may be larger or smaller than that in the sample. The divergence of plausible regression lines is much greater where *J* = 50; the interval becomes something like 67–93 (26 points wide). Although spreading confidence bands such as this can be calculated by means of a long-known formula, that calculation is almost never made. Rather, readers must recognize intuitively that greater uncertainty attends predictions at the extremes of the range than predictions at the mean.

Comparisons of regression slopes in two treatments played a large part in Snow's research and hence in this book. Interaction effects are best judged by the separation of sample regression lines at a moderate distance from the predictor mean, rather than at the extremes. That is the justification for the intuitive summary device ("Net") laid out in Exhibit Ptr.

References

Ablard, K. E., & Lipschultz, R. E. (1998). Self-regulated learning in high-achieving students: Relations to advanced reasoning, achievement goals, and gender. *Journal of Educational Psychology, 90,* 94–101.

Ach, N. (1910). *Über den Willensakt und das Temperament.* Leipzig, Germany: Quelle Meyer.

Ackerman, P. L. (1986). Individual differences in information processing: An investigation of intellectual abilities and task performance during practice. *Intelligence, 10,* 101–139.

Ackerman, P. L. (1988). Determinants of individual differences during skill acquisition: Cognitive abilities and information processing. *Journal of Experimental Psychology: General, 117,* 284–318.

Ackerman, P. L. (1989). Individual differences in skill acquisition. In P. L. Ackerman, R. J. Sternberg, & R. Glaser (Eds.), *Learning and individual differences: Advances in theory and research* (pp. 164–217). New York: Freeman.

Ackerman, P. L. (1996). A theory of adult intellectual development: Process, personality, interests, and knowledge. *Intelligence, 22,* 227–237.

Ackerman, P. L., & Heggestad, E. D. (1997). Intelligence, personality, and interests: Evidence for overlapping traits. *Psychological Bulletin, 121,* 219–245.

Ackerman, P. L., & Kanfer, R. (1993). Integrating laboratory and field study for improving selection: Development of a battery for predicting air traffic controller success. *Journal of Applied Psychology, 78,* 413–432.

Ackerman, P. L., & Lohman, D. F. (1990). *An investigation of the effect of practice on the validity of spatial tests* (Final Report; NPRDC Contract N66001-88C-0291). Minneapolis, MN: Personnel Decisions Research Institute.

Aiken, L. S., West, S. G., Schwalm, D. E., Carroll, J., & Hsiung, S. (1998). Comparison of a randomized and two quasi-experiments in a single outcome evaluation: Efficacy of a university-level remedial writing program. *Evaluation Review, 22,* 207–244.

Ainley, M. D. (1993). Styles of engagement with learning: Multidimensional assessment of their relationship with strategy use and school achievement. *Journal of Educational Psychology, 85,* 395–405.

Allison, R. B., Jr. (1960). Learning parameters and human abilities (Doctoral dissertation, Educational Testing Service and Princeton University, 1960). *Dissertation Abstracts, 21,* 2375.

Allport, G. W. (1961). *Pattern and growth in personality.* New York: Holt, Rinehart & Winston.

Ames, C. (1990). Motivation: What teachers need to know. *Teachers College Record, 91,* 409–421.

Ames, C. (1992). Classrooms: Goals, structures, and student motivation. *Journal of Educational Psychology, 84,* 261–271.

Anderson, J. R. (1983). *The architecture of cognition.* Cambridge, MA: Harvard University Press.

Anderson, J. R. (1991). The adaptive nature of human categorization. *Psychological Review, 98,* 409–429.

Anderson, J. R. (1993). Problem solving and learning. *American Psychologist, 48,* 35–44.

Anderson, J. R., Reder, L. M., & Simon, H. (1996). Situated learning and education. *Educational Researcher, 25*(4), 5–11.

Anderson, J. R., Reder, L. M., & Simon, H. (1997). Situative versus cognitive perspective: Form versus substance. *Educational Researcher, 26*(1), 18–21.

Anderson, L. W., & Krathwohl, D. R. (Eds.), with Airasian, P. W., Cruikshank, K. A., Mayer, R. E., Pintrich, P. R., & Raths, J. (2001). *A taxonomy for learning, teaching and assessing: A revision of Bloom's taxonomy of educational objectives.* New York: Longman.

Atkinson, J. W. (1974). Motivational determinants of intellective performance and cumulative achievement. In J. W. Atkinson & J. O. Raynor (Eds.), *Motivation and achievement* (pp. 389–410). Washington, DC: Winston.

Atkinson, J. W., Lens, W., & O'Malley, P. M. (1976). Motivation and ability: Interactive psychological determinants of intellective performance, educational achievement, and each other. In W. H. Sewell, R. M. Hauser, & D. L. Featherman (Eds.), *Schooling and achievement in American society* (pp. 29–60). New York: Academic Press.

Atkinson, J. W., & Raynor, J. O. (Eds.). (1974). *Motivation and achievement.* Washington, DC: Winston.

Au, K. (1980). Participation structures in a reading lesson with Hawaiian children. *Anthropology and Education Quarterly, 11,* 91–115.

Averbach, E., & Coriell, A. S. (1961). Short-term memory in vision. *Bell System Technical Journal, 40,* 309–328.

Baddeley, A. D. (1986). *Working memory.* Oxford, England: Oxford University Press.

Baddeley, A. D. (1996). Exploring the central executive. *Quarterly Journal of Experimental Psychology: Human Experimental Psychology, 49A,* 5–28.

Baker, S. C., Rogers, R. D., Owen, A. M., Frith, C. D., Dolan, R. J., Frackowiak, R. S. J., & Robbins, T. W. (1996). Neural systems engaged by planning: A PET study of the Tower of London task. *Neuropsychologia, 34,* 515–526.

Bargh, J. A., & Chartrand, T. L. (1999). The unbearable automaticity of being. *American Psychologist, 54,* 462–479.

Barker, R. G., & Gump, P. V. (1964). *Big school, small school: High school size and student behavior.* Stanford, CA: Stanford University Press.

Baron, J., & Sternberg, R. J. (Eds.). (1987). *Teaching thinking skills.* New York: Freeman.

Bartlett, F. C. (1932). *Remembering: A study in experimental and social psychology.* London: Cambridge University Press.

Bartlett, F. C. (1948). The measurement of human skill. *Occupational Psychology, 22,* 30–38.

Battistich, V., Solomon, D., Kim, D., Watson, M., & Schaps, E. (1995). Schools as communities, poverty levels of student populations, and students' attitudes, motives, and performance: A multilevel analysis. *American Educational Research Journal, 32,* 627–658.

Belmont, J. M., & Mitchell, D. W. (1987). The general strategies hypothesis as applied to cognitive theory in mental retardation. *Intelligence, 11,* 91–105.

Bereiter, C. (1990). Aspects of an educational learning theory. *Review of Educational Research, 60,* 603–624.

Bereiter, C., & Scardamalia, M. (1987). *The psychology of written composition.* Hillsdale, NJ: Lawrence Erlbaum Associates.

Berliner, D. C. (1983). Developing conceptions of classroom environments: Some light on the T in classroom studies of ATI. *Educational Psychologist, 18,* 1–13.

Bethell-Fox, C. E., Lohman, D. F., & Snow, R. E. (1984). Adaptive reasoning: Componential and eye movement analysis of geometric analogy performance. *Intelligence, 8,* 205–238.

Binet, A. (1899). Attention et adaptation. *L'année Psychologique, 6,* 248–404.

Bingham, W. V. (1937). *Aptitudes and aptitude testing.* New York: Harper and Brothers.

Block, J. (1995). A contrarian view of the five-factor approach to personality description. *Psychological Bulletin, 117,* 187–215.

Bloom, B. S. (Ed.). (1956). *Taxonomy of educational objectives: The cognitive domain.* New York: Longman.

Blumenfeld, P. C. (1992). Classroom learning and motivation: Clarifying and expanding goal theory. *Journal of Educational Psychology, 84,* 272–281.

Boekaerts, M. (1987). Situation-specific judgments of a learning task versus overall measures of motivational orientation. In E. DeCorte, H. Lodewijks, R. Parmentier, & P. Span (Eds.), *Learning and instruction: European research in an international context* (Vol. 1, pp. 169–179). Leuven, Belgium: Leuven University Press and Pergamon.

Boekaerts, M. (1993). Being concerned with well-being and with learning. *Educational Psychologist, 28,* 149–167.

Boekaerts, M. (1996). Personality and the psychology of learning. *European Journal of Personality, 10,* 377–404.

Bossert, S. T. (1978, January). *Activity structures and student outcomes.* Paper presented at the National Institute of Education Conference on School Organization and Effects, San Diego.

Bower, G. H. (1981). Mood and memory. *American Psychologist, 36,* 129–148.

Breiman, J. H., Olshen, R. A., & Stone, C. J. (1984). *Classification and regression trees.* Belmont, CA: Wadsworth & Brooks/Cole.

Brogden, H. E. (1957). New problems for old solutions. *Psychometrika, 22,* 301–309.

Bronfenbrenner, U. (1993). The ecology of cognitive development: Research models and fugitive findings. In R. H. Wozniak & K. W. Fischer (Eds.), *Development in context* (pp. 3–44). Hillsdale, NJ: Lawrence Elrbaum Associates.

Brophy, J. (1998). *Motivating students to learn.* Boston: McGraw-Hill.

Brown, A. L. (1992). Design experiments: Theoretical and methodological challenges in creating complex interventions in classroom settings. *Journal of the Learning Sciences, 2,* 141–178.

Brown, A. L. (1994). The advancement of learning. *Educational Researcher, 23*(8), 4–12.

Brown, A. L., & Campione, J. C. (1990). Communities of learning and thinking, or a context by any other name. *Contributions to Human Development, 21,* 108–126.

Brown, A. L., Campione, J, G., Webber, L. S., & McGilly, K. (1992). Interactive learning environments: A new look at assessment and instruction. In B. R. Gifford & M. C. O'Connor (Eds.), *Changing assessments: Alternative views of aptitude, achievement, and instruction* (pp. 121–211). Boston: Kluwer.

Brunswik, E. (1956). *Perception and the representative design of psychological experiments.* Berkeley: University of California Press.

Buss, A. H., & Plomin, R. (1975). *A temperament theory of personality development.* New York: Wiley-Interscience.

Buss, A. H., & Plomin, R. (1984). *Temperament: Early developing personality traits.* Hillsdale, NJ: Lawrence Erlbaum Associates.

Cacioppo, J. T., Petty, R. E., Feinstein, J. A., & Jarvis, W. B. G. (1996). Dispositional differences in cognitive motivation: The life and times of individuals varying in need for cognition. *Psychological Bulletin, 119,* 197–253.

Calfee, R. C. (1982). Cognitive models of reading: Implications for assessment and treatment of reading disability. In R. N. Malatesha & P. G. Aaron (Eds.), *Reading disorders: Varieties and treatments* (pp. 151–176). New York: Academic Press.

Calfee, R. C., & Norman, K. A. (1998). Psychological perspectives on the early reading wars: The case of phonological awareness. *Teachers College Record, 100,* 242–274.

Callahan, R. E. (1962). *Education and the cult of efficiency.* Chicago: University of Chicago Press.

Campbell, D. T., & Fiske, D. W. (1959). Convergent and discriminant validation by the multitrait-multimethod matrix. *Psychological Bulletin, 56,* 81–105.

Campbell, F. A., & Ramey, C. T. (1994). Effects of early intervention on intellectual and academic achievement: A follow-up study of children from low-income families. *Child Development, 65,* 684–698.

Campbell, F. A., & Ramey, C. T. (1995). Cognitive and school outcomes for high-risk African-American students at middle adolescence: Positive effects of early intervention. *American Educational Research Journal, 32,* 743–772.

Cappon, L. J. (Ed.). (1959). *Adams-Jefferson letters.* Chapel Hill: University of North Carolina Press.

Cardelle, M., & Corno, L. (1981). Effects on second language learning of variations in homework written feedback. *TESOL Quarterly, 15,* 251–261.

Cardelle-Elawar, M. (1982). *Effects of training Venezuelan teachers in providing feedback on mathematics homework* (Doctoral dissertation, Stanford University, 1982). *Dissertation Abstracts International, 43A,* 1508.

Carpenter, P. A., Just, M. A., & Shell, P. (1990). What one intelligence test measures: A theoretical account of the processing in the Raven Progressive Matrices Test. *Psychological Review, 97,* 404–431.

Carroll, J. B. (1974). The aptitude–achievement distinction: The case of foreign language aptitude and proficiency. In D. R. Green (Ed.), *The aptitude-achievement distinction* (pp. 286–303). Monterey, CA: CTB/McGraw-Hill.

Carroll, J. B. (1976). Psychometric tests as cognitive tasks: A new "structure of intellect." In L. Resnick (Ed.), *The nature of intelligence* (pp. 27–56). Hillsdale, NJ: Lawrence Erlbaum Associates.

Carroll, J. B. (1993). *Human cognitive abilities: A survey of factor-analytic studies.* Cambridge, England: Cambridge University Press.

Carroll, J. B. (1995). Reflections on Stephen Jay Gould's *The mismeasure of man: A retrospective review. Intelligence, 21,* 121–134.

Carroll, J. B. (1996). A three-stratum theory of intelligence: Spearman's contribution. In I. Dennis & P. Tapsfield (Eds.), *Human abilities: Their nature and measurement* (pp. 1–17). Mahwah, NJ: Lawrence Erlbaum Associates.

Case, R., & Bereiter, C. (1984). From behaviourism to cognitive development: Steps in the evolution of instructional design. *Instructional Science, 13,* 141–158.

Cattell, R. B. (1987). *Intelligence: Its structure, growth and action.* Amsterdam: North-Holland.

Cattell, R. B, Eber, H. W., & Tatsuoka, M. M. (1970). *Handbook for the Sixteen Personality Factor questionnaire (16 PF) in clinical, educational, industrial, and research psychology, for use with all forms of the test.* Champaign, IL: Institute for Personality and Ability Testing.

Ceci, S. J. (1990). *On intelligence ... more or less: A bioecological treatise on intellectual development.* Englewood Cliffs, NJ: Prentice-Hall.

Ceci, S. J. (1991). How much does schooling influence general intelligence and its cognitive components? A reassessment of the evidence. *Developmental Psychology, 27,* 703–722.

Chastain, R. L. (1992). Adaptive processing in complex learning and cognitive performance. (Doctoral dissertation, Stanford University, 1992). *Dissertation Abstracts International, 53A,* 2296.

Chinn, C. A., & Anderson, R. D. (1998). The structure of discussions intended to promote reasoning. *Teachers College Record, 100,* 315–368.

Chipman, S. F., Segal, J. W., & Glaser, R. (Eds.). (1985). *Thinking and learning skills: Vol. II. Research and open questions.* Hillsdale, NJ: Lawrence Erlbaum Associates.

Clark, C. M., Gage, N. L., Marx, R. W., Peterson, P. L., Stayrook, N. G., & Winne, P. H. (1979). A factorial experiment on teacher structuring, soliciting, and reacting. *Journal of Educational Psychology, 71,* 534–553.

Cohen, J. (1988). *Statistical power analysis for the behavioral sciences* (2nd ed.). Hillsdale, NJ: Lawrence Erlbaum Associates.

Cohen, J. (1994). The earth is round (*p* < .05). *American Psychologist, 49,* 997–1003.

Cole, M. (1985). Mind as a cultural achievement: Implications for IQ testing. In E. Eisner (Ed.), *Learning and teaching the ways of knowing* (pp. 218–249) (Eighty-fourth yearbook of the National Society for the Study of Education, Part II). Chicago: University of Chicago Press.

Collins, A., Brown, J. S., & Newman, S. E. (1989). Cognitive apprenticeship: Teaching the craft of reading, writing, and mathematics. In L. B. Resnick (Ed.), *Knowing, learning, and instruction: Essays in honor of Robert Glaser* (pp. 453–494). Hillsdale, NJ: Lawrence Erlbaum Associates.

Collins, J. (1998, October 19). Seven kinds of smart. *Time, 152*(16), 94–96.

Collis, J., & Messick, S. (Eds.). (2001). *Intelligence and personality: Bridging the gap in theory and measurement*. Mahwah, NJ: Lawrence Erlbaum Associates.

Converse, P. E. (1986). Generalization and the social psychology of "other worlds." In D. W. Fiske & R. A. Schweder (Eds.), *Metatheory in social science* (pp. 42–60). Chicago: University of Chicago Press.

Cooper, H., & Hedges, L. V. (Eds.). (1994). *The handbook of research synthesis*. New York: Russell Sage Foundation.

Corno, L. (1979). A hierarchical analysis of selected naturally occurring aptitude-treatment interactions in the third grade. *American Educational Research Journal, 16*, 391–410.

Corno, L. (1986). The metacognitive control components of self-regulated learning. *Contemporary Educational Psychology, 11*, 333–346.

Corno, L. (1988). More lessons from aptitude-treatment interaction theory. *Educational Psychologist, 23*, 353–356.

Corno, L. (1989). Self-regulated learning: A volitional analysis. In B. Zimmerman & D. Schunk (Eds.), *Self-regulated learning and academic achievement: Theory, research and practice* (pp. 111–142). New York: Springer.

Corno, L. (1992). Encouraging students to take responsibility for learning and performance. *Elementary School Journal, 93*, 69–84.

Corno, L. (1993). The best-laid plans: Modern conceptions of volition and educational research. *Educational Researcher, 22*(2), 14–22.

Corno, L., & Mandinach, E. B. (1983). The role of cognitive engagement in classroom learning and motivation. *Educational Psychologist, 18*, 88–108.

Cronbach, L. J. (1957). The two disciplines of scientific psychology. *American Psychologist, 12*, 671–684.

Cronbach, L. J. (1960). *Essentials of psychological testing* (2nd ed.) New York: Harper & Row.

Cronbach, L. J. (1967a). How can instruction be adapted to individual differences? In R. M. Gagné (Ed.), *Learning and individual differences* (pp. 23–39). Columbus, OH: Merrill.

Cronbach, L. J. (1967b). Year-to-year correlations of mental tests: A review of the Hofstaetter analysis. *Child Development, 38*, 284–289.

Cronbach, L. J. (1975). Five decades of public controversy over mental testing. *American Psychologist, 30*, 1–14.

Cronbach, L. J. (1982). *Designing evaluations of educational and social programs*. San Francisco: Jossey-Bass.

Cronbach, L. J. (1990). *Essentials of psychological testing* (5th ed.) New York: Harper & Row.

Cronbach, L. J., & Gleser, G. C. (1957). *Psychological tests and personnel decisions*. Urbana: University of Illinois Press.

Cronbach, L. J., & Snow, R. E. (1977). *Aptitudes and instructional methods: A handbook for research on interactions*. New York: Irvington.

Csikszentmihalyi, M. (1975). *Beyond anxiety and boredom: The experience of play in work and games*. San Francisco: Jossey-Bass.

Csikszentmihalyi, M. (1997). *Finding flow: The psychology of engagement in everyday life*. New York: Basic Books.

Csikszentmihalyi, M., Rathund, K., & Whalen, S. (1993). *Talented teenagers: The roots of success and failure*. Cambridge, England: Cambridge University Press.

Damasio, A. R. (1994). *Descartes' error: Emotion, reason, and the human brain.* New York: Putnam.

Daneman, M., & Carpenter, P. A. (1980). Individual differences in working memory and reading. *Journal of Verbal Learning and Verbal Behavior, 19,* 450–466.

Deary, I. J., & Stough, C. (1996). Intelligence and inspection time. *American Psychologist, 51,* 599–608.

DeCorte, E. (1995). Fostering cognitive growth: A perspective from research on mathematics learning and instruction. *Educational Psychologist, 30,* 37–46.

Demetriou, A., Gustafsson, J.-E., Efklides, A., & Platsidou, M. (1992). Structural systems in developing cognition, science, and education. In A. Demetriou, M. Shayer, & A. Efklides (Eds.), *Neo-Piagetian theories of cognitive development* (pp. 79–103). London: Routledge.

Detterman, D. K. (1986). Human intelligence is a complex system of separate processes. In R. J. Sternberg & D. K. Detterman (Eds.), *What is intelligence?: Contemporary viewpoints on its nature and definition* (pp. 57–61). Norwood, NJ: Ablex.

Dewey, J. (1966). *Democracy and education.* New York: The Free Press. (Original work published 1916)

Digman, J. M. (1990). Personality structure: Emergence of the five-factor model. *Annual Review of Psychology, 41,* 417–440.

Domino, G. (1968). Differential predictions of academic achievement in conforming and independent settings. *Journal of Educational Psychology, 59,* 256–260.

Domino, G. (1971). Interactive effects of achievement orientation and teaching style on academic achievement. *Journal of Educational Psychology, 62,* 427–431.

Domino, G. (1974, August). *Aptitude by treatment interaction effects in college instruction.* Paper presented at the meeting of the American Psychological Association, Albuquerque, NM.

Dowaliby, F., & Schumer, A. (1973). Teacher-centered versus student-centered mode of college classroom instruction as related to manifest anxiety. *Journal of Educational Psychology, 64,* 125–132.

DuBois, P. H. (Ed.). (1947). *The classification program* (Army Air Forces Psychology Program Research Reports, No. 2). Washington, DC: U.S. Government Printing Office.

Dweck, C. S. (1986). Motivational processes affecting learning. *American Psychologist, 41,* 1040–1048.

Dweck, C. S., & Leggett, E. L. (1988). A social-cognitive approach to motivation and personality. *Psychological Review, 95,* 256–273.

Eccles, G., & Wigfield, A. (1995). In the mind of the actor: The structure of adolescents' achievement task values and expectancy-related beliefs. *Personality and Social Psychology Bulletin, 21,* 215–225.

Eisenberger, R. (1992). Learned industriousness. *Psychological Review, 99,* 248–267.

Elawar, M. C., & Corno, L. (1985). A factorial experiment in teachers' written feedback on student homework: Changing teacher behavior a little rather than a lot. *Journal of Educational Psychology, 77,* 162–173.

Elshout, J. J. (1985, June). *Problem solving and education.* Paper presented at the meeting of the European Association for Research on Learning and Instruction, Leuven, Belgium.

Embretson, S. E. (1986). Intelligence and its measurement: Extending contemporary theory to existing tests. In R. J. Sternberg (Ed.), *Advances in the psychology of human intelligence* (Vol. 3, pp. 335–368). Hillsdale, NJ: Lawrence Erlbaum Associates.

English, H. B., & English, A. C. (1958). *A comprehensive dictionary of psychological and psychoanalytical terms.* New York: Longmans Green.

Entwistle, N. (1987). Explaining individual differences in school learning. In E. DeCorte, H. Lodewijks, R. Parmentier, & P. Span (Eds.), *Learning and instruction: European research in an international context* (Vol. 1, pp. 69–88). Leuven, Belgium: Leuven University Press.

Entwistle, N. (1988). Motivational factors in students' approaches to learning. In R. R. Schmeck (Ed.), *Learning styles and strategies* (pp. 21–51). New York: Plenum.

Entwistle, N. J., & Ramsden, P. (1983). *Understanding student learning.* London: Croom Helm.

Epstein, J. (1989). Family structures and student motivation: A developmental perspective. In C. Ames & R. Ames (Eds.), *Research on motivation in education. Vol. 3: Goals and cognitions* (pp. 259–295). San Diego: Academic Press.

Ericsson, K. A., & Smith, J. (Eds.). (1991). *Toward a general theory of expertise: Prospects and limits.* Cambridge, England: Cambridge University Press.

Estes, W. K. (1974). Learning theory and intelligence. *American Psychologist, 29,* 740–749.

Feuerstein, R., Klein, P. S., & Tannenbaum, A. J. (Eds.). (1991). *Mediated learning experience (MLE): Theoretical, psychosocial and learning implications.* London: Freund.

Flavell, J. (1963). *The developmental psychology of Jean Piaget.* Princeton, NJ: Van Nostrand.

Fleishman, E. A., & Reilly, M. E. (1992). *Handbook of human abilities: Definitions, measurements, and job task requirements.* Palo Alto, CA: Consulting Psychologists Press.

Flynn, J. R. (1984). The mean IQ of Americans: Massive gains 1932 to 1978. *Psychological Bulletin, 95,* 29–51.

Flynn, J. R. (1987). Massive IQ gains in 14 nations: What IQ tests really measure. *Psychological Bulletin, 101,* 171–191.

Ford, M. E., & Tisak, M. S. (1983). A further search for social intelligence. *Journal of Educational Psychology, 75,* 196–206.

Frederiksen, J. R., & Warren, B. M. (1987). A cognitive framework for developing expertise in reading. In R. Glaser (Ed.), *Advances in instructional psychology* (Vol. 3, pp. 1–39). Hillsdale, NJ: Lawrence Erlbaum Associates.

Frederiksen, N., Carlson, S., & Ward, W. C. (1984). The place of social intelligence in a taxonomy of cognitive abilities. *Intelligence, 8,* 315–337.

French, E. G. (1958). Effects of the interaction of motivation and feedback on task performance. In J. W. Atkinson (Ed.), *Motives in fantasy, action* (pp. 400–408). Princeton, NJ: Van Nostrand.

Fuster, J. M. (1997). Network memory. *Trends in Neurosciences, 20,* 451–459.

Gage, N. L. (1985). *Hard gains in the soft sciences: The case of pedagogy.* Bloomington, IN: Phi Delta Kappan.

Gagné, R. M., Briggs, L. J., & Wagner, W. W. (1988). *Principles of instructional design* (3rd ed.). New York: Holt, Rinehart & Winston.

Gale, A., Strelau, J., & Farley, F. H. (1986). Introduction: Overview and critique. In J. Strelau, F. H. Farley, & A. Gale (Eds.), *The biological bases of personality and behavior* (Vol. 2, pp. 1–22). Washington, DC: Hemisphere.

Galton, F. (1869). *Hereditary genius: An inquiry into its laws and consequences.* London: Macmillan.

Galton, F. (1883). *Inquiries into human faculty and its development.* London: Macmillan.

The gaming of violence. (1999, April 30). *The New York Times,* p. A30.

Gardner, H. (1983). *Frames of mind: The theory of multiple intelligences.* New York: Basic Books.

Gardner, H. (1985). *The mind's new science: A history of the cognitive revolution.* New York: Basic Books.

Gardner, H. (1993). *Multiple intelligences: The theory in practice.* New York: Basic Books.

Gardner, H. (1999). What is intelligence? [Response to letters to the editor]. *Atlantic Monthly, 283*(5), 13.

Gibson, J. J. (1979). *The ecological approach to visual perception.* Boston: Houghton Mifflin.

Gibson, J. J. (1986). *The senses considered as perceptual systems.* Boston: Houghton Mifflin.

Gibson, J. T., & Haritos-Fatouros, M. (1985). The education of a torturer. *Psychology Today, 20*(11), 50–58.

Gitomer, D. H., Curtis, M. E., Glaser, R., & Lensky, D. B. (1987). Processing differences as a function of item difficulty in verbal analogy performance. *Journal of Educational Psychology, 79,* 212–219.

Goldman-Rakic, P. S. (1987). Circuitry of the prefrontal cortex and the regulation of behavior by representational memory. In F. Plum & V. Mountcastle (Eds.), *Handbook of physiology: Sec. 1. The nervous system* (Vol. 5, pp. 373–417). Bethesda. MD: American Physiological Society.

Goleman, D. (1995). *Emotional intelligence: Why it can matter more than IQ.* New York: Bantam.

Gollwitzer, P. M. (1996). The volitional benefits of planning. In P. M. Gollwitzer & J. A. Bargh (Eds.), *The psychology of action: Linking cognition and motivation to behavior* (pp. 287–312). New York: Guilford.

Gollwitzer, P. M. (1999). Implementation intentions: Strong effects of simple plans. *American Psychologist, 54,* 493–503.

Gollwitzer, P. M., & Brandstatter, V. (1997). Implementation intentions and effective goal pursuit. *Journal of Personality and Social Psychology, 73,* 186–199.

Gordon, L. V. (1953). *Gordon Personal Profile Manual.* Yonkers, NY: World Book.

Gough, H. G. (1987). *California Psychological Inventory* (3rd ed.). Palo Alto: Consulting Psychologists Press.

Gould, S. J. (1981). *The mismeasure of man.* New York: Norton.

Gould, S. J. (1994, November 28). Curveball [Review of R. J. Herrnstein & C. Murray, *The bell curve: Intelligence and class structure in American life*]. *The New Yorker, 70*(39), 139–149.

Gould, S. J. (2000). Deconstructing the "science wars" by reconstructing an old mold. *Science, 287,* 253–261.

Greeno, J. G. (1978). A study of problem solving. In R. Glaser (Ed.), *Advances in instructional psychology* (Vol. 1, pp. 13–75). Hillsdale, NJ: Lawrence Erlbaum Associates.

Greeno, J. G. (1994). Gibson's affordances. *Psychological Review, 101*, 336–342.

Greeno, J. G. (1997). Theories and practices of thinking and learning to think. *American Journal of Education, 106*, 85–126.

Greeno, J. G., Collins, A. M., & Resnick, L. B. (1996). Cognition and learning. In D. C. Berliner & R. C. Calfee (Eds.), *Handbook of educational psychology* (pp. 15–46). New York: Macmillan.

Greeno, J. G., & the Middle School Mathematics Theory Application Project. (1998). The situativity of knowing, learning, and research. *American Psychologist, 53*, 5–26.

Grigorenko, E. L., & Sternberg, R. J. (1993). Thinking styles. In D. H. Saklofske & M. Zeidner (Eds.), *International handbook of personality and intelligence* (pp. 205–229). New York: Plenum.

Grigorenko, E. L., & Sternberg, R. J. (1997). Styles of thinking, abilities, and academic performance. *Exceptional Children, 63*, 295–312.

Grigorenko, E. L., & Sternberg, R. (1998a). Dynamic testing. *Psychological Bulletin, 124*, 75–111.

Grigorenko, E. L., & Sternberg, R. (1998b). "Dynamic testing": Erratum. *Psychological Bulletin, 124*, 443.

Grossman, D. (1996). *On killing: The psychological cost of learning to kill in war and society*. New York: Little, Brown.

Guilford, J. P. (1967). *The nature of human intelligence*. New York: McGraw-Hill.

Guilford, J. P. (1981). Higher-order structure-of-intellect abilities. *Multivariate Behavioral Research, 16*, 411–435.

Guilford, J. P. (1985). The structure of intellect model. In B. B. Wolman (Ed.), *Handbook of intelligence: Theories, measurements, and applications* (pp. 225–266). New York: Wiley.

Guilford, J. P., & Zimmerman, W. S. (1949). *The Guilford–Zimmerman Temperament Survey*. Beverly Hills, CA: Sheridan Supply Co.

Gustafsson, J.-E. (1988). Hierarchical models of the structure of cognitive abilities. In R. J. Sternberg (Ed.), *Advances in the psychology of human intelligence* (Vol. 4, pp. 35—71). Hillsdale, NJ: Lawrence Erlbaum Associates.

Gustafsson, J.-E. (1999). Measuring and understanding G: Experimental and correlational approaches. In P. L. Ackerman, P. C. Kyllonen, & R. D. Roberts (Eds.), *Learning and individual differences: Process, trait, and content determinants* (pp. 275–289). Washington, DC: American Psychological Association.

Gustafsson, J.-E. (2001). Measurement from a hierarchical point of view. In H. Braun, D. N. Jackson, & D. E. Wiley (Eds.), *Under construction: The role of constructs in psychological and educational measurement*. Mahwah, NJ: Lawrence Erlbaum Associates.

Gustafsson, J.-E. (2001). On the hierarchical structure of personality and ability. In J. Collis & S. Messick (Eds.), *Intelligence and personality: Bridging the gap in theory and measurement* (pp. XXX–XXX). Mahwah, NJ: Lawrence Erlbaum Associates.

Gustafsson, J.-E., & Balke, G. (1993). General and specific abilities as predictors of school achievement. *Multivariate Behavioral Research, 28*, 407–434.

Gustafsson, J.-E., & Undheim, J. O. (1996). Individual differences in cognitive functions. In D. C. Berliner & R. C. Calfee (Eds.), *Handbook of educational psychology* (pp. 186–242). New York: Macmillan.

Guttman, L. (1954). A new approach to factor analysis: The radex. In P. F. Lazarfield (Ed.), *Mathematical thinking in the social sciences* (pp. 258–348) Glencoe, IL: The Free Press.

Guttman, L. (1965). The structure of interrelations among intelligence tests. In *Proceedings of the 1964 Invitational Conference on Testing Problems* (pp. 25–36). Princeton, NJ: Educational Testing Service.

Hamilton, L. S., Nussbaum, E. M., Kupermintz, H., Kerkhoven, J. I. M., & Snow, R. E. (1995). Enhancing the validity and usefulness of large-scale educational assessments: II. NELS:88 science achievement. *American Educational Research Journal, 32,* 555–581.

Hamilton, L. S., Nussbaum, E. M., & Snow, R. E. (1994). Interview procedures for validating science assessments. *Applied Measurement in Education, 10,* 181–200.

Haritos-Fatouros, M. (1983a). *Antecedent conditions leading to the behavior of a torturer: Fallacy or reality?* Unpublished report, University of Thessaloniki, Greece.

Haritos-Fatouros, M. (1983b). *The official torturer: Learning mechanisms involved in the process: Relevance to democratic and totalitarian regimes today.* Unpublished report, University of Thessaloniki, Thessaloniki, Greece.

Harlow, L. L., Mulaik, S. A., & Steiger, J. H. (1997). *What if there were no significance tests?* Mahwah, NJ: Lawrence Erlbaum Associates.

Hartshorne, H., & May, M. A. (1928). *Studies of the nature of character: I. Studies in deceit.* New York: Macmillan.

Heckhausen, H. (1991). *Motivation and action.* Berlin: Springer.

Heckhausen, H., & Kuhl, J. (1985). From wishes to action: The dead ends and short-cuts on the long way to action. In M. Frese & J. Sabini (Eds.), *Goal-directed behavior: Psychological theory and research on action* (pp. 134–160). Hillsdale, NJ: Lawrence Erlbaum Associates.

Heckhausen, H., Schmalt, H. D., & Schneider, R. (1985). *Achievement motivation in perspective.* Orlando, FL: Academic Press.

Hepburn, L., & Eysenck, M. W. (1989). Personality, average mood and mood variability. *Personality and Individual Differences, 10,* 975–983.

Hilgard, E. R. (1980). The trilogy of mind: Cognition, affection, and conation. *Journal of the History of Behavioral Sciences, 16,* 107–117.

Hirschfeld, L. A., & Gelman, S. A. (Eds.). (1994). *Mapping the mind.* Cambridge, England: Cambridge University Press.

Hoban, C. F., Jr., & Van Ormer, E. B. (1950). *Instructional film research (rapid mass learning), 1918–1950* (Tech. Rep. No. SDC 269-7-19). Port Washington, NY: U.S. Navy Special Devices Center.

Hofstadter, R. (1955). *Social Darwinism in American thought* (Rev. ed.). Boston: Beacon.

Hofstee, W. K. B., DeRadd, B., & Goldberg, L. R. (1992). Integration of the Big Five and circumplex approaches to trait structure. *Journal of Personality and Social Psychology, 63,* 146–163.

Horn, J. L. (1989). Cognitive diversity: A framework of learning. In P. L. Ackerman, R. J. Sternberg, & R. Glaser (Eds.), *Learning and individual differences* (pp. 61–116). New York: Freeman.

Horn, J. L., & Cattell, R. B. (1966). Refinement and test of the theory of fluid and crystallized general intelligences. *Journal of Educational Psychology, 57,* 253–270.

Horn, J. L., Donaldson, G., & Engstrom, R. (1981). Apprehension, memory, and fluid intelligence decline in adulthood. *Research on Aging, 3*, 33–84.

Horn, J., & Noll, J. (1994). A system for understanding cognitive capabilities: A theory and the evidence on which it is based. In D. K. Detterman (Ed.), *Theories of intelligence* (pp. 151–204). Norwood, NJ: Ablex.

Humphreys, L. G. (1971). Theory of intelligence. In R. Cancro (Ed.), *Intelligence: Genetic and environmental influences* (pp. 31–42). New York: Grune & Stratton.

Humphreys, L. G. (1979). The construct of general intelligence. *Intelligence, 3*, 105–120.

Humphreys, L. G. (1984). A rose is not a rose: A rival view of intelligence. *Behavioral and Brain Sciences, 7*, 292–293.

Hunt, E. B., Frost, N., & Lunneborg, C. (1973). Individual differences in cognition: A new approach to intelligence. In G. Bower (Ed.), *The psychology of learning and motivation* (Vol. 7, pp. 87–122). New York: Academic Press.

Hunt, E., & Lansman, M. (1982). Unified model of attention and problem solving. *Psychological Review, 93*, 446–461.

Hunt, E., & MacLeod, C. M. (1978). The sentence-verification paradigm: A case study of two conflicting approaches to individual differences. *Intelligence, 2*, 129–144.

Hunt, J. M. (1961). *Intelligence and experience.* New York: Ronald.

Huttenlocher, J., Levine, S., & Vevea, J. (1998). Environmental input and cognitive growth: A study using time-period comparisons. *Child Development, 69*, 1012–1029.

Isen, A., Daubman, K. A., & Gorgolione, J. M. (1987). The influence of positive affect on cognitive organization: Implication for education. In R. E. Snow & M. J. Farr (Eds.), *Aptitude, learning, and instruction* (Vol. 3, pp. 143–162). Hillsdale, NJ: Lawrence Erlbaum Associates.

Jackson, D. N. (1984). *Personality Research Form.* Port Huron, MI: Sigma Assessment Systems.

James, W. (1983). *The principles of psychology.* Cambridge, MA: Harvard University Press. (Original work published 1890)

Jefferson, T. (1955). *Notes on the State of Virginia.* Chapel Hill: University of North Carolina Press. (Original work published 1787)

Jenkins, J. J. (1989). The more things change, the more they stay the same: Comments from an historical perspective. In R. E. Kanfer & P. L. Ackerman (Eds.), *Abilities, motivation, and methodology: The Minnesota Symposium on Learning and Individual Differences* (pp. 475–491). Hillsdale, NJ: Lawrence Erlbaum Associates.

Jensen, A. R. (1982). The chronometry of intelligence. In R. J. Sternberg (Ed.), *Advances in the psychology of human intelligence* (Vol. 1, pp. 255–310) Hillsdale, NJ: Lawrence Erlbaum Associates.

Jensen, A. R. (1992). Commentary: Vehicles of *g. Psychological Science, 3*, 275–278.

Jensen, A. R. (1998). *The g factor.* Westport, CT: Praeger.

John, O. P. (1990). The "Big Five" factor taxonomy: Dimensions of personality in the natural language and in questionnaires. In L. A. Pervin (Ed.), *Handbook of personality theory and research* (pp. 66–100). New York: Guilford.

Kanfer, R. (1996). Self-regulatory and other non-ability determinants of skill acquisition. In P. M. Gollwitzer & J. A. Bargh (Eds.), *The psychology of ac-*

tion: Linking cognition and motivation to behavior (pp. 404–423). New York: Guilford.

Kanfer, R., & Ackerman, P. L. (1989a). Dynamics of skill acquisition: Building a bridge between intelligence and motivation. In R. J. Sternberg (Ed.), *Advances in the psychology of human intelligence* (Vol. 5, pp. 83–134), Hillsdale, NJ: Lawrence Erlbaum Associates.

Kanfer, R., & Ackerman, P. L. (1989b). Motivation and cognitive abilities: An integrative/aptitude-treatment interaction approach to skill acquisition. *Journal of Applied Psychology, 74,* 657–690.

Kanfer, R., Ackerman, P. L., & Cudeck, R. (Eds.). (1989). *Abilities, motivation, and methodology: The Minnesota Symposium on Learning and Individual Differences.* Hillsdale, NJ: Lawrence Erlbaum Associates.

Kanfer, R., Dugdale, B., & McDonald, B. (1994). Empirical findings on the Action Control Scale in the context of complex skill acquisition. In J. Kuhl & J. Beckmann (Eds.), *Volition and personality: Action versus state orientation* (pp. 61–77). Göttingen, Germany: Hogrefe.

Kelso, J. A. S. (1995). *Dynamic patterns: The self-organization of brain and behavior.* Cambridge, MA: MIT Press.

Kimberg, D. A., & Farah, M. J. (1993). A unified account of cognitive impairments following frontal lobe damage: The role of working memory in complex, organized behavior. *Journal of Experimental Psychology: General, 122,* 411–428.

Kirk, R. E. (1996). Practical significance: A concept whose time has come. *Educational and Psychological Measurement, 56,* 746–759.

Kleckley, K. (1997). The intelligences, in Gardner's words. *Educational Leadership, 55(1),* 12.

Klinger, E. (1996). Emotional influences on cognitive processing, with implications for theories of both. In P. M. Gollwitzer & J. A. Bargh (Eds.), *The psychology of action: Linking cognition and motivation to behavior* (pp. 168–189). New York: Guilford.

Klonowicz, T. (1986). Reactivity and performance: The third side of the coin. In J. Strelau, F. H. Farley, & A. Gale (Eds.), *The biological bases of personality and behavior* (Vol. 2, pp. 119–126). Washington, DC: Hemisphere.

Krathwohl, D. R., Bloom, B. S., & Masia, B. (1964). *Taxonomy of educational objectives: The affective domain.* New York: McKay.

Kuhl, J. (1981). Motivational and functional helplessness: The moderating effect of state versus action orientation. *Journal of Personality and Social Psychology, 40,* 155–170.

Kuhl, J. (1982). The expectancy-value approach in the theory of social motivation: Elaborations, extensions, critique. In N. T. Feather (Ed.), *Expectations and actions: Expectancy-value models in psychology* (pp. 125–160). Hillsdale, NJ: Lawrence Erlbaum Associates.

Kuhl, J. (1984). Volitional aspects of achievement motivation and learned helplessness: Toward a comprehensive theory of action control. In B. A. Maher (Ed.), *Progress in experimental personality research* (Vol. 12, pp. 99–170). New York: Academic Press.

Kuhl, J. (1985). Volitional mediators of cognition-behavior consistency: Self-regulatory processes and action versus state orientation. In J. Kuhl & J. Beckman (Eds.), *Action control: From cognition to behavior* (pp. 101–128). New York: Springer.

Kuhl, J. (1993). The Self-Regulation-Test-for-Children (SRTC). In F. E. Weinert & W. Schneider (Eds.), *The Munich longitudinal study on the genesis of individual competencies (LOGIC)* (Rep. No. 9, pp. 12–19). Munich, Germany: Max Planck Institute for Psychological Research.

Kuhl, J. (2000). A functional-design approach to motivation and volition: The dynamics of personality systems interactions. In M. Boekaerts, P. R. Pintrich, & M. Zeidner (Eds.), *Self-regulation: Directions and challenges for future research* (pp. 111–169). San Diego: Academic Press.

Kuhl, J., & Kazén-Saad, M. (1989). Volition and self-regulation: Memory mechanisms mediating the maintenance of intentions. In W. A. Hersberger (Ed.), *Volitional action* (pp. 387–407). Dordrecht, Netherlands: Martinus Nijhoff.

Kuhl, J., & Kraska, K. (1989). Self-regulation and metamotivation: Computational mechanisms, development, and assessment. In R. Kanfer, P. L. Ackerman, & R. Cudeck (Eds.) *Abilities, motivation, and methodology: The Minnesota Symposium on Learning and Individual Differences* (pp. 343–374). Hillsdale, NJ: Lawrence Erlbaum Associates.

Kulik, J. A. (1981, April). *Integrating findings from different levels of instruction.* Paper presented at the annual meeting of the American Educational Research Association, Los Angeles.

Kupermintz, H., Ennis, M. N., Hamilton, L. S., Talbert, J. E., & Snow, R. E. (1995). Enhancing the validity and usefulness of large-scale educational assessments: I. NELS:88 mathematics achievement. *American Educational Research Journal, 32,* 525–554.

Kyllonen, P. C., & Christal, R. E. (1990). Reasoning ability is (little more than) working-memory capacity? *Intelligence, 14,* 389–433.

Kyllonen, P. C., Lohman, D. F., & Woltz, D. J. (1984). Componential modeling of alternative strategies for performing spatial tasks. *Journal of Educational Psychology, 76,* 1325–1345.

Kyllonen, P. C., & Shute, V. J. (1989). A taxonomy of learning skills. In P. L. Ackerman, R. J. Sternberg, & R. Glaser (Eds.), *Learning and individual differences* (pp. 117–163). New York: Freeman.

Lajoie, S. P. (1986). Individual differences in spatial ability: A computerized tutor for orthographic projection tasks (Doctoral dissertation, Stanford University, 1986). *Dissertation Abstracts International, 47A,* 3370.

Lajoie, S. P., & Lesgold, A. M. (1992). Apprenticeship training in the workplace: Computer-coached practice environment as a new form of apprenticeship. In M. J. Farr & J. Psotka (Eds.), *Intelligent instruction by computer: Theory and practice* (pp. 15–36). Philadelphia: Taylor & Francis.

Lambrechts, L. (n.d.). *Psychological selection of divers.* Oostende: Belgium: Belgian Navy Hyperbaric Medical Center.

Lander, E. S., & Weinberg, R. A. (2000). Genomics. *Science, 287,* 1777–1782.

Langer, E. J. (1989). *Mindfulness.* Reading, MA: Addison-Wesley.

Lenning, O. T. (1975). *Predictive validity of the ACT tests at selective colleges* (ACT Research Rep. No. 69). Iowa City: American College Testing Program.

Lidz, C. S. (Ed.). (1987). *Dynamic assessment.* New York: Guilford.

Lidz, C. S. (1991). *Practitioner's guide to dynamic testing.* New York: Guilford.

Lohman, D. F. (1979). Spatial ability: Individual differences in speed and level (Doctoral dissertation, Stanford University, 1979). *Dissertation Abstracts International,* 40A, p. 3898. (NTIS ERIC ED 195 573; No. AD-A075 973)

Lohman, D. F. (1988). Spatial abilities as traits, processes, and knowledge. In R. J. Sternberg (Ed.), *Advances in the psychology of human intelligence* (Vol. 4, pp. 181–248). Hillsdale, NJ: Lawrence Erlbaum Associates.

Lohman, D. F., & Rocklin, T. (1995). Current and recurring issues in the assessment of intelligence and personality. In H. D. Saklofske & M. Zeidner (Eds.), *International handbook of personality and intelligence* (pp. 447–474). New York: Plenum.

Lubinsky, D. (2000). Scientific and social significance of assessing individual differences: Sinking shafts at a few critical points. *Annual Review of Psychology, 51,* 405–444.

Lubinsky, D., & Benbow, C. P. (1995). An opportunity for empiricism [Review of *Multiple intelligences*]. *Contemporary Psychology, 40,* 935–937.

Maehr, M., & Midgley, C. (1991). Enhancing student motivation: A schoolwide approach. *Educational Psychologist, 26,* 399–427.

Magnusson, D., & Endler, N. S. (Eds.). (1977). *Personality at the crossroads: Current issues in interactional psychology.* Hillsdale, NJ: Lawrence Erlbaum Associates.

Mandinach, E. B. (1984). The role of strategic planning and self-regulation in learning an intellectual computer game. (Doctoral dissertation, Stanford University, 1984). *Dissertation Abstracts International, 45A,* 1693.

Mandinach, E. B. (1987). Clarifying the "A" in CAI for learners of different abilities. *Journal of Educational Computing Research, 3,* 113–128.

Mandinach, E. B., & Corno, L. (1985). Cognitive engagement variations among students of different ability level and sex in a computer problem solving game. *Sex Roles, 13,* 241–251.

Marshalek, B., Lohman, D. F., & Snow, R. E. (1983). The complexity continuum in the radex and hierarchical models of intelligence. *Intelligence, 7,* 107–128.

Martin, B. L., & Reigeluth, C. M. (1999). Affective education and the affective domain: Implications for instructional design theories and models. In C. M. Reigeluth (Ed.), *Instructional design theories and models: Vol. II. A new paradigm of instructional theory* (pp. 485–510). Mahwah, NJ: Lawrence Erlbaum Associates.

Marton, F., Hounsell, D. S., & Entwistle, N. J. (1984). *The experience of learning.* Edinburgh: Scottish Academic Press.

Mayr, E. (1982). *The growth of biological thought.* Cambridge, MA: Belknap.

McKay, H., Sinisterra, L., McKay, A., Gomez, B., & Lloreda, P. (1978). Improving cognitive ability in chronically deprived children. *Science, 200,* 270–278.

Meichenbaum, D. (1977). *Cognitive-behavior modification: An integrative approach.* New York: Plenum.

Messick, S. (1987). Structural relationships across cognition, personality, and style. In R. E. Snow & M. J. Farr (Eds.), *Aptitude, learning, and instruction: Vol. 3. Conative and affective process analysis* (pp. 35–76). Hillsdale, NJ: Lawrence Erlbaum Associates.

Messick, S. (1992). Multiple intelligences or multilevel intelligence? Selective emphasis on distinctive properties of hierarchy: On Gardner's *Frames of mind* and Sternberg's *Beyond IQ* in the context of theory and research on the structure of human abilities. *Psychological Inquiry, 3,* 365–384.

Messick, S. (1994). The matter of style: Manifestations of personality in cognition, learning, and teaching. *Educational Psychologist, 29,* 121–136.

Michaels, C. F., & Carello, C. (1981). *Direct perception.* New York: Appleton–Century–Crofts.

Middleton, M. J., & Midgley, C. (1997). Avoiding the demonstration of lack of ability: An underexplored aspect of goal theory. *Journal of Educational Psychology, 89,* 710–718.

Miller, N. E. (1957). Graphic communication and the crisis in education [Special issue]. *Audio Visual Communication Review, 5*(3).

Mischel, W., & Shoda, Y. (1995). A cognitive-affective system theory of personality: Reconceptualizing situations, dispositions, dynamics, and invariance in personality structure. *Psychological Review, 102,* 246–68.

Mischel, W., & Shoda, Y. (1998). Reconciling processing dynamics and personality dispositions. *Annual Review of Psychology, 49,* 229–258.

Moos, R. H. (1979). *Evaluating educational environments.* San Francisco: Jossey-Bass.

Mulholland, T. M., Pellegrino, J. W., & Glaser, R. (1980). Components of geometric analogy solution. *Cognitive Psychology, 12,* 252–284.

Murray, H. A. (1938). *Explorations in personality.* New York: Oxford University Press.

Murtha, T. C., Kanfer, R., & Ackerman, P. L. (1996). Toward an interactionist taxonomy of personality and situations: An integrative situational-dispositional representation of personality traits. *Journal of Personality and Social Psychology, 71,* 193–207.

Namiki, H. (1997). *Interaction between individuality and educational environments: A task for educational psychology.* Tokyo: Baifukan.

Newell, A. (1980). Reasoning, problem-solving, and decision processes: The problem space as a fundamental category. In R. Nickerson (Ed.), *Attention and performance VIII* (pp. 693–718). Hillsdale, NJ: Lawrence Erlbaum Associates.

Newell, A., & Simon, H. A. (1961). Computer simulation of human thinking. *Science, 134,* 2011–2017.

OSS Assessment Staff. (1948). *Assessment of men.* New York: Holt, Rinehart & Winston.

Oxford English Dictionary. (1971). Oxford, England: Oxford University Press.

Pace, C. R., & Stern, G. G. (1958). An approach to the measurement of psychological characteristics of college environments. *Journal of Educational Psychology, 49,* 269–277.

Pascarella, E. T. (1978). Interactive effects of prior mathematics preparation and level of instructional support in college calculus. *American Educational Research Journal, 15,* 275–285.

Pellegrino, J. W. (1985). Inductive reasoning ability. In R. J. Sternberg (Ed.), *Human abilities: An information-processing approach* (pp. 195–225). San Francisco: Freeman.

Pellegrino, J. W., & Glaser, R. (1980). Components of inductive reasoning. In R. E. Snow, P.-A. Federico, & W. F. Montague (Eds.), *Aptitude, learning, and instruction: Vol. 1. Cognitive process analyses of aptitude* (pp. 177–217). Hillsdale, NJ: Lawrence Erlbaum Associates.

Pellegrino, J. W., & Glaser, R. (1982). Analyzing aptitudes for learning: Inductive reasoning. In R. Glaser (Ed.), *Advances in instructional psychology* (Vol. 2, pp. 269–345). Hillsdale, NJ: Lawrence Erlbaum Associates.

Pellegrino, J. W., & Lyon, D. R. (1979). The components of a componential analysis [Review of the book *Intelligence, information processing and ana-*

logical reasoning: The componential analysis of human abilities]. *Intelligence, 3,* 169–186.

Perkins, D. N., Jay, E., & Tishman, S. (1993). New conceptions of thinking: From ontology to education. *Educational Psychologist, 28,* 67–85.

Pervin, L. A. (1994). A critical analysis of current trait theory. *Psychological Inquiry, 5,* 103–113.

Peterson, P. L. (1976). Interactive effects of student anxiety, achievement orientation, and teacher behavior on student achievement and attitude (Doctoral dissertation, Stanford University, 1976). *Dissertation Abstracts International, 37A,* 2750.

Peterson, P. L. (1977). Interactive effects of student anxiety, achievement orientation, and teacher behavior on student achievement and attitude. *Journal of Educational Psychology, 69,* 779–792.

Peterson, P. L. (1979). Aptitude × treatment interaction effects of teacher structuring and student participation in college instruction. *Journal of Educational Psychology, 71,* 521–533.

Peterson, P. L. (1988). Selecting students and services for compensatory education: Lessons from aptitude-treatment interaction research. *Educational Psychologist, 23,* 313–352.

Piaget, J. (1969). *Judgment and reasoning in the child.* New York: Harcourt Brace. (Original work published 1928)

Pintrich, P. R. (1989). The dynamic interplay of student motivation and cognition in the college classroom. In C. Ames & M. L. Maehr (Eds.), *Advances in motivation and achievement: Motivation-enhancing environments* (Vol. 6, pp. 117–160). Greenwich, CT: JAI Press.

Pintrich, P. R., & DeGroot, E. V. (1990). Motivational and self-regulated learning components of classroom academic performance. *Journal of Educational Psychology, 82,* 33–40.

Pintrich, P. R., & Garcia, T. (1991). Student goal orientation and self-regulation in the college classroom. In M. L. Maehr & P. R. Pintrich (Eds.), *Advances in motivation and achievement* (Vol. 7, pp. 371–402). Greenwich, CT: JAI.

Pintrich, P. R., & Schunk, D. H. (1996). *Motivation in education: Theory, research, and applications.* Englewood Cliffs, NJ: Prentice-Hall.

Porteus, A. W. (1976). Teacher-centered vs. student-centered instruction: Interactions with cognitive and motivational aptitudes (Doctoral dissertation, Stanford University, 1976). *Dissertation Abstracts International, 37A,* 6376.

Posner, M. I., & Mitchell, R. F. (1967). Chronometric analysis of classification. *Psychological Review, 74,* 392–409.

Potter, S. C. (Ed.). (1996). Multiple intelligences. *Bulletin of the National Association of Secondary School Principals, 80,* 1–86.

Prabhakaran, V., Smith, J. A. L., Desmond, J. E., Glover, G. H., & Gabrieli, J. D. E. (1997). Neural substrates of fluid reasoning: An IMRI study of neocortical activation during performance of the Raven's Progressive Matrices Test. *Cognitive Psychology, 33,* 43–63.

Pressley, M., Goodchild, F., Fleet, J., Zajchowski, R., & Evans, D. E. (1989). The challenge of classroom strategy instruction. *Elementary School Journal, 89,* 301–342.

Quartz, S., & Sejnowski, T. J. (1997). The neural basis of cognitive development: A constructivist manifesto. *Behavioral and Brain Sciences, 20,* 537–596.

Ramey, C. T., & Campbell, F. A. (1984). Preventive education for high-risk children: Cognitive consequences of the Carolina Abecedarian Project. *American Journal of Mental Deficiency, 88,* 515–523.

Ramist, L., Lewis, C., & McCamley, L. (1990). Implications of using freshman GPA as the criterion for the predictive validity of the SAT. In W. W. Willingham, C. Lewis, R. Morgan, & L. Ramist, *Predicting college grades: An analysis of institutional trends over two decades* (pp. 253–288). Princeton, NJ: Educational Testing Service.

Ramist, L., Lewis, C., & McCamley-Jenkins, L. (1994). *Student group differences in predicting college grades: Sex, language, and ethnic groups* (College Board Report No. 93-1). New York: College Entrance Examination Board.

Randi, J., & Corno, L. (2000). Teacher innovations in self-regulated learning. In M. Boekaerts, P. R. Pintrich, & M. Zeidner (Eds.), *Handbook of self-regulation* (pp. 651–686). San Diego: Academic Press.

Ree, M. J., & Earles, J. A. (1997). Predicting occupational criteria: Not much more than *g.* In I. Dennis & P. Tapsfield (Eds.), *Human abilities: Their nature and measurement* (pp. 151–165). Mahwah, NJ: Lawrence Erlbaum Associates.

Reigeluth, C. M. (Ed.). (1983). *Instructional design theories and models: Vol. 1. An overview of their current status.* Hillsdale, NJ: Lawrence Erlbaum Associates.

Reigeluth, C. M. (Ed.). (1999). *Instructional design theories and models: Vol. II. A new paradigm of instructional theory.* Mahwah, NJ: Lawrence Erlbaum Associates.

Resnick, L. B. (1987). *Education and learning to think.* Washington, DC: National Academy Press.

Resnick, L. B. (1994). Situated rationalism: Biological and social preparation for learning. In L. A. Hirschfeld & S. A. Gelman (Eds.), *Mapping the mind: Domain specificity in cognition and culture* (pp. 474–493). New York: Cambridge University Press.

Risemberg, R., & Zimmerman, B. J. (1992). Self-regulated learning in gifted students. *Roeper Review, 15,* 98–101.

Roberts, R. D. (1995). *Speed of processing within the structure of human cognitive abilities.* Unpublished doctoral dissertation, University of Sydney, Sydney, Australia.

Ross, S. M., & Rakow, E. A. (1981). Learner control versus program control as adaptive strategies for selection of instructional support on math rules. *Journal of Educational Psychology, 73,* 745–753.

Rubin, L. J. (1973). *Facts and feelings in the classroom: Views on the role of the emotions in successful learning.* New York: Viking.

Salomon, G. (1981). *Communication and education: Social and psychological interactions.* Beverly Hills, CA: Sage.

Salomon, G. (1983). The differential investment of mental effort in learning from different sources. *Educational Psychologist, 18,* 42–50.

Salomon, G. (1984). Television is "easy" and print is "tough": The differential investment of mental effort in learning as a function of perceptions and attributions. *Journal of Educational Psychology, 76,* 647–658.

Salomon, G., & Leigh, T. (1984). Predispositions about learning from print and television. *Journal of Communication, 20,* 119–135.

Salthouse, T. A., Babcock, R. L., Mitchell, D. R., Palmon, R., & Skovronek, E. (1990). Sources of individual differences in spatial visualization ability. *Intelligence, 14,* 187–230.

Schank, R. C. (1978). *Interestingness: Controlling inferences* (Computer Science Research Rep. No. 145). New Haven, CT: Yale University.

Schank, R. C. (1980). How much intelligence is there in artificial intelligence? *Intelligence, 4,* 1–14.

Schank, R. C. (1984). *The explanation game* (Computer Science Research Rep. No. 307). New Haven, CT: Yale University.

Schank, R. C., & Joseph, D. M. (1998). Intelligent schooling. In R. M. Sternberg & W. M. Williams (Eds.), *Intelligence, instruction, and assessment* (pp. 67–94). Mahwah, NJ: Lawrence Erlbaum Associates.

Scheffler, I. (1985). *Of human potential.* Boston: Routledge & Kegan Paul.

Schmeck, R. R., Ribich, F., & Ramanaiah, N. V. (1977). Development of a self-report inventory for assessing individual differences in learning processes. *Applied Psychological Measurement, 1,* 413–431.

Schmitt, A. P., & Crocker, L. (1981, April). *Improving examinee performance on multiple choice tests.* Paper presented at the annual meeting of the American Educational Research Association, Los Angeles.

Schoenfeld, A. H. (1999). Looking toward the 21st century: Challenges of educational theory and practice. *Educational Researcher, 28*(7), 4–14.

Schunk, D. H., & Rice, J. M. (1985). Verbalizations of comprehension strategies: Effects on children's achievement outcomes. *Human Learning: Journal of Practical Research Applications, 4,* 1–10.

Schunk, D. H., & Zimmerman, B. J. (Eds.). (1994). *Self-regulation of learning and performance: Issues and educational applications.* Hillsdale, NJ: Lawrence Erlbaum Associates.

Schunk, D. H., & Zimmerman, B. J. (Eds.). (1998). *Self-regulated learning: From teaching to self-reflective practice.* New York: Guilford.

Schwarz, N., & Bohner, G. (1996). Feelings and their motivational implications: Moods and the action sequence. In P. M. Gollwitzer & J. A. Bargh (Eds.), *The psychology of action: Linking cognition and motivation to behavior* (pp. 119–145). New York: Guilford.

Seibert, W. F., & Snow, R. E. (1965). *Studies in cine-psychometry: I. Preliminary factor analysis of visual cognition and memory* (Final Report, USOE Grant 7-12-0280-184.) Lafayette, IN: Purdue University, Audio Visual Center. (ERIC Document Reproduction Service No. ED 003 624)

Seligman, M. E. P. (1975). *Helplessness: On depression, development, and death.* San Francisco: Freeman.

Sfard, A. (1998). On two metaphors for learning and the dangers of choosing just one. *Educational Researcher, 27*(2), 4–13.

Shoda, Y., Mischel, W., & Peake, P. K. (1990). Predicting adolescent cognitive and self-regulatory competencies from preschool delay of gratification: Identifying diagnostic conditions. *Developmental Psychology, 26,* 978–986.

Shoda, Y., Mischel, W., & Wright, J. C. (1994). Intraindividual stability in the organization and patterning of behavior: Incorporating psychological situations into the idiographic analysis of personality. *Journal of Personality and Social Psychology, 67,* 674–687.

Shrout, P. E., & Fiske, S. T. (Eds.). (1995). *Personality research, methods, and theory: A festschrift honoring Donald W. Fiske.* Hillsdale, NJ: Lawrence Erlbaum Associates.

Simon, D. P., & Simon, H. A. (1978). Individual differences in solving physics problems. In R. S. Siegler (Ed.), *Children's thinking: What develops?* (pp. 325–348). Hillsdale, NJ: Lawrence Erlbaum Associates.

Simon, H. A. (1969). *The sciences of the artificial.* Cambridge, MA: MIT Press.

Simon, H. A. (1976). Identifying basic abilities underlying intelligent performance of complex tasks. In L. B. Resnick (Ed.), *The nature of human intelligence* (pp. 65–98). Hillsdale, NJ: Lawrence Erlbaum Associates.

Simon, H. A. (1982). *Models of bounded rationality.* Cambridge, MA: MIT Press.

Simon, H. A., & Kotovsky, K. (1963). Human acquisition of concepts for sequential patterns. *Psychological Review, 70,* 534–546.

Slavin, R. (1995). *Cooperative learning* (2nd ed.). Boston: Allyn & Bacon.

Smail, W. M. (1938). *Quintilian on education.* Oxford, England: Clarendon.

Snow, R. E. (1963). Effects of learner characteristics on learning from instructional films (Doctoral dissertation, Purdue University, 1963). *Dissertation Abstracts International, 25,* 30.

Snow, R. E. (1973). Theory construction for research on teaching. In R. M. W. Travers (Ed.), *Second handbook of research on teaching* (pp. 77–112). Chicago: Rand McNally.

Snow, R. E. (1974). Representative and quasi-representative designs for research on teaching. *Review of Educational Research, 44,* 265–291.

Snow, R. E. (1977). Individual differences and instructional theory. *Educational Researcher, 6*(10), 11–15.

Snow, R. E. (1978a). Research on aptitudes: A progress report. In L. S. Shulman (Ed.), *Review of research in education* (Vol. 4, pp. 50–105). Itasca, IL: Peacock.

Snow, R. E. (1978b). Theory and method for research on aptitude processes: A prospectus. *Intelligence, 2,* 225–278.

Snow, R. E. (1980a). Aptitude and achievement. In W. B. Schrader (Ed.), *Measuring achievement: Progress over a decade. Proceedings of the 1979 ETS Invitational Conference.* San Francisco: Jossey-Bass. (*New directions for testing and measurement,* No. 5, pp. 39–60)

Snow, R. E. (1980b). Aptitude processes. In R. E. Snow, P.-A. Federico, & W. E. Montague (Eds.), *Aptitude, learning, and instruction: Vol. I. Cognitive process analyses of aptitude* (pp. 27–63). Hillsdale, NJ: Lawrence Erlbaum Associates.

Snow, R. E. (1981). Toward a theory of aptitude for learning: I. Fluid and crystallized abilities and their correlates. In M. P. Friedman, J. P. Das, & N. O'Connor (Eds.), *Intelligence and learning* (pp. 345–362). New York: Plenum.

Snow, R. E. (1984). More on the psychology of divers. *European Scientific Notes, 38,* 524–526.

Snow, R. E. (1985). *Frames of mind: The theory of multiple intelligences* by Howard Gardner. *American Journal of Education, 94,* 109–112.

Snow, R. E. (1987). Aptitude complexes. In R. E. Snow & M. J. Farr (Eds.), *Aptitude, learning, and instruction: Vol. 3. Conative and affective process analyses* (pp. 11–34). Hillsdale, NJ: Lawrence Erlbaum Associates.

Snow, R. E. (1989a). Aptitude-treatment interaction as a framework for research on learning and individual differences. In P. L. Ackerman, R. J. Sternberg, & R. Glaser (Eds.), *Learning and individual differences* (pp. 13–59). New York: Freeman.

Snow, R. E. (1989b). Cognitive-conative aptitude interactions in learning. In R. Kanfer, P. L. Ackerman, & R. A. Cudeck (Eds.), *Abilities, motivation, and methodology: The Minnesota Symposium on Learning and Individual Differences* (pp. 435–474). Hillsdale, NJ: Lawrence Erlbaum Associates.

Snow, R. E. (1990). Progress and propaganda in learning assessment [Review of Lidz, *Dynamic assessment*]. *Contemporary Psychology, 35,* 1134–1136.

Snow, R. E. (1991). The concept of aptitude. In R. E. Snow & D. F. Wiley (Eds.), *Improving inquiry in social science* (pp. 249–284). Hillsdale, NJ: Lawrence Erlbaum Associates.

Snow, R. E. (1992). Aptitude theory: Yesterday, today, and tomorrow. *Education Psychologist, 27,* 5–32.

Snow, R. E. (1994). Abilities in academic tasks. In R. J. Sternberg & R. K. Wagner (Eds.), *Mind in context: Interactionist perspectives on human intelligence* (pp. 3–37). Cambridge, England: Cambridge University Press.

Snow, R. E. (1995). Individual differences and instruction. In T. Husen & T. N. Postlethwaite (Eds.), *International encyclopedia of education* (2nd ed., Vol. 5, pp. 2759–2769). Oxford, England: Pergamon.

Snow, R. E. (1996a). Aptitude development and education. *Psychology, Public Policy, and Law, 2,* 536–560.

Snow, R. E. (1996b). Self-regulation as meta conation? *Learning and Individual Differences, 8,* 261–267.

Snow, R. E. (1997). Aptitudes and symbol systems in adaptive classroom teaching. *Phi Delta Kappan, 78,* 354–360.

Snow, R. E. (1998). Abilities as aptitudes and achievements in learning situations. In J. McArdle & R. Woodcock (Eds.), *Human cognitive abilities in theory and practice* (pp. 93–112). Mahwah, NJ: Lawrence Erlbaum Associates.

Snow, R. E., Corno, L, & Jackson, D., III. (1996). Individual differences in affective and conative functions. In D. C. Berliner & R. C. Calfee (Eds.), *Handbook of educational psychology* (pp. 243–310). New York: Macmillan.

Snow, R. E., & Farr, M. J. (Eds.). (1987). *Aptitude, learning, and instruction: Vol. 3. Conative and affective process analyses.* Hillsdale, NJ: Lawrence Erlbaum Associates.

Snow, R. E., Federico, P.-A., & Montague, W. E. (Eds.). (1980a). *Aptitude, learning, and instruction: Vol. 1. Conative process analyses of aptitude.* Hillsdale, NJ: Lawrence Erlbaum Associates.

Snow, R. E., Federico, P.-A., & Montague, W. E. (Eds.). (1980b). *Aptitude, learning, and instruction: Vol. 2. Conative process analyses of aptitude.* Hillsdale, NJ: Lawrence Erlbaum Associates.

Snow, R. E., & Jackson, D., III. (1997). *Individual differences in conation: Selected constructs and measures* (CSE Tech. Rep. No. 447). Los Angeles: University of California, Center for the Study of Evaluation.

Snow, R. E., Kyllonen, P. C., & Marshalek, B. (1984). The topography of ability and learning correlations. In R. J. Sternberg (Ed.), *Advances in the psychology of human intelligence* (pp. 47–103). Hillsdale, NJ: Lawrence Erlbaum Associates.

Snow, R. E., & Lohman, D. F. (1984). Toward a theory of cognitive aptitude for learning from instruction. *Journal of Educational Psychology, 76,* 347–376.

Snow, R. E., & Lohman, D. F. (1989). Implications of cognitive psychology for educational measurement. In R. L. Linn (Ed.), *Educational measurement* (3rd ed., pp. 263–332). New York: Macmillan.

Snow, R. E., & Mandinach, E. B. (1999). *Integrating assessment and instruction for classrooms and courses: Programs and prospects for research.* Princeton, NJ: Educational Testing Service.

Snow, R. E., Tiffin, J., & Seibert, W. F. (1965). Individual differences and instructional film effects. *Journal of Educational Psychology, 56,* 315–326.

Snow, R. E., & Yalow, E. (1982). Education and intelligence. In R. J. Sternberg (Ed.), *Handbook of human intelligence* (pp. 493–585). New York: Cambridge University Press.

Solomon, D., Watson, M., Battistich, V., Schaps, E., & DeLucchi, K. (1992). Creating a caring community: Educational practices that promote children's prosocial development. In F. K. Oser, A. Dick, & J.-L. Patry (Eds.), *Effective and responsible teaching: The new synthesis* (pp. 383–390). San Francisco: Jossey-Bass.

Spearman, C. E. (1927). *The abilities of man.* London: Macmillan.

Spearman, C., & Wynn-Jones, L. (1950). *Human ability.* London: Macmillan.

Sperling, G. (1960). Negative afterimage without prior positive image. *Science, 131,* 1613–1614.

Stake, R. E. (1961). Learning parameters, aptitudes, and achievement. *Psychometric Monographs,* No. 9.

Stankov, L. (1988). Single tests, competing tasks and their relationship to broad factors of intelligence. *Personality and Individual Differences, 9,* 25–33.

Sternberg, R. J. (1975). The componential analysis of human abilities: Intelligence, information processing, and analogical reasoning (Doctoral dissertation, Stanford University, 1975). *Dissertation Abstracts International, 36B,* 4741.

Sternberg, R. J. (1977). *Intelligence, information processing, and analogical reasoning: The componential analysis of human abilities.* Hillsdale, NJ: Lawrence Erlbaum Associates.

Sternberg, R. J. (1985). *Beyond IQ: A triarchic theory of human intelligence.* Cambridge, England: Cambridge University Press.

Sternberg, R. J. (1986). Toward a unified theory of human reasoning. *Intelligence, 10,* 281–314.

Sternberg, R. J. (1990). *Metaphors of mind: Conceptions of the nature of intelligence.* New York: Cambridge University Press.

Sternberg, R. J. (1996). Matching abilities, instruction, and assessment: Reawakening the sleeping giant of ATI. In I. Dennis & P. Tapsfield (Eds.), *Human abilities: Their nature and measurement* (pp. 167–181). Mahwah, NJ: Lawrence Erlbaum Associates.

Sternberg, R. J. (1998). Applying the triarchic theory of human intelligence in the classroom. In R. J. Sternberg & W. M. Williams (Eds.), *Intelligence, instruction, and assessment: Theory into practice.* Mahwah, NJ: Lawrence Erlbaum Associates.

Sternberg, R. J., & Grigorenko, E. L. (1995) Styles of thinking in the school. *European Journal for High Ability, 6,* 201–219.

Sternberg, R. J., & Grigorenko, E. L. (1997). Are cognitive styles still in style? *American Psychologist, 52,* 700–712.

Sternberg, R. J., Grigorenko, E. L., Ferrari, M., & Clinkenbeard, P. A. (2000). Triarchic analysis of an aptitude-treatment interaction. *European Journal of Psychological Assessment, 15,* 3–13.

Sternberg, R. J., & Wagner, R. K. (1986). *Practical intelligence: Nature and origins of competence in the everyday world.* Cambridge, England: Cambridge University Press.

Strelau, J. (1983). *Temperament-personality-activity.* New York: Academic Press.

Strelau, J., Zawadski, B., & Piotrowska, A. (2000). Temperament and intelligence: A psychometric approach to the links between both phenomena. In J. Collis & S. Messick (Eds.), *Intelligence and personality: Bridging the gap in theory and measurement.* Mahwah, NJ: Lawrence Erlbaum Associates.

Swiney, J. F., Jr. (1985). A study of executive processes in intelligence (Doctoral dissertation, Stanford University, 1985). *Dissertation Abstracts International, 46A,* 957.

Tellegen, A. (1985). Structures of mood and personality and their relevance to assessing anxiety, with an emphasis on self-report. In A. H. Tuma & J. D. Maser (Eds.), *Anxiety and the anxiety disorders* (pp. 681–716). Hillsdale, NJ: Lawrence Erlbaum Associates.

Tendan, D. J. (1961). *Preparation and evaluation in use of a series of brief films of selected demonstrations from the introductory college physics course.* Lafayette, IN: Purdue Research Foundation.

Tendan, D. J., & McLeod, R. R. (1962). Production of instructional films with university facilities. *American Journal of Physics, 30,* 517–521.

Tendan, D. J., McLeod, R. R., & Snow, R. E. (1962). An experimental evaluation of the use of instructional films in college physics. *American Journal of Physics, 30,* 594–601.

Terman, L. M. (1916). *The measurement of intelligence.* Boston: Houghton Mifflin.

Thomas, A., Chess, S., & Birch, H. G. (1968). *Temperament and behavior disorders in children.* New York: New York University Press.

Thomson, G. H. (1916). A hierarchy without a general factor. *British Journal of Psychology, 8,* 271–281.

Thorndike, R. L., & Hagen, E. P. (1993). *Cognitive abilities test* (Form 5). Chicago: Riverside.

Thurstone, L. L. (1938). Primary mental abilities. *Psychometric Monographs,* No. 1.

Thurstone, L. L. (1947). *Multiple factor analysis.* Chicago: University of Chicago Press.

Thurstone, L. L., & Thurstone, T. G. (1941). Factorial studies of intelligence. *Psychometric Monographs,* No. 2.

Treffers, A. (1987). *Three dimensions: A model of goal and theory description in mathematics instruction—The Wiskobas project.* Dordrecht, Netherlands: Riedel.

Tyler, L. E. (1976). The intelligence we test—An evolving concept. In L. B. Resnick (Ed.), *The nature of intelligence* (pp. 13–26). Hillsdale, NJ: Lawrence Erlbaum Associates.

Urdan, T. (1997). Achievement goal theory: Past results, future directions. In P. R. Pintrich & M. L. Maehr (Eds.), *Advances in motivation and achievement* (Vol. 10, pp. 99–142). Greenwich, CT: JAI.

Urdan, T., Midgley, C., & Anderman, E. M. (1998). The role of classroom goal structure in students' use of self-handicapping strategies. *American Educational Research Journal, 35,* 101–122.

Vauras, M., Lehtinen, E., Kinnunen, R., & Salonen, P. (1992). Socio-emotional coping and cognitive processes in training learning-disabled children. In B. Wong (Ed.), *Intervention research in learning disabilities: An international perspective* (pp. 163–189). New York: Springer.

Vernon, P. E. (1950). *The structure of human abilities*. London: Methuen.

von Neumann, J. (1966). *Theory of self-reproducing automata*. Urbana: University of Illinois Press.

Vygotsky, L. S. (1978). *Mind in society* (M. Cole, V. John-Steiner, S. Scribner, & E. Souberman, Eds.). Cambridge, MA: Harvard University Press.

Walberg, H. J. (1977) Psychology of learning environments: Behavioral, structural, or perceptual? In L. S. Shulman (Ed.), *Review of research in education* (Vol. 4, pp. 142–178). Itasca, IL: Peacock.

Webb, E. (1915). *Character and intelligence*. Cambridge, England: Cambridge University Press.

Webb, N. (1978). Learning in individual and small group settings (Doctoral dissertation, Stanford University, 1977). *Dissertation Abstracts International, 38A*, 7248–7249.

Webb, N. (1983). Predicting learning from student interaction: Defining the interaction variables. *Educational Psychologist, 18*, 33–41.

Webb, N. M., Nemer, K. M., Chizhik, A. W., & Sugrue, B. (1998). Equity issues in collaborative group assessment: Group composition and performance. *American Educational Research Journal, 35*, 607–651.

Weiner, B. (1990). History of motivational research in education. *Journal of Educational Psychology, 82*, 616–622.

White, B. Y., & Frederiksen, J. R. (1998). Inquiry, modeling, and metacognition: Making science accessible to all students. *Cognition and Instruction, 16*, 3–118.

Whitener, E. M. (1989). A meta-analytic review of the effect on learning of the interaction between prior achievement and instructional support. *Review of Educational Research, 59*, 65–86.

Wigfield, A. (1994). Expectancy-value theory of achievement motivation: A developmental perspective. *Educational Psychology Review, 6*(1), 49–78.

Wijnen, W. H. F. W., & Snow, R. E. (1975). *Implementing an evaluation system for medical education* (Tech. Rep. No. 1). Maastricht, Netherlands: Medische Faculteit.

Wilkinson, L., & the Task Force on Statistical Inference. (1999). Statistical methods in psychology journals: Guidelines and explanations. *American Psychologist, 54*, 594–604.

Willingham, W. (1985). *Success in college*. New York: College Board.

Winne, P. H. (1995). Self-regulation is ubiquitous but its forms vary with knowledge. *Educational Psychologist, 30*, 223–228.

Winne, P. H. (1997). Experimenting to bootstrap self-regulated learning. *Journal of Educational Psychology, 89*, 397–410.

Winne, P. H., & Hadwin, A. L. (1998). Studying as self-regulated learning. In D. J. Hacker & J. Dunlosky (Eds.), *Metacognition in educational theory and practice* (pp. 277–304). Mahwah, NJ: Lawrence Erlbaum Associates.

Wolf, T. H. (1973). *Alfred Binet*. Chicago: University of Chicago Press.

Wolters, C. A. (1998). Self-regulated learning and college students' regulation of motivation. *Journal of Educational Psychology, 90*, 224–235.

Young, M. (1958). *The rise of the meritocracy, 1870–2033*. London: Thames & Hudson.

Zajonc, R. B. (1976). Family configuration and intelligence. *Science, 192,* 227–236.

Zajonc, R. B., & Mullally, P. R. (1997). Birth order: Reconciling conflicting effects. *American Psychologist, 52,* 685–699.

Zimmerman, B. (1988). Academic studying and the development of personal skill: A self-regulatory perspective. *Educational Psychologist, 33,* 73–86.

Zimmerman, B. J. (1990). Self-regulating academic learning and achievement: The emergence of a social cognitive perspective. *Educational Psychology Review, 2,* 173–201.

Zimmerman, B., & Bandura, A, (1984) Impact of self-regulatory influences on writing course attainment. *American Educational Research Journal, 31,* 845–862.

Zimmerman, B. J., Bandura, A., & Martinez-Pons, M. (1992). Self-motivation for academic attainment: The role of self-efficacy beliefs and personal goal setting. *American Educational Research Journal, 29,* 663–676.

Zimmerman, B. J., & Martinez-Pons, M. M. (1986). Development of a structured interview for assessing student use of self-regulated learning strategies. *American Educational Research Journal, 23,* 614–629.

Zimmerman, B. J., & Schunk, D. H. (Eds.). (1989). *Self-regulated learning and academic achievement.* New York: Springer.

Zimmerman, W. S. (1954). The influence of item complexity upon the factor composition of a spatial visualization test. *Educational and Psychological Measurement, 14,* 106–119.

Author Index

Subject Index

A

Ability-Grouping, 100
ACT (adaptive control of thought), 133
  declarative and procedural knowledge, 134
Affcon
  definition, 4, 82–84
  development, 200–210
    social/emotional education, 201, 202–204
    teaching self-regulation, 204–205
    collaborative learning, 206–207
    feedback as tool for motivational development, 208–209
    training in coping, 173, 209–210
Affect,
  taxonomy, 82–87
    and cognition, 168–174
    and conation (affcon), 165, 167, 170–171
    and effort, 168, 171, 174

in learning and performance, 167, 169, 172–174
    anxiety, 167–169
    mood, 169–170
    reactivity, 171, 172–174
Affordances, 43, 53–55, 163, 215
Approaches to learning
    participant vs. acquisition metaphors, 35–36
    situative perspective, 38–41
    social dimension, 36
Aptitude, definitions
    and individual differences, 9–11, 20–30
    and multiple abilities, 16–20. 76–80
    and readiness, 211
    as a-in-p-in-s, 42, 211–214
    complexes, 116–117, 221
    historical conceptions, 6–11
    versus ability, 4–6, 11–15
    versus a-in-p, 42
    versus achievement, 46, 49
    versus propensity, 42, 47–55, 59–60, 212–214, 221–222
Aptitude theory
    construct validation, 228–229

285